ALEX GROBMAN

the Palestinian Right to Israel

Balfour Books

Icon Publishing Group, LLC
Noble, Oklahoma 73068
www.iconpublishinggroup.com

First Edition, First Impression. Printed in Canada.

Library of Congress Cataloging-in-Publication Data:

Grobman, Alex
The Palestinian Right to Israel / Alex Grobman
ISBN: 978-1-60725-588-8

For information about other books by this author, please visit:
www.balfourstore.com

CONTENTS

The Palestinian Right to Israel

Judging by the attention the Arab-Israeli conflict generates in the international media and at the United Nations,[1] the dispute is clearly among the most inexorable clashes in the world today. Few, if any other, conflicts in modern history have remained so central for so long. No problem has aroused "the conscience of humanity" as the "problem of Israel in its land," observed former Israeli Ambassador to the UN Yaacov Herzog.[2]

Seven Nobel Peace Prizes have been awarded to individuals for their contributions to Arab-Israeli peacemaking: UN mediator Ralph Bunche in 1950, Canadian prime minister Lester Pearson in 1957, UN Secretary General Dag Hammarskjold in 1961, Egyptian president Anwar Sadat and Israeli prime minister Menachem Begin in 1978, the UN Peace Keeping Force in 1988, Chairman of the Palestine Liberation Organization (P.L.O.) Yasser Arafat, Israeli foreign minister Shimon Peres and Israeli prime minister Yitzhak Rabin in 1994, and former United States president Jimmy Carter in 2002.[3]

In addition, from the time of the British Mandate in Palestine to the present, numerous British, American and European government commissions and official emissaries have come to the region to investigate the underlying causes of the dispute. Academics and journalists have added their own analyses. International attempts at solving the Arab-Israeli conflict include: the King-Crane Commission (1919), Shaw Commission Report (1930), Peel Commission report

(1937), Woodhead Commission (1938), the Anglo-American Committee of Inquiry (1946), the United Nations partition resolutions (1947), the Bernadotte plan (1948), the Lausanne Conference (1948-49), Security Council Resolution 242 (1967), the Rodgers Plan (1970), the Jarring Mission (1971), the Camp David "framework for peace" (1978), the Madrid conference (1991), the Oslo Declaration of Principles (1993), the Wye Summit (1997), the Camp David Summit (2000), the Sharm-el-Sheikh Summit (2000), the Taba Conference (2001), the Quartet Road Map (2003), and the Annapolis Summit (2007).[4] Their recommendations and insights fill volumes,[5] yet the ability to reconcile this clash between two national movements—Zionism and Arab nationalism—remains as elusive as ever.[6]

The purpose of this work is to present a historical narrative of the Arab-Israeli conflict.

Chapter One analyzes the connection of the Jewish people to the land of Israel after the end of Jewish sovereignty in 70 CE. Before 1948, Palestine was never considered an independent state and was at times considered part of Syria. Jerusalem was first sacred to Jews and Christians, and did not become holy to Muslims until 692, with the construction of the Dome of the Rock on the Temple Mount. Firsthand accounts of the region ranging throughout the centuries describe Palestine as a desolate, lawless place.

During the various eras of Muslim and Christian rule, Jews had an uninterrupted presence in the land, with hope of messianic redemption driving Jewish immigration from the Diaspora. In spite of the hardships faced by Jews at the hands of either Muslim or Christian persecutors, Jews never gave up hope of re-establishing their sovereignty in Palestine, a goal that began to be realized during the early Zionist period in the late 19th century.

Chapter Two explores the Arab claim that Palestine is a "twice promised land," because the British pledged it to both the Arabs and the Jews. Arabs base their argument on their interpretation of the Sir Henry McMahon/King Hussein correspondence, in which, they allege, they were given the guarantee that if they helped the British fight the Turks during WWI, they would be given Palestine.

Chapter Three examines Arab reaction to the Balfour Declaration and Jewish immigration to Palestine. Arabs responded by staging protests, which were often violent, and by sending Arab diplomatic delegations to England to plead their case before British officials. On April 19, 1936, the Arab Rebellion began for control of Palestine. The British responded by issuing the MacDonald White Paper on May 17, 1939, restricting Jewish immigration. This established a precedent for dealing with Arabs that continues to this day.

Chapter Four examines Arab activities during WWII to thwart an Allied victory, especially the actions of Haj Amin el-Husseini, the Grand Mufti of Jerusalem and the titular head of the Muslim community in Palestine. Given the Arab attempts to claim Palestine as their own, it is important to expose the Mufti's role in collaborating with the Nazis in Germany during the war. His broadcasts, which implored Arabs and Muslims to enlist in the German army and to engage in sabotage, yielded significant results.

Chapter Five considers the role played by the Jewish community in Palestine *(Yishuv)* in both World Wars. While Arabs attempted to prevent Allied victories, the *Yishuv* vigorously supported the Allies.

After Turkey joined the Central Powers in 1914, members of the *Yishuv* feared this would prevent the establishment of a Jewish state. This concern led to the founding of NILI, a pro-British spy ring that provided vital intelligence about the state of the Turkish military and domestic conditions in the area.

During WWII more than 26,000 Jewish men and women from Palestine were serving in the British Air Force, Navy, and Army. The *Yishuv* provided technical assistance to the British military and assembled military production lines. The staff of the Hebrew University's Hadassah Hospital presented weekly lectures on how to deal with local medical issues affecting the British in the region.

Contrasting the *Yishuv's* role with that of the Arabs provides a historical perspective on the conflict that is often omitted.

Chapter Six demonstrates how the Arabs have never accepted the right of Jews to re-establish their sovereignty in the land of Israel. Refuting the Jewish connection to the Land of Israel, especially the city of Jerusalem, is an ongoing process sanctioned by the Palestinian Authority (PA), and is promoted in their media and textbooks. Some tactics used by Israel's detractors toward substantiating this claim are: the destruction of Temple Mount artifacts to eliminate any evidence of a Jewish past; the accusation that Israeli archeologists manipulate authentic archeological evidence to justify the Jewish people's right to Israel; and finally, the charge that the Jews are not a people at all, and are consequently not entitled to a country of their own.

For many years, there was no need to defend Israel's right to exist as a Jewish state. The League of Nations and later the U.N. had affirmed its legitimacy. However, questioning Israel's right to exist today is seen as a valid exercise, which is why it is necessary to explain how Israel was created.

SUMMATION

In the absence of a solution, a number of distortions proliferate about the conflict. American playwright David Mamet suggests it is futile to respond to these fabrications:

The effort to combat psychotic prejudice with reasonable counterarguments is only not an act of folly, but a capitulation... One cannot reason a lunatic, or a congeries of the same, out of their delusion, for the delusion is the absence of reason.[7]

In essence, one cannot reason with people who do not wish to be swayed by facts. But what about those who genuinely seek the objective truth? This book is addressed to them.

CHAPTER 1

An Uninterrupted Jewish Presence

PALESTINE AS AN INDEPENDENT STATE

From the destruction of the Second Commonwealth by the Romans in 70 CE until the establishment of the modern state of Israel in 1948, Palestine was neither a home for any other people, nor ever been considered a separate geopolitical entity. When the Muslims invaded Palestine in 634, ending four centuries of conflict between Persia and Rome, they found direct descendants of Jews who had lived in the country since the time of Joshua bin Nun, who led the Jews into Canaan. For 2,000 years, Jews and Christians constituted the majority of the population, while the Bedouins were the ruling class.[1]

Diaspora Jews, particularly believers in messianic redemption, returned to Palestine throughout the centuries, making *aliyah* (immigration to Israel) and settling the land.[2]

Starting in the year 1240 (5000 on the Hebrew calendar), there was a mystical expectation at the beginning of each century that Jews could be redeemed if they returned to their land. Although these groups were never more than a small percentage of world Jewry, the fact that they involved leading Jewish figures from around the world had a profound effect on the majority of the Jews who remained behind.[3]

The messianic impetus for *aliyah* and the centrality of the land of Israel became a vital part of Jewish spiritual life. Although modern Zionism rejected the messianic tradition, it still embodied the belief in national redemption and the yearning for return to the land and even the re-establishment of sovereignty.[4] The existence of the pre-modern Zionist *aliyah* movement from the thirteenth to the nineteenth centuries demonstrates that a number of Jews were not content only to pray for the return to Zion, but also saw *aliyah* as a realistic objective. In view of the difficulties of the journey, the uncertainty of finding employment and of being able to live in peaceful surroundings, it is understandable that more people did not go.[5]

After 750, the Muslims ruled the country. Muhammad believed the Day of Judgment was near for the wicked of the world, and ordered the invasion of Palestine to spread the word of God to the righteous—the Muslims—who would soon inherit the entire world.[6]

Aside from the 90 years during which the country was under the rule of Damascus, Palestine was far from a seat of power. The rulers in Damascus viewed it as part of Syria. Subsequent rulers in Baghdad and Egypt saw this neglected area as having only limited value, a source for tax revenue and some military functions.

Despite vast distances in reaching the country and other problems, the Christians remained connected to Palestine, especially Jerusalem and their churches and monasteries. Their hold on the country steadily waned, apart from Jerusalem, where their members became further impoverished. On the eve of the first Crusades in 1095, the situation was quite desperate. Palestine continued to play a major role in only the lives of the Jews.

The Muslim conquest constituted a defining moment in the history of Jerusalem and of the Jewish population in the country. Jews returned to the city more than 500 years after expulsion (135-638) and established a Jewish quarter there. The Romans had forbidden them to enter Jerusalem, and killed any Jew caught trespassing. As a compromise between the demands of Jewish families and the restriction imposed by the Christian patriarch, the Muslim authorities permitted 70 Jewish families to inhabit Jerusalem. Muslims and Jews cleaned up the Temple Mount, which had been used by the Romans as a garbage dump. A number of Jews were then appointed to keep the place clean.[7]

The decision to allow Jews to return to Jerusalem is consistent with Muslim tradition that accepted the Jewish connection to the holy places. Jerusalem was considered the city of the Children of Israel, of the Prophets and of Kings David and Solomon. In a classic display of realpolitik, the Muslims sought a Jewish presence in Jerusalem in order to reduce Christian control of the city, which existed for 300 years.[8]

The accounts of Bar-Sawma, a Christian monk, are a significant source of Palestine's demographics in the Byzantine era. In his biography he wrote that the heathens and Jews comprised the majority in Palestine, Arabia and Phoenicia. Christians were still few in number. An anti-Jewish treatise written at the start of the Muslim invasion of Palestine, suggests there were large numbers of Jews in Acre and Haifa.[9]

A comparatively large number of Jews also lived in Ramla after moving from Lod following the Muslim conquest. Arabic sources also refer to an accord reached by Muhammad in 630 with several Jewish settlements, indicating a considerable Jewish presence in southern Palestine. Arabic sources additionally describe the city of Eilat and its environs as having a large Jewish population.[10]

In the northern part of the Arabian Peninsula, Medina was identified in Muslim sources as a Jewish city. Arab tribes eventually settled in the city, but were not involved in agricultural activities. Jews were known as exceptional farmers who cultivated the land on their plantations. During his final years, Muhammad forced Arab tribes, who were viewed as idolaters and heathens, living on the border of

Palestine to adopt Islam and become part of a unified Islamic rule. Those who accepted Islam were permitted to keep their lands, and become "members of the Islamic ascendancy." Those who refused were killed.[11]

After establishing a new order, Muhammad made a covenant with the Arab tribes compelling every member of the clan to accept his authority, thus facilitating his ability to ultimately destroy the Jewish community of Medina. Some Jews were forbidden to remain in the city; others were killed. Jewish homes and land were confiscated and given to his impoverished followers, who had come from Mecca. Stolen Jewish property was also used to create a war chest to build a formidable military, which had never existed on the Arabian Peninsula.[12]

In 628, the Muslims conquered the Khaybar region, approximately 150 miles north of Medina, another agricultural area in which Jews lived. Jews were forced to give the Muslims half of their annual date crop, and their palm trees became the property of the Muslim community. The Jews of Fadak and those living in Wadi'l-Qura (Valley of the Villages) on the border of Palestine suffered the same fate of becoming Muslim tenants.[13]

Muhammad's attitude toward the Jews changed during the Tabuk campaign that lasted from mid-October to mid-December 630, as he encamped on the border of Palestine. Instead of taking their possessions and expelling them from their lands, he offered to protect the Jews and their property in return for special taxes to be determined in agreements, thus precluding the need for the Jews to maintain a military presence. These treaties became the legal basis within Islam for defining its relationship towards non-Muslims and became a key part of Islamic martial law.[14]

By the summer of 634, most of the cities in Palestine were conquered. In a sermon on Christmas, the Jerusalem patriarch Sophronius described how the Arabs "plunder cities, despoil the fields, burn the villages, destroy holy monasteries." Wary of attacks by the Muslim armies, Jerusalem Christians did not travel to Bethlehem to celebrate the holiday.[15]

FALESTIN IS NOT AN ARABIC NAME

Once in power, the Arabs began renaming cities and places in Palestine. Some were given names in Arabic, but most were based on different pronunciations of the original names. Falestin, for example, which is not Arabic, is a distortion of Greek and Latin. The name is derived from the Philistines who lived on the coastal strip in Biblical times. Epiphanius, who wrote about the Christian Church in its early years and who died in May 402 explained that, "The seed of Abraham is widespread in the land of Canaan, that is the Jewish land [Ioudaia] and in the land of the Philistines [Philistiaia], that which is now called Palaistine."[16]

JERUSALEM TRANSFORMED INTO A SACRED CITY

In the early years of Islam, Jerusalem was called Iliya, with Muslims using the name even in the tenth century. It was also known as *Madinat Bayt al-Maqdis*, city of the temple. The Arabs began to use the name al-Quds only in the eleventh century. The city did not become sacred to the Muslims until the Umayyad period (661-750). Until then, it was holy only to the Jews.[17]

The transformation of Jerusalem into a Muslim holy city began after Caliph Abd al-Malik built the Dome of the Rock on the Temple Mount, completed in four years in 692. The al-Aqsa mosque, which was also built on the Temple Mount by Abd al-Malik's sons, took about ten years to construct, from 706-717. Once completed, the Dome of the Rock and the al-Aqsa mosque attracted thousands of Muslims on route to Mecca, conferring a religious and spiritual quality to them. In turn, traditions around this holy site were born, tied to the Koran and the *hadith* [Muslim tradition of pronouncements and decisions alleged to have originated from Muhammad himself]. According to the *hadith*, the angel Gabriel carried Muhammad to Jerusalem from where he ascended to heaven.[18]

Eventually, the whole city of Jerusalem became sacred. An extensive literature of traditions ascribed to Muhammad, known as the eulogies of Jerusalem, was produced. The holiness of the city required Muslims to come and pray at these holy shrines. Uttering one prayer in Jerusalem was 500 times more valuable than in any other place according to one calculation. Jerusalem, along with Mecca and Medina, were the three places that Muhammad gave the Koran. Jerusalem would be where all the mosques would gather at the End of the Days, and where the trumpet for the resurrection of the dead would be blown. Palestine also warranted praise because the Koran calls it the sanctified land.[19]

Arab sources differ about the purpose of these magnificent buildings. Several objectives have been suggested: Abd al-Malik wanted to redirect attention from Mecca to Jerusalem where he reigned; to show the religious importance of Jerusalem to Muslims; to surpass the Christian churches and monasteries in beauty, and thus convey the superiority of Islam. One recent study avers the objective was to influence the Jews and Christians to become Muslims.[20]

At the time of the Crusaders, Jews and Christians were the dominant inhabitants in Palestine. The Arab tribes lived in the border areas. There were large Jewish communities in Tiberias, Tyre, Acre, Haifa, Ascalon, Gaza, Hebron, Rafiah, and Eilat. Jewish communities also existed in Safed, Jaffa, the Galilee and the Golan. There were more

Jews in Ramla than Jerusalem. Tiberias was the site of the Sanhedrin, also known as the yeshiva of Palestine, and Jewish spiritual life. Rural areas were predominately Christian, while Jerusalem was mainly inhabited by Christians and Jews. Muslims residing in the city were mostly religious personalities or individuals who had come from far-away lands because they believed in its sanctity.[21]

In Gaza there was an institution of learning of some kind, although its exact nature is unknown. The presence in the region of the indigo plant used for dyes in textiles made this an important area for Jewish merchants.[22]

Hebron, where an organized Jewish community existed with a synagogue near the tomb of the patriarchs is "almost never" referred to in Muslim literature before the 10th century, an indication that the city was not considered that significant. Hebron is not mentioned either in any of the Muslim traditions about the Crusades. In the 10th century, Muslim geographers described the graves of the patriarchs Abraham, Isaac and Jacob as well as an inn, supported with funds from the *Waqfs* (religious endowments), that offered hospitality to those who came to pray at the graves in keeping with Abraham's tradition of providing assistance to guests. During the Crusades, many Jews fled to Ascalon and to Egypt.[23]

Even before the Crusades, the Jews of Palestine experienced a number of invasions and internal conflicts. In 969, the Fatimids, who had controlled most of northwest Africa and claimed to be descendants of Fatima, Muhammad's daughter, captured Egypt and then went on to Syria and Ramla in their quest to conquer the whole Muslim world. The war in Palestine, conducted in a number of phases and with different adversaries, devastated the country and especially the Jews. Synagogues were destroyed, Jews were forced to wear distinguishing attire, and they were taxed to the point of impoverishment. Those residing in villages and small towns were compelled to find sanctuary in the cities after the Bedouin uprising in 981. Other groups followed, bringing further destruction and killings in their wake. From 634 to 1099, Palestine was a land of continual unrest and turmoil.[24]

CRUSADES END 465 YEARS OF MUSLIM RULE

In 1099, the First Crusades and the conquest of Jerusalem ended 465 years of Muslim rule in Palestine. Jews were expelled, sold into captivity, or killed all across Palestine. Synagogues and institutions of learning were ransacked and burned. The synagogue in Hebron was converted into a church.[25]

The Crusades lasted until 1291. Throughout the period of the Crusades, Jews still longed for the land of their forefathers. Spanish-born Judah Halevi, the foremost Hebrew poet of his era, expressed this deep feeling when writing about Jerusalem:

> Beautiful heights,
> Joy of the world,
> City of a great king,
> For you my soul yearns,
> From the lands of the west,
> My pity collects and is aroused
> When I remember the past:
> Your story in exile,
> Your temple destroyed.
> I shall cherish your stones and kiss them,
> And your earth will be sweeter
> Than honey to my taste.[26]

Halevi left for the land of Israel in 1140, but was killed, according to legend, as he approached the walls of Jerusalem.[27]

From 1099 to 1187, Jerusalem was under Crusader rule. Jews were brutally forced out of the Jewish quarter of the city, and Christian

Arab tribes from the east side of the Jordan River were brought in to reside in their homes.[28]

In 1187, Saladin, the Ayyubid sultan of Egypt, captured Jerusalem and all the Crusader cities and strongholds. Saladin invited Jews throughout the world to return to Jerusalem. Jews viewed these events as the realization of the divine promise that the land of Israel would not allow any outside conquerors to possess the land, and that this clash between Christians and Muslims would inevitably allow Jews to "return to Zion." The Muslim rulers were perceived as having contributed to this process.[29]

By 1211, sizable numbers of Torah scholars from Europe and North Africa immigrated to Palestine. Called the *"aliyah of the three hundred rabbis"* because of its composition and amount of Jews it attracted, the *aliyah* included Rabbi Samson of Schantz, a foremost French Talmudic scholar, Rabbi Jonathan Hacohen of Lunel of Provence, and Rabbi Moses ben Nahman (Nahmanides), Spanish-born philosopher and scholar. Little is known about this *aliyah* except that some Jews settled in Jerusalem.[30]

When Acre fell to the Muslims in 1291, they destroyed its considerable Jewish community along with the yeshiva of Rabbi Yehiel of Paris. The constant battles and fluctuations of rule between Muslim and Crusaders was a key reason why the Jewish communities in Palestine had so much difficulty in establishing themselves. Tragically, the *aliyah* failed. Although another *aliyah* was not attempted for a while, it set the precedent for future immigration.[31]

Christian travelers visiting the Holy Land often used Jews as guides for their competent knowledge of the land. Jacques of Verona, a monk who visited in 1335, wrote about the deep-rooted Jewish community he found in Jerusalem near Mount Zion:

A pilgrim who wished to visit ancient forts and towns in the Holy Land would have been unable to locate these without a good guide who knew the Land well or without one of the Jews who lived there. The Jews were able to recount the history of these places since this knowledge had been handed down from their forefathers and wise men. So when I journeyed overseas I often requested and managed to obtain an excellent guide among the Jews who lived there.[32]

Following the surge of persecution in Europe, the immigration of large numbers of Jews from Italy prompted a papal order in 1428 forbidding sea captains from transporting Jews to Palestine, followed by similar proclamations in Venice and Sicily.[33]

The Vatican feared an increase of Jews in the Holy Land because the Jews of Jerusalem had tried to wrest control of the Tomb of King David on Mount Zion from the Franciscan order by obtaining the site from the Muslim authorities. The dispute ended with the Franciscans being removed and the Jews failing to keep their hold on the site. Still the Jews managed to buy a large amount of property in a new area of Jerusalem on the "Street of the Jews' Synagogue," known today as the Jewish Quarter of the Old City. Building a synagogue, which was a violation of Islamic law, demonstrated Jewish confidence. According to a document from 1245, an Islamic court accepted a Jewish claim that a synagogue existed on the site many years before and agreed that it remain in possession of the Jews.[34]

Throughout the 15th century, a Jewish presence in the Holy Land impressed Christian observers. In 1486, Bernhard von Breidenbach, Dean of Mainz Cathedral, remarked that Jews in Hebron and Jerusalem "will treat you in full fidelity—more so than anyone else in those countries of the unbelievers."[35]

Life under the Muslims had become severe and intolerant noted Martin Kabtanik, a pilgrim from Bohemia, while on a visit to Jerusalem. In his *Journey to Jerusalem*, he wrote:

> There are not many Christians but there are many Jews, and these the Moslems persecute in various ways. Christians and Jews go about in Jerusalem in clothes considered fit only for wandering beggars.
>
> The Moslems know that the Jews think and even say that this is the Holy Land which has been promised to them and that those Jews who dwell there are regarded as holy by Jews elsewhere, because in spite of all the troubles and sorrows inflicted on them by the Moslems, they refuse to leave.[36]

The growth in the Jewish community in Jerusalem was short-lived. A prohibitive increase in taxes compelled many Jews to sell their property. After Muslims were unable to persuade the Mameluke sultan in Cairo to demolish the synagogue on the Street of the Jews, they simply razed it themselves in 1474. Had it not been for the government of Egypt, the Muslims would have thrown the Jews out of the city as well. Jewish hopes that this period would usher in their impending redemption ended with this and other actions against the community.[37]

JEWISH MYSTICISM AND THE CODE OF JEWISH LAW

The most well known messianic *aliyah*, involving the migration of thousands of families from Europe to the northern town of Safed, occurred during the years prior to 1540.[38] By 1530, there were 10,000 Jews living around the city, mostly Sephardim.[39] This number grew to about 20,000 in the early 17th century and may have even reached 30,000, according to some sources.[40] In Jerusalem , the Jews built four synagogues where Jews worshiped continuously for 400 years, destroyed only in the 1948 war.[41]

A new group of immigrants, who were centered in Safed, produced some of the most significant works of Judaism: the *Shulhan Aruch* and *Beit Yosef*, the authoritative code of Jewish law, by Rabbi Joseph Karo, and the Kabalistic work of Rabbi Isaac Luria (the "Ari") that transformed Jewish mysticism and became the foundation of the Hasidic movement in the 18th century.[42]

Other leading scholars and Kabalists left their mark, as well. Rabbi Jacob Berab, one of the greatest Spanish scholars of the period, attempted to reinstitute rabbinic ordination *(semicha)* through which the Sanhedrin could be restored in preparation for redemption. *Semicha* was prerequisite for appointment to the Sanhedrin. With the approval of 25 of the foremost rabbis in Safed, Berab was ordained in 1538. Opposition by Rabbi Levi ibn Habib of Jerusalem, and the possibility of incarceration forced Rabbi Berab to seek refuge in Cairo. Before fleeing, he ordained four scholars in Safed, including Rabbi Karo, who became the leader of the community.[43]

Rabbi Karo had come to Safed with Rabbi Solomon Alkabetz and a group of Kabalists. He became a leading spiritual figure of Safed, where he wrote works on Kabala and prayers, including the *Lecha Dodi, Come My Beloved*, which became part of the Friday Sabbath service. In one prayer, he asked God to redeem the Jewish people, contending that by making *aliyah*, he and his contemporaries had demonstrated their commitment and thus merited divine support.[44]

Safed became one of the foremost Jewish intellectual and spiritual centers "since the redaction of the Talmud" because of the belief that the Messiah would appear first in the Galilee, the absence of Muslim and Christian institutions in the city, the local textile industry and the beneficial economic ties with Syria which offered the opportunity to earn an income.[45] The city was also close to many graves of the *tannaim* (Jewish sages) buried in the Galilee, including that of Shimon bar Yohai, the author of the *Zohar* (mystical commentary on the Torah). Jews who traveled to the Holy Land from the northwestern part of the Ottoman Empire came through Safed, the closest Jewish center near Syria.[46] Within ten years of the arrival of the first Jews, the Galilee and Safed became a successful economic hub that exported sheep, wool, grain and fruit.[47]

This economic prosperity did not last long. Toward the end of the 16th century, a serious financial crisis that battered the country hurt Safed's wool industry. Government leaders, who had become increasingly antagonistic to the Jews, tried to banish 1,000 families to Cyprus. As a pretext for persecuting the Jews in Safed, the authorities claimed that they had not obtained government consent to build their synagogues in the city. This crisis, which ended the life of the Jewish community in Safed, and which was felt throughout Palestine, did not stop Jews from returning a number of decades later.[48]

A new movement of immigration that included major rabbinic figures and their families arrived in Palestine prior to 1648, the year the redemption was to begin with the resurrection of the dead according to a passage in the *Zohar*. The majority of the rabbis were Kabalists, including Rabbi Isaiah Horowitz, author of *Shnei Luhot Habrit*, and known as the "Shelah," because of the acronym of his famous work.

Settling the land was essential to bring the redemption, the Shelah claimed adamantly, and was profoundly disturbed that Jews did not fulfill this mission.

> For my heart burned continually when I saw the children of Israel building houses like princely fortresses, making permanent homes in the world in an impure land…which seems, heaven

forbid, as if they were turning their minds away from the redemption.[49]

Arriving in 1622, Rabbi Horowitz remained in Safed for a short time before moving to Jerusalem, where he believed the redemption would come.

Between 1625 and 1627, the Ibn Farukh family ruled Jerusalem after buying control of it from the Ottoman government. The poor in Jerusalem were forced to pay high taxes, and those not able to do so were penalized. The Jews were singled out because they had no political power, and aid sent from the Diaspora for their support was easily confiscated.[50] As part of their persecution, religious objects were destroyed, Torah scrolls were used for cloths and bags, liens were placed on synagogues and religious courts and schools were shut down. Those who could flee sought refuge outside the reach of the governor. In 1624, there were 2,500 to 3,000 Jews living in Jerusalem, and by 1627 only a few hundred remained.[51]

The messianic fervor that preceded Ibn Farukh did not wane after the end of his reign. Eugene Roger, a Christian traveler, who visited the region between 1629 and 1634, saw several attempts by Jews to welcome the Messiah. He described two such occasions where he saw more than 2,000 Jews on Shavuot in 1630, and again in 1633.[52]

The attempt by Shabtai Tzvi to bring large numbers of Jews to Palestine failed in 1666, after this false messiah converted to Islam. However, a new movement began in 1700 under Rabbi Judah Hasid. The expectation that in the year 1740 the Messiah would come precipitated another messianic movement. Within a decade, several thousand Jews, mostly from the Ottoman Empire and Italy, settled in Jerusalem and Tiberias. In 1740, the Ottoman authorities asked Rabbi Haim Abulafia, the rabbi of Izmir, to rebuild Tiberias.

He used the opportunity to encourage Jews to believe the Messiah would arrive soon.

During this period, Jews began arriving in such great numbers that the Muslims began to complain that "Behold the people of the children of Israel are too numerous to count, and there are ten thousand Jewish men."[53] Their arrival forced the price of food and housing to increase radically. This influx precipitated the need to establish eight new yeshivot, build new synagogues and repair the old ones. Among the leading rabbinic leaders who came were Rabbi Moses Haim Luzzatto, author of *Mesilat Yesharim (Path of The Just-Self Perfection and Cleaving to the Divine)*; the Kabalist Rabbi Haim ben Atar, author of Or Hahaim, one of the fundamental mystical texts; Elazar Rokeah, chief rabbi of Brody and Amsterdam; Rabbi Gershon of Kutow; Rabbi Gedaliah Hayun and R. Shalom Sharabi (known as Rashash), who were the heads of the Beth-El yeshiva in Jerusalem.[54]

Rabbi Israel Ba'al Shem Tov, founder of the Hasidic movement, attempted to move to the Holy Land to work together with Rabbi Haim ben Atar, in the hope that they might bring about the redemption through mystical powers. From 1740-1781, many of the Ba'al Shem Tov's closest friends and followers made *aliyah*. Rabbi Menahem Mendel of Vitebsk (a disciple of Rabbi Dov Baer of Mezrich, the "Magid of Mezrich"), led the largest group of about 300, arriving in 1777.[55]

Significantly, Elijah of Vilna, the "Vilna Gaon," the leading rabbinic leader of Lithuanian Jewry in the 18th century who was known for his mastery of the Talmud and Kabala and as an opponent of Hasidism, also attempted to immigrate to Palestine. After reaching The Netherlands, he was forced to turn back home. Had he succeeded in reaching his destination, he had planned to write a "new *Shulhan Aruch*."[56]

Toward the end of the 18th century, there was a decline in messianic *aliyah* and a deterioration of Jewish life in Palestine. The Ottoman authorities and the local Muslims instituted economic restrictions, the Jews suffered violent attacks at the hands of the local Arabs, and there were internecine clashes within the Jewish leadership. A significant number of Jews decided to emigrate rather than tolerate such abuse. The approximately 3,000 Jews remaining in Jerusalem studied the Torah, while the rabbis wrote Halahkic Responsa, commentaries, homiletics and Kabala that were published by Western European and Ottoman Empire publishers.[57]

The Jewish community in Palestine remained in contact with the Diaspora, which provided financial and diplomatic support enabling the *Yishuv* (Jewish settlement in Palestine) to endure and grow. Awareness of the *Yishuv* throughout the world during the first half of the 19th century made Diaspora Jews view the land of Israel as a place of future relocations. Jewish life in Palestine, which was considerably influenced by a messianic fidelity to the land of Israel, had laid the foundation for the influx of Jews that would soon be arriving.[58]

To be sure, there were significant and substantive distinctions between the messianic *aliyot* and the new form of Zionism that followed. Yet the profound yearning for Zion—the fervent belief in the possibility of physical and spiritual redemption of the land— which finally compelled the waves of Jewish immigrants to immigrate to Palestine, was at the core for this return to their ancestral home. Thus, one can regard the messianic migration and secular Zionism "as milestones on the same historical path, different chapters in an ongoing national story."[59]

During the Jewish Diaspora, Palestine never became a state for another people. For centuries, far-away caliphs controlled the region. The territory had been conquered many times by numerous nations including the Egyptians, Assyrians, Babylonians, Persians,

Greeks, Romans, Arabs, Seljuks, Crusaders, Mamelukes, Ottomans and English. Each conquest left in its wake soldiers, slaves and their offspring who were compelled to accept Islam or suffer the consequences. By the 19th century, Palestine was a mélange of nations, linguistic, religious and ethnic groups.[60]

RE-ESTABLISHMENT OF ISRAEL: CONDITION OF JEWS IN PALESTINE

Hostility toward the Jews before the 19th century was often a result of religious and social differences, while violence against them (particularly during war) occurred when they and Christians were assumed to be assisting the enemy—or when enmity against an adversary could be more practically aimed against their vulnerable and abhorred Jewish communities.[61]

After Napoleon conquered Egypt in 1799, he launched an attack on Gaza and Jaffa. Fear that Napoleon would succeed in an assault on Jerusalem precipitated panic among the Muslims. The Jews of Jerusalem were terrified of being killed by their Arab neighbors who wrongly accused them of being "spies and traitors" for having entered into a treaty with Napoleon to "deliver the city into his hands, through fraud and cunning." The Muslims "secretly resolved… to kill all the Jewish inhabitants," as soon as Napoleon marched on Jerusalem." The crisis was averted when the Jews learned of the threat and helped the Muslims fortify the city. Once they saw Jews actively participating in the defense of Jerusalem, the Muslims recognized that it was "nothing but calumny and falsehood to accuse the Jews of a treasonable intention."[62]

Shortly after the French retreated from Safed in 1799, which they held with limited armed forces, the resident Muslims demolished the Jewish quarter, murdered a number of Jews and ordered the remaining inhabitants to pay 50,000 piastres in penalties. During

Napoleon's Syrian campaign, Jews in Palestine were seen as traitors and the enemy was regarded as being part Jewish.[63]

In 1834, the Jews in Tiberias and Safed suffered in the anti-Egyptian revolt against the occupation of Palestine and Syria by Muhammad Ali's Egyptian soldiers. The Jews were confined in Tiberias until they paid the rebels 50,000 piastres. In Safed, Jews were killed, their wives and daughters were raped and Torah scrolls were vandalized. During the Crimean War (1853-1856), a number of Ashkenazi Jews in Jerusalem were charged with being spies, while the Russo-Turkish War of 1877 precipitated anti-Christian riots in Lydda. It was during these turbulent periods that Muslim loathing and contempt for the *dhimmis* would be manifest.[64]

Travelers going through Nablus on their way to or from Jerusalem during the first half of the 19th century were urged to do so with a guard or in a group. *Murray's Handbook for Travelers* described the Muslim residents of Nablus as having "a bad character and deserve it. They have long been notorious for fanaticism and turbulence... Travelers, and especially ladies, in passing through the streets are exposed to the most wanton insolence."[65] Foreigners reported being cursed and threatened with stones. Most of the perpetrators were children, apparently with the approval of their parents. James Finn, the British Consul in Jerusalem, observed that Nablus was "mostly inhabited by fanatic Muslims" that "are distinguishable by a mean and cruel cast of countenance" and "notoriously one of the most turbulent and fanatical places in Syria."[66]

Finn found that except for Reverend John Bowen and Reverend J. Mills, who spent 12 months and three months respectively in Nablus, "no one from our land has remained, even for a few days, in this most interesting district, visited and passed through by hundreds of British travelers, for pleasure, but cared for by none."[67]

After visiting Nablus, John Lewis Burckhardt, a Swiss citizen and orientalist, concluded:

> The inhabitants of Nablous [sic] are governed by their own chiefs, who are invested by the Pasha [governor of Damascus]. It is said that the villages belonging to the district can raise an army of five thousand men. They are a restless people, continually in dispute with each other, and frequently in insurrection against the Pasha. Djezzar never succeeded in completely subduing them, and Junot, with a corps of fifteen hundred French soldiers, was defeated by them.[68]

Hebron was hardly better. Walter Keating Kelly, a lawyer and historian, said that "There is little to detain" a person in the city. "The present inhabitants are the wildest, most lawless, and desperate people in the Holy Land…The Muslims in Hebron are exceedingly bigoted." When Kelly and a Jewish companion paused to admire the marble staircase leading to the tomb of the patriarch Abraham, a Turk emerged from the bazaar and "with furious gesticulations" summoned a crowd that surrounded them. The Jew and the Christian "were driven with contempt from the sepulchre of the patriarch whom they both revered."[69]

One particular blood libel episode in March 1847 epitomized the treacherous life faced by Jews in Palestine. After having been hit with a stone by a Greek pilgrim boy, a little Jewish boy struck the Greek with another stone, drawing blood from his ankle. Fearing a repeat of the blood libel affairs in Rhodes and Damascus in February 1840, Finn intervened. A mob of pilgrims and others called for vengeance against all Jews "for having stabbed (they said) an innocent Christian child with a knife in order to get his blood for mixing in their Passover biscuits."[70]

The case was brought before the Pasha but was dismissed as being too trivial. Three days later, the Christian clergy exaggerated the nature of the wound and attempted to use Jewish sacred texts to prove to him that Jews are "addicted" to this "cannibal practice, either for purposes of necromancy or out of hatred of Christians." The Jews were then ordered to defend their position two days later.[71] Finn maintained that the "unexpected revival of so monstrous and false accusation," was almost certainly a result of "the desire of both Greeks and Turks to get possession of some Jewish money."[72]

Finn wrote in his memoirs…

> In the interval, both Greeks and Armenians went out in the streets insulting and menacing the Jews, both men and women, sometimes drawing their hands across the throat, sometimes showing the knives which they generally carry about with them, and among other instances brought to my notice, was that of a party of six catching hold of the son of the late Chief Rabbi of London (Herschell) and shaking him, elderly man that he was by the collar, crying out, 'Ah Jew, have you got the knives ready for our blood.'[73]

CONDITION OF JEWS IN PALESTINE AND THE CHRISTIAN COMMUNITY

Palestinian Jews suffered discrimination and persecution from both Muslims and Christians. In a May 25, 1839 letter to Viscount Palmerston, British State Secretary for Foreign Affairs, William Tanner Young, the first British Vice-Consul in Jerusalem (1838-1841 and consul from 1841-1845), explained the situation of the Jews in the city. Although they enjoy "more peace and tranquility," than ever before, he noted, "scarcely a day passes," that he does not hear "of some act of tyranny and oppression against a Jew—chiefly by [Turkish] soldiers, who enter their Houses and borrow whatever they require without asking any permission—sometimes they return the article, but more frequently not."[74]

Young described the behavior of the Turkish Governor toward the Jews as "savage" after hearing an account of how his punishment of an innocent Jew led to the Jew's death. He thought the governor was "superior to such wanton inhumanity—but it was a Jew without friends or protection…"[75]

Local Muslims forced Jews to pay taxes to enable them to pray at their holy sites. For the privilege of praying at the Western Wall, for example, Jews had to provide a yearly payment to the Effendi, whose house was next to the Wall; the villagers of Siloam were paid a stipend for not vandalizing the graves on the slopes of the Mount of Olives; the Ta'amra Arabs were bribed so they would not damage Rachel's Tomb near Bethlehem; and Sheikh Abu Gosh received money each year for "not molesting" travelers on the road to Jaffa, even though he received a significant sum yearly from the Turkish government as "Warden of the road."[76]

With regard to Christians, Young reported that…

If a Jew…were to attempt to pass the door of the Church of the Holy Sepulchre, it would in all probability cost him his life—this is not very Christian like, considering Christ Himself was a Jew. And were a Jew to fly for safety, he would seek it sooner in a Mussulman's house than in that of a Christian.[77]

What the Jew has to endure, at all hands, is not to be told. Like the miserable dog without an owner he is kicked by one because he crosses his path, and cuffed by another because he cried out—to seek redress he is afraid, lest it bring worse upon him; he thinks it better to endure than to live in the expectation of his complaint being revenged upon him. Brought up from infancy to look upon his civil disabilities everywhere as a mark of degradation,

his heart becomes the cradle of fear and suspicion—he finds
he is trusted by none—and therefore he lives himself without
confidence in any.[78]

"Until the English Consulate was established in Jerusalem," asserted
James Finn, "there was no other jurisprudence in the country than that
of the old fashioned corruption and self-will of the Mohammedans,
and for many ages but very few (often none) of the European Jews
ventured to make an abode in Palestine."[79]

The relationship between the local churches and the Jews was
described by H.H. Jessup, a leading personality in the American
Presbyterian church in Beirut:

> They are hated intensely by all sects, but more especially by the
> Greeks and the Latins. In the gradations of Oriental cursing, it
> is tolerably reasonable to call a man a donkey, somewhat more
> severe to call him a dog, contemptuous to call him a swine, but
> withering to the last degree to call him a Jew. The animosity of
> the nominal Christian sects against the Jews is most relentless
> and unreasoning.[80]

Local Christian attitudes toward Jews thus provided fertile ground
for European antisemitism. The Russian Imperial Orthodox Palestine
Society, which began operating in 1882, barred Jews from their medical
clinics, reflecting the negative views of the Tsarist government in
Russia. All other segments of the local population were admitted.[81]

Another source of anti-Jewish sentiment emanated from members of
the consular corps, especially those from the Austrian and Russian
Consulates. Economic competition concerned the Deutsches Palastina
Bank, Credit Lyonnais and other foreign banks and merchants. The
thousand or so Protestants ("Templars") from Germany who lived
in Palestine shared this fear and the possibility that they might be

included in the restraints placed on the Jews. In 1890, Jerusalem already had a German antisemitic club.[82]

In 1897, Père Henri Lammens, a Belgium scholar who taught at the Jesuit University in Beirut, wrote an article entitled "Zionism and the Jewish Colonies," in the anti-Jewish and anti-Zionist Jesuit journal *Etudes*. Lammens described the Jews of Jerusalem as easily "recognizable...by their repulsive grubbiness and above all that famous Semitic nose, which is not, like the Greek nose, a pure myth."[83]

CONDITION OF JEWS IN PALESTINE: EARLY ZIONIST ERA

During the 1880's, Sultan Abdul Hamid saw Zionism as another national movement endangering his empire, but not the most threatening when compared to nationalistic fervor in Armenia and the Balkans. The Jews were a tolerated and inferior community who he would not allow to possess Islamic lands, especially Jerusalem, Islam's holy city. "Why should we accept Jews whom the civilized European nations do not want in their countries and whom they had expelled," he asked. "It is not expedient to do so, especially at a time when we are dealing with the Armenian subversion."[84]

Though not outwardly worried about Zionism, the sultan did not want a large number of foreigners, particularly with nationalistic interests, settling in his territory. Jews were specifically banned from immigrating, and new laws were enacted whenever ambiguities were detected in enforcing them. Yet between 1881-1882 and 1890, the *Yishuv* population doubled to 50,000 people, mostly due to immigration.

Relations with Jews improved after the Committee of Union and Progress (CPU) took control of Turkey in 1909, but there was no government consensus on how to proceed. Following the Balkan wars of 1912-1913, Pasha Talaat turned to the Zionists for financial aid. Talaat expected that the Zionists would be able to influence worldwide Jewry to provide loans to Turkey in exchange for eliminating restrictions on immigration and property ownership in Palestine. As a sign of friendship, the Young Turks in September 1914 abolished the "Red Slip," the temporary residence permit that had been in effect since 1901, as well as restrictions on Jewish settlement.[85]

THE FIRST ALIYAH

At the end of the 19th century, Palestine was a small area far from the heart of Europe but governed by the consulates of Britain, the United States, France, Prussia, Sardinia, Austria, Spain and Russia. Increased immigration from Europe by Ashkenazic Jews changed Muslim-Jewish relations as European powers intervened to protect their citizens from Turkish or Arab persecution under capitulation agreements negotiated with the Ottoman Empire.[86]

The consul's extraterritorial rights meant that he had ultimate power over the assets and lives of the nationals residing within the territorial boundaries of his command. Each consulate even had its own prison room.[87] In turn, the capitulation agreements permitted the Great Powers to increase their political presence in Palestine and "institutionalize" their missionary work. The protection reluctantly won the Jews respect from the Arabs, while also stirring resentment against them.[88]

In the early 1850's, 5,000 Ashkenazim were under the protection of foreign consuls: 3,000 by Austria, 1,000 by the British, and the rest were registered with the American, Prussian, Dutch and Russian consulates.[89]

By championing the rights of foreign Jews[90] and endorsing Jewish resettlement in Palestine, the British established and expanded their consulate in Palestine, which they hoped to use to counter Russia's expanding influence in the Levant.[91]

The British also took a special interest in the welfare of the Jews, *The Times of London* noted, because "...no people on the face of the earth has been so little understood and so grossly misinterpreted as the Jewish...A new era is however commencing."[92]

Until war broke out in 1914, the British consulate in Jerusalem served as the place where every Jew in Palestine, no matter their nationality, could receive advice and protection. When William T. Young began his work as Vice-Consul in 1838, his first dispatch instructed him to protect the Jews in Palestine and report on their present condition.[93]

Protestant missionaries in Palestine, also protected by the British, made common cause with the Jews as they were passionate believers in the "restoration of the Jews" to the Holy Land. Restoration gained worldwide interest in the 19th century as Protestants from around the world initiated projects to bring Jews to Palestine. Rather than convert the Jews, they sought to repatriate them to Palestine, which they believed would hasten the return of the Messiah. This movement further strengthened the bond between the British and Palestine.[94]

According to David Ben-Gurion, Israel's first prime minister, the creation of the Jewish state began with the founding of Mikveh Israel in 1870, when *Alliance Israelite Universelle*, the French philanthropic organization, established the first agricultural training school for Jewish youth and an elementary research center outside Jaffa.[95] The Zionists needed to establish a Jewish majority in the country and create a separate Jewish national community secured by economic, political, social and even military protection or the movement would lose its *raison d'être*. The experience of Jews in the Diaspora had long exposed the inherent danger of being a permanent minority.[96]

During the years leading up to 1840, messianic fervor played a role in inspiring a mass movement of tens of thousands of traditional Jews from Europe to Palestine, drastically altering the demography of the Jewish community there. When the first Zionists began arriving at the end of the 19th century, "the land of Israel was already the host to its largest and most vibrant Jewish community" than there had been in many centuries.[97]

Followers of the Vilna Gaon purchased land in Palestine in order to fulfill the religious commandments relating to the land of Israel though cultivation. Developing the land would be a sure sign of God's love for his people, according to the Talmudic interpretation (Sanhedrin 98a) of the verse in Ezekiel (36:8): "But you, O mountains of Israel, shall shoot forth your branches, and yield your fruit to my people Israel—there is no better sign than this."[98]

Palestinian Jewry ascribed enormous importance to agriculture, as can be seen in a letter sent by the Sephardic and Ashkenazic leaders in 1839 to Moses Montefiore, the English philanthropist, after learning that he wanted to buy land for rural Jewish colonies. "...We await and anticipate the divine salvation through Moses, the faithful one of his house, to say when he shall begin this beginning of the redemption," it read.[99]

Three years earlier Rabbi Tzvi Hirsch Kalischer asked Baron Anshel Rothschild to buy the Temple Mount from the ruler of Egypt, Muhammad Ali, so the Jews could begin the sacrificial service once again. Restoring sacrifices on the Temple Mount, Rabbi Kalischer believed, would accelerate the redemption and the coming of the Messiah. In the letter the rabbi noted:

> And particularly at a time like this, when the province of the land of Israel is not under the rule of a powerful regime as it was in former times...he may well sell you the city of Jerusalem

and its surroundings. From this too there will spring forth a horn of salvation, if we have the power and authority to seek the place of the altar and to offer acceptable burnt offerings to the God of Eternity, and from this may Judah be delivered in an eternal deliverance.[100]

The Jews in Palestine also sought to rebuild "earthly Jerusalem" by restoring the ruins of the "Court of the Ashkenazim," where Jews lived, prayed, studied and conducted business. Donors in Europe were approached for funds, but it took twenty years before they received permission to begin rebuilding. There were also attempts to reinstate the Sanhedrin, a prerequisite for reinstituting *semicha*. As in Safed hundreds of years before, they encountered the same religious issues that doomed the earlier effort.[101]

The Jews faced continuous assaults by local Arabs and Muslim authorities that made life unbearable for them. In 1834, when Arab farm workers revolted against the regime of Muhammad Ali, Jews were attacked in the major cities.[102] In Safed, they stole Jewish property, destroyed homes, and defiled synagogues. Some Jews were raped, beaten and murdered. A report by Rabbi Shumel Heller of Safed assessed the tragedy that ensued:

> For forty days, day after day, from the Sunday following Shavuot, all of the people of our holy city, men, women, and children have been like refuse upon the field. Hungry, thirsty, naked, barefoot, wandering to and fro in fear and confusion like lambs led to the slaughter...They [the Arab marauders] removed all the Torah scrolls and thrust them contemptuously to ground, and they ravished the daughters of Israel—woe to the ears that hear it— and the great study they burned to its foundations...And the entire city was destroyed and laid ruin, they did not leave a single

wall whole; they dug and sought treasures, and the city stood ruined and, desolate without a single person...[103]

Although many Jews left Palestine under such difficult conditions, the majority remained—aided by Montefiore, the Rothschild family, and other Jewish philanthropic institutions. Jews were often protected by Jewish organizations in the Diaspora and by European nations, whose consuls in the region insisted that the Jews be reimbursed for the losses they sustained in the riots of 1834. Jews were less exposed than in previous times, enabling continued settlement of the land and the subsequent waves of immigration beginning in the 1880s.[104]

THE DEMOGRAPHIC COMPOSITION OF PALESTINE

By 1900, Palestine was home to nearly 600,000 inhabitants. The population was overwhelmingly Arab Muslim, but also included large Jewish, Arab Christian, and Druze communities. However, through steady immigration, the Jewish population increased markedly over the next half century. While in 1880 Jews numbered 6,700 and Arabs 268,000, a ratio of 1:40, by 1947 Jews numbered 630,000 and Arabs 1.31 million, a ratio of 1:2.[105] As the Nazis and other fascist movements gained strength in Europe, Jews fled in large numbers to Palestine. In 1929, they comprised 17 percent of the population, but had increased to 31 percent by 1936.[106]

Within the minority Jewish community, there were two distinct entities: the old *Yishuv* and the new one. The old *Yishuv* was mainly composed of Ashkenazi Orthodox Jews from Europe, who lived the holy cities of Jerusalem, Safed, Hebron, and Tiberias, and had been the largest religious group in Jerusalem since the middle of the 19th century. Although they were in the minority, Sephardic Jewish communities from Asian and African countries also predated the new wave of immigrants fleeing European antisemitism.[107]

In 1878, following the increased persecution, Romanian Jews began arriving in large numbers. The first group came as an organized body, according to an agreed upon plan, and settled in Zikhron Ya'akov.[108] In 1882, Jews from czarist Russia began arriving in Palestine. Pogroms and persecution had forced them to flee, as did their desire to help build a new society in the country as part of *Hibbat Zion* (Love of Zion), the national renaissance movement.[109]

During the winter of 1882, several hundred Jews from Yemen also arrived. They had been immigrating to *Eretz Israel* (the land of Israel) in small numbers since the 15th century, if not before. They lived in Jerusalem and were Ottoman subjects. In the coming years, famine and oppression drove many more toward Palestine.[110]

This wave of immigration, known as the *First Aliyah*, continued until 1903 and brought 30,000 Jews to the country. A group of mostly Russian middle-aged religious families established 20 *moshavot* (colonies) from the Galilee in the north to Judea in the south. Hadera was established by a small group of secular Jews as a prototype for the future Jewish society.[111]

From 1904-1914, the *Second Aliyah* arrived in Palestine "to show the way to independence."[112] Almost equal in number to the first wave of immigrants, this group consisted of thousands of young, idealistic people, motivated by the desire to create egalitarian and agricultural societies. Much of Israel's future political leadership arrived in this wave, including future prime ministers David Ben-Gurion, Moshe Sharett and Levi Eshkol; Yitzhak Ben-Zvi, the second president of Israel and Berl Katznelson, the spiritual leader of the labor movement; and Yitzhak Tabenkin, a founder and one of the leaders of the kibbutz movement.[113]

THE LAND

There were about 26.3 dunams of land in Palestine in the 19th and early 20th centuries, of which less than a third were deemed cultivable. [A metric dunam equals 1,000 square meters or ¼ acre.] The rest of the land was "dotted by intermittent mountain ranges, sand dunes, bleak terrain, alkaline soils, semiarable mountain regions, obstructed water courses, and marshlands."[114] An interim report presented to the British Parliament in August 1921 on the civil administration of Palestine, commented on the condition of Palestine after World War I:

It is obvious to every passing traveler...that the country was before...War[I], and is now, undeveloped and under-populated. The methods of agriculture are for the most part primitive; the area of laud[sic] now cultivated could yield a far greater product. Other large cultivable areas have remained untilled. The hills are suitable to grow trees, but there are no forests. Miles of sand dunes that could be redeemed, are untouched...The Jordan and the Yarmuk offer an abundance of water-power, but it is unused. Some industries—fishing and the culture and manufacture of tobacco are examples—have been killed by Turkish laws; none have been encouraged; the markets of Palestine...are supplied almost wholly from Europe. The seaborne commerce, such as it is, is loaded and discharged in the open roadsteads of Jaffa and Haifa: there are no harbours...

The country is under-populated because of this luck [sic] of development. There are now in the whole of Palestine hardly 700,000 people, a population much less than that of the province of the Gallilee (sic) alone during the time of Christ.[115]

And yet, wherever Jews touched the land, this changed. Russian Jews, for example, came to escape persecution and established agriculture colonies where they grew oranges, manufactured and exported wine, planted eucalyptus trees, and used modern agriculture methods.

Every traveler in Palestine who visits them is impressed by the contrast between these pleasant villages, with the beautiful stretches of prosperous cultivation about them and the primitive conditions of life and work by which they are surrounded.[116]

CHAPTER 2

Palestine: A Twice Promised Land?

On November 2, 1917 the British government issued the Balfour Declaration, which Lord Curzon called "the Magna Carta of the Zionists," stating that, "His Majesty's Government views with favour the establishment in Palestine of a national home for the Jewish people and will use their best endeavours to facilitate the achievement of the object, it being clearly understood that nothing shall be done which may prejudice the civil and religious rights of existing non-Jewish communities in Palestine, or the rights and political status enjoyed by Jews in any other country."

From a strictly legal perspective, Arab views on the Balfour Declaration were irrelevant since the area was under Turkish rule, not Arab sovereignty. Palestine was not a separate administrative entity, and the Arabs were not a recognized body. William Ormsby-Gore, who during World War I served in Egypt and became an assistant secretary to the British Cabinet in 1917, found in Palestine and Syria a "kaleidoscope of races and creeds" with virtually no national traditions, history or sentiment.[1]

T.E. Lawrence (Lawrence of Arabia), the leading advocate of the pan-Arab cause, confirmed this assessment in 1915 when he wrote that in Syria: "There is no national feeling. Between town and town, village and village, family and family, creed and creed, exist intimate jealousies, sedulously fostered by the Turks to render spontaneous union impossible. The largest indigenous political entity in settled

Syria is only the village under its sheikh, and in patriarchal Syria the tribe under its chief...All the constitution above them is the artificial bureaucracy of the Turk...By accident and time the Arabic language has gradually permeated the country, until it is now almost the only one in use; but this does not mean that Syria—any more than Egypt is an Arabian country. On the sea coast there is little, if any, Arabic feeling or tradition; on the desert edge there is much."[2]

Before and after the British issued the Balfour Declaration, Arab nationalists consistently opposed using the name "Palestine" or "Palestinian," to distinguish themselves from other Arabs in the area. Every pronouncement from 1880 onward focused on "the unity of Syria," with no mention of Palestine other than "south Syria." The General Syrian Congress made this point in Damascus on July 2, 1919: "We ask that there should be no separation of the southern part of Syria, known as Palestine, nor of the littoral western zone which includes Lebanon, from the Syrian country. We desire that the unity of the country should be guaranteed against partition under whatever circumstances."[3]

When the First Congress of Muslim-Christian Associations met in Jerusalem in February 1919 to select Palestinian Arab representatives for the Paris Peace Conference, they adopted the following resolution: "We consider Palestine as part of Arab Syria, as it has never been separated from it at any time. We are connected with it by national, religious, linguistic, natural, economic and geographical bonds."[4]

Also in 1919, the Arab Congress met in Jerusalem to formulate an Arab Covenant stating: "[T]he Arab lands are a complete and individual whole, and the divisions of whatever nature to which they have been subjected are not approved or recognized by the Arab nation."[5]

In his testimony before the Peel Commission in 1937, Auni Bey Abdul-Hadi, a local leader asserted: "There is no such country [as Palestine]!

'Palestine' is a term the Zionists invented! There is no Palestine in the Bible. Our country was for centuries part of Syria."[6]

Haj Amin el-Husseini, the Mufti of Jerusalem and the head of the Muslim community in Palestine, initially challenged the British Mandate because it separated Palestine from Syria. For the Mufti, no difference existed between Syrian and Palestinian Arabs in terms of their distinctive national and communal characteristics. Even as late as May 1947, the representative of the Arab Higher Committee to the United Nations reminded the General Assembly "Palestine was part of the Province of Syria...Politically, the Arabs of Palestine were not independent in the sense of forming a separate political entity."[7]

The Arab Ba-ath Party, whose primary principles are secularism, socialism, and pan-Arab unity, affirmed in its constitution that the "Arabs form one nation. This nation has the natural right to live in a single, independent state and to be free to direct its own destiny," and compared the fight against colonialism to the "struggle to gather all the Arabs in a single, independent Arab state." The only mention of Palestine is as a reference to it being seized Syrian land.[8]

Ahmed ash-Shukairy, founder the Palestine Liberation Organization (P.L.O.) in 1964, readily admitted to the U.N. Security Council on May 31, 1956 "it is common knowledge that Palestine is nothing but southern Syria."[9]

Significantly, the British concurred with Arab assessments of Palestine. In a report to the Council of the League of Nations on the administration of Palestine and Trans-Jordan for the year 1938, they noted: "Palestine is not a State but is the name of a geographical area."[10]

Since Arabs were not hosts of Palestine, their approval was not needed to establish the Jewish National Home. The historian Arnold J. Toynbee believed the Zionists had "as much right to this no-man's land as the Arabs, or more."[11] Lord Robert Cecil, the Under-Secretary of State for Foreign Affairs, an original backer of the Balfour Declaration, believed that no Arab state had any justification to criticize this policy. In acknowledging the right of Jews to their national homeland, this had been "part of the terms on which the Arab State was brought into existence, subject of course, to the rights of individual Arabs being fully protected."[12]

Lord Arthur James Balfour reiterated this point by noting that it was the British who had created an independent kingdom, along the current western Saudi Arabian coast: "I hope they will remember that it is we who desire in Mesopotamia [Iraq] to prepare the way for the future of a self-governing, autonomous Arab State, and I hope that, remembering all that, they will not grudge that small notch—for it is no more than that geographically, whatever it may be historically—that small notch in what is now Arab territories being given to the people who for all these hundreds of years have been separated from it."[13]

THE GREAT ARAB REVOLT THAT NEVER WAS

While many Arabs fought with the Ottoman Empire against the British in World War I, Hussein Ibn Ali of the Hashemite family—the Sharif of Mecca—and the British agreed that he would lead an Arab revolt against the Ottoman Empire in exchange for significant areas of the disintegrating Ottoman Empire. Relations between the Sharif, a descendant of Mohammed, and Istanbul had greatly deteriorated following government centralization and a Young Turk effort to depose him.[14]

Sir Arthur Henry McMahon, British High Commissioner in Egypt, began negotiations with the Sharif after Sir Ian Hamilton, the Commander in Chief of the Mediterranean Expeditionary Force, "begged" the British Foreign Office "to take immediate action and draw the Arabs out of the war." The British launched a naval assault in the Gallipoli Peninsula on February 19, 1915 to seize Constantinople, the capital of the Ottoman Empire. After sustaining heavy losses, Hamilton sought the Foreign Office's assistance.[15]

McMahon was "a lackluster middle-aged civil servant of a legendary slowness of mind."[16] He appreciated the decision was "a purely military" one, but this brought him little comfort. He reported that a considerable number of Turkish forces at Gallipoli and practically all of the forces in Mesopotamia were Arabs. Substantial sums of money were being invested by the Germans to enlist the support of the remaining Arabs, and he questioned whether the British could provide some "guarantee of assistance in the future to justify their splitting with the Turks." The British instructed him to begin negotiations "at once and in that way" McMahon saw himself as having "started the Arab movement."[17]

Reports poured in from British officials in Egypt and Sudan documenting increasing Muslim hostility towards the British following Ottoman-British battles. They recommended that a public agreement with the Sharif would do much to dispel the notion that the British were engaging in an anti-Muslim conflict.[18]

The ultimate goal of the British officials in Khartoum and Cairo, who aggressively pushed this accord, was explained in a letter of August 26, 1915 from Sir Reginald Wingate, Governor-General of the Sudan, to Lord Hardings, then viceroy of India. The Indian Office, the government of India and others had voiced their opposition to the Sharif. Because of their unique position within the Islamic world, Wingate argued, the Arabs could counter the fear of the British in the Ottoman Empire, which would intensify at the end of the war. Wingate appreciated that creating a pan-Arab federation to counter this antagonistic pan-Islamism would not be simple, but envisaged that "a federation of semi-independent Arab states might exist under

European guidance and supervision, linked together by racial and linguistic bonds, owing spiritual allegiance to a single Arab primate, and looking to Great Britain as its patron and protector."[19]

The underlying assumption was that the Arab movement would not be as much of a threat to British interests since it was "less religious than national." The idea that nationalist movements are more benevolent and constructive than religious ones was a basic tenet of "Gladstonian Liberalism" espoused by William Ewart Gladstone, British Liberal Party statesman and Prime Minister (1868-1874, 1880-1885, 1886, 1892-1892). Such a "beguiling contrast between 'Moslem fanaticism' and nationalism was wrong in theory as it was useless in practice" insisted British historian Elie Kedourie. It introduced a creed that "served, in an incalculable and far-reaching manner, to distort and falsify the calculations of policy."[20]

The British Foreign Office and the India Office opposed any pan-Arab proposal under British patronage, and viewed the Sharif's movement as illusory. Such a scheme would be worthless, an albatross and prevent any agreement with France after the end of the war.[21]

In any event, the "Great Arab Revolt" failed to materialize in any significant way because Hussein failed to command widespread support. Many understood that Hussein was not attempting to oust the Ottomans for the good of his people, but to replace the Ottoman Empire with his own empire. In varying degrees, opposition to the Sharif was widespread. There was no popular support in the Levant. The political leadership in Syria objected to the rebellion, and a similar situation existed in Palestine, which did not have any sense of national identity. In late 1914 and early 1915 when the Turks were about to attack the Suez Canal, there were all types of parades and festivities in Palestine anticipating their victorious entry into Egypt.[22]

One day in Jaffa, a camel, a dog and a bull, adorned respectively with a Russian, French and English flag, were driven through the streets where the Arabs hit and threw waste on them to demonstrate their utter disdain for the Allies. The Reverend Dr. Otis Allan Glazebrook, the American Consul in Jerusalem, witnessed this contemptible demonstration of scapegoats with "pain and disgust."[23]

The Sharif initiated his revolt on June 1, 1916 without informing the British and without adequate preparation. He launched the attack after his duplicitous attempt to secure a separate deal with the Ottoman authorities failed. In the autumn of 1917, he came under the command of General Sir Edmund Allenby, the commander of the Egyptian Expeditionary Force. With his limited military and political support,[25] the Sharif provided such insignificant assistance that by June 1918 Sir Reginald Wingate, the high commissioner in Egypt, observed that any Arab achievements "must be attributed almost entirely to the unsparing efforts of the British and Allied officers attached to the Sherifian forces."[26]

Such was the deceit of the Arabs that on December 1, 1917, Colonel Richard Meinertzhagen, first General Allenby's Chief Political Officer and later involved in the creation of the British Mandate, recorded in his diary:

> [A] large batch of Turkish prisoners of war was being marched through the village [of Ramleh], but they were not preceded by their British Guard. The Arabs, thinking it was the return of the Turkish Army, turned out in force, yelling with delight and waving Turkish flags; it was not till the end of the column appeared and they saw British soldiers with fixed bayonets that they realized their mistake and great was their confusion.

Their faces fell with a bump and they sank disconsolate to their hovels.[24]

The British had no illusions about the danger the officers faced. As Lieutenant-Colonel W.F. Sterling explained:

> We realized that if Allenby's forces failed, we should have little or no chance of escaping...The Arabs would be sure to turn on us.

T.E. Lawrence contemptuously noted that the Arabs in Syria and Palestine would have rather have the Judean Hills stained with the blood of British soldiers than to choose sides in the war for their own independence.[27]

Meinertzhagen concurred:

> The Arabs of Palestine, far from contributing anything towards ultimate victory [during the First World War] actively opposed us and deserve no better treatment than others...And my advice to the Jews is never to lose sight of the fact that Palestine includes the area from Dan to Beersheba...[28]

Philip Graves, a correspondent for *The London Times* in the Middle East who served in the British Army from 1915-1919, was disturbed that the Arabs in Palestine, who either helped the Turks or were not involved in General Allenby's military campaign in Palestine and Syria, tried to take credit for helping the British to bolster their claim for Palestine. "Most annoying," he said, "to anyone who has served with the British forces or the Sherifian Arab forces in the Palestine campaign...are the pretensions of the Arabs in Palestine to have rendered important military services to the Allies in the Great War." The Palestinians "confined themselves to deserting in large numbers to the British, who fed and clothed and paid for the maintenance of many thousand such prisoners of war, few indeed of whom could be induced to obtain their liberty by serving in the Sherifian Army."[29]

Historian Arnold Toynbee, who served with the Intelligence department of the British Foreign Office during World War I and became Director of Studies at the Royal Institute of International Affairs (Chatham House), also took issue with the Arabs who sought to romanticize their role in defeating the Turks. "The militant peoples of Islam," he said, "obtained political concessions, out of all proportion to their military achievements." Yet they had the audacity to ascribe these military successes "to their own prowess and drew thence encouragement to continue in the same militant course" against the Allies who freed them.[30]

McMAHON-HUSSEIN CORRESPONDENCE

Arab failure to uphold their agreement with the British, and even active support of British enemies did not prevent the Arabs from attempting to claim their reward. The claim is based on the conditions of the accord reached between the Grand Sharif, who became King Hussein, and Sir Henry McMahon in 1915.

In June 1915, almost a year after the First World War began, the British still entertained the possibility of leaving the Ottoman Empire intact. By October, Hussein had persuaded McMahon that his help was critical in the conflict against the Ottoman Empire. Foreign Secretary Edward Grey directed McMahon not to obligate the British government to any territorial demands outside of the Arabian Peninsula to secure Hussein's assistance, unless it was essential: "The simplest plan would be to give assurance of Arab independence saying that we will proceed at once to discuss boundaries if they will send representatives for that purpose."[31]

Yet in a series of letters that were vague and qualified, McMahon acknowledged Hussein's request for an Arab empire. In a letter of November 5, 1915, Hussein adamantly protested that the "two *vilayets* [districts] of Aleppo and Beirut and their sea coasts are purely Arab *vilayet*," and that they be included in the empire. On December 5, McMahon pointed out that Britain's French ally had an interest in Aleppo and Beirut and that "the question will require careful consideration and further communication on the subject will be addressed to you in due course." With regard to the provinces in Mesopotamia and the *vilayet* of Baghdad, he claimed that it required "much fuller and more detailed consideration than the present situation and the urgency of these negotiations permit."[32] He continued:

> It is most essential that you should spare no effort to attach all the Arab peoples to our united cause, [and] urge them to afford no assistance to our enemies. It is on the success of these efforts and on the more active measures which the Arabs may hereafter take in support of our cause, when the time for action comes, that the permanence and strength of our agreement must depend.[33]

On January 1, 1916, Hussein responded acidly: "I do not find it necessary to draw your attention to the fact that our plan is of greater security to the interests and protection of the rights of Great Britain than it is to us, and will necessarily be so whatever may happen… Consequently, it is impossible to allow any derogation that gives France, or any other Power, a span of land in those regions." Should such a situation arise, the Arabs might be compelled "to undertake new measures which may exercise Great Britain, certainly not less than her present troubles…" With regard to "the northern parts and their coasts," Hussein was prepared to postpone his claim during the war in order not to "injure the alliance of Great Britain and France," but at the end of the conflict, he was determined to raise the issue in earnest.[34]

Rather than respond to Hussein's condescending remarks, McMahon assured him, "We take note of your remarks concerning the *vilayet* of Baghdad, and will take the question into careful consideration when the enemy has been defeated and the time for peaceful settlement arrives." Concerning...

...the northern parts, we note with satisfaction your desire to avoid anything which might possibly injure the alliance of Great Britain and France. It is, as you know, our fixed determination that nothing shall be permitted to interfere in the slightest degree with our united prosecution of this war to a victorious conclusion. Moreover, when the victory has been won, the friendship of Great Britain and France will become yet more firm and enduring, cemented by the blood of Englishmen and Frenchmen who have died side by side fighting for the cause of right and liberty.[35]

Why did McMahon appear to acquiesce to Hussein's demands in light of Grey's instructions not to commit the British government to any territorial changes before Hussein demonstrated his ability perform as promised, and in violation of an agreement signed by the Entente Powers (Great Britain, France and Russia) on September 4, 1914 to coordinate their peace terms? Historian Efraim Karsh suggests that McMahon and his superiors in London saw this correspondence as part of the process of negotiation, and not the final product of their deliberations.

A tentative thread is clear throughout the ten letters that began July 14, 1915 and ended on March 10, 1916. The British were in a fluid situation in which they were influenced by the vicissitudes of the war and by their alliance with the French. Communications between Hussein and McMahon never ended in any formal agreement, as had been the case when the British concluded accords with their other Arab allies: Sheikh Mubarak of Kuwait (1899), Abd al-Aziz Ibn Saud of Najd (1915), or Muhammad al-Idrisi of Asir (1915). There wasn't even an informal understanding except that the Sharif would enlist Arab support against the Ottoman Empire and, in return, would receive monetary, military and territorial compensation. The absence of any final and clearly defined declaration, which the British did not want in any case, caused misunderstandings, accusations and condemnations.[36]

Another explanation for McMahon's willingness to make territorial concessions was that he thought they were ambiguous enough to please the Sharif while allowing "as free a hand as possible to His Majesty's Government in the future." This point was made clear in his letter to Grey on October 4. "I have been definite enough," McMahon wrote,

> ...in stating that Great Britain will recognize the principle of Arab independence in purely Arab territory, this being the main point on which [the] agreement depends, but have been equally definite in excluding Mersina, Alexandretta and those districts on the north coast of Syria, which cannot be said to be Arab, and where I understand that French interests have been recognized. I am not aware of the extent of French claims in Syria, nor of how far His Majesty's Government have agreed to recognize them. Hence, while recognizing the towns of Damascus, Hama, Homs and Aleppo as being within the circle of Arab countries, I have endeavored to provide for possible French pretensions to those places by a general modification to the effect [that] His Majesty's Government can only give assurances in regard to those territories 'in which she can act without detriment to the interests of her ally France.[37]

More than anything else, McMahon reflected the attitude of Sir Reginald Wingate, Sir Ronald Storrs, Oriental Secretary of the British Agency in Cairo between 1907 and 1917, Sir Gilbert Clayton, head of military intelligence, and Lord Horatio Herbert Kitchener, secretary of war, who concluded that one way to ensure allied victory was to separate the Arabic speaking subjects of the Ottoman Empire from the rest of the population. Hussein was seen as the best leader to achieve this objective without jeopardizing Britain's interests in the region.[38]

Ironically, McMahon's promises of establishing an empire, which were ambiguous and a starting point for negotiations, became a source of Arab animosity toward the West. The biggest problem McMahon created was with regard to Palestine.[39]

Beginning in 1920, the British asserted that Palestine was not included in the empire because it was west of the Ottoman district of Damascus, which was to become the Emirate of Transjordan. At a meeting in London in March 1921, Faisal, Hussein's third son, claimed…

> …if His Majesty's Government relied upon the strict interpretation of the word *vilayet*, [a Turkish term for a province or main administrative division] as applied to Damascus, they must also interpret the word to mean the same with regard to Homs and Hama. There was not, and never had been, a velayet [sic] of Homs and Hama…[Hence] as the Arabic stood, it would clearly be interpreted by any Arab, and had been so interpreted by King Hussein, to refer to the four towns and their immediate surroundings. Palestine did not lie to the west of the four towns, and was therefore in his opinion, included in the area for which His Majesty's Government had given pledges to his father.[40]

Officials in Cairo and London did translate the four "districts" to mean "towns," but not in the way the Arabs have asserted. The British considered the towns to be part of the potential Arab empire in Syria, which excluded Palestine. At the meeting in London, Faisal disputed British understanding of McMahon's assurances, but indicated "he was quite prepared to accept…that it had been the original intention of His Majesty's Government to exclude Palestine."[41]

In a letter to Sir John Shuckburgh of the Middle East Division in the Colonial Office on March 12, 1922, McMahon explained, "It was my intention to exclude Palestine from independent Arabia, and I hoped that I had so worded the letter as to make this sufficiently clear for all practical purposes." Inexplicably, the British government did not use this letter to substantiate its case, and did not permit the letter to be published.[42]

The decision to restrict Arab claims to Homs, Hama, Damascus and Aleppo most likely came from Ronald Storrs. Damascus and Aleppo were not generally significant cities and Homs and Hama were provincial towns. The most plausible explanation for presenting "this odd and extraordinary proposal," was the result "of a literary reminiscence." A citation in chapter 58 of Edward Gibbon's *Decline and Fall of the Roman Empire* is probably the source: "[T]he four cities of Hems, Hamah, Damascus, and Aleppo were the only relics of the Mohammedan conquests in Syria."[43]

The only other time this rationale was found in official British documents was in a memo sent to Prime Minister David Lloyd George in February 1919 by Arnold J. Toynbee and Sir Louis Mallet, a member of the British delegation in Paris. They maintained, "during the period of the crusades...Aleppo, Hama, Homes and Damascus were never included in the boundaries of the Latin principalities..."[44] Although the memorandum was found in the papers of Lloyd George, we do not know if he used the information. It is doubtful that Toynbee or anyone else used this history to explain McMahon's letter.[45]

That the British wanted to preserve Palestine for themselves to advance their own agenda was clear, and they had no illusion that they could grant the area to anyone—especially "to a *potential junior partner*"—without creating havoc in their relations with the French and the Russians.[46] The unique position of Palestine was acknowledged by the De Bunsen Committee chaired by Sir Maurice de Bunsen, assistant Under-Secretary of State at the Foreign Office, in its report of June 30, 1915. Established to consider what the British expected to gain in "Turkey-in-Asia" should they win the war, the committee understood the need to rise above the regular pattern of power politics when it said, "Palestine must be recognized as a country whose destiny must be the subject of special negotiations, in which both belligerents and neutrals are alike interested."[47]

> I feel it is my to duty to state, and to do so definitely and emphatically, that it was not intended by me in giving this pledge to King Hussein to include Palestine in the area in which Arab independence was promised. I also had every reason to believe at the time that the fact that Palestine was not included in my pledge was well understood by King Hussein.[48]

In response to the attacks against the Jews and the Palestine Government that began in the middle of April 1936, the British Government appointed a commission to investigate how the Mandate for Palestine was being implemented, and to determine whether the grievances were legitimate. The Arabs wanted national independence and expressed their apprehension and loathing of the establishment of the Jewish National Home. In support of their argument, they referred to the McMahon-Hussein correspondence. The Commission rejected their contention, "We think it sufficient for the purposes of this Report to state that the British Government have never accepted the Arab case." When it was first formally presented by the Arab Delegation in London in 1922, the Secretary of State for the Colonies (Mr. Churchill) replied as follows:

> That letter [Sir H. McMahon's letter of the 24th October, 1915] is quoted as conveying the promise to the Sherif of Mecca to recognize and support the independence of the Arabs within the territories proposed by him. But this promise was given subject to a reservation made in the same letter, which excluded from its scope, among other territories, the portions of Syria lying to

the west of the district of Damascus. This reservation has always been regarded by His Majesty's Government as covering the *vilayet* of Beirut and the independent Sanjak of Jerusalem. The whole of Palestine west of the Jordan was thus excluded from Sir H. McMahon's pledge.

It was in the highest degree unfortunate that, in the exigencies of war, the British Government was unable to make their intention clear to the Sherif. Palestine, it will have been noticed, was not expressly mentioned in Sir Henry McMahon's letter of the 24th October 1915. Nor was any later reference made to it. In the further correspondence between Sir Henry McMahon and the Sherif the only areas relevant to the present discussion which were mentioned were the *vilayet*s of Aleppo and Beirut. The Sherif asserted that these *vilayet*s were purely Arab; and, when Sir Henry McMahon pointed out that French interests were involved, he replied that, while he did not recede from his full claims in the north, he did not wish to injure the alliance between Britain and France and would not ask 'for what we now leave to France in Beirut and its coasts' till after the War. There was no more bargaining over boundaries. It only remained for the British Government to supply the Sherif with the monthly subsidy in gold and the rifles, ammunition and foodstuffs he required for launching and sustaining the revolt.[49]

At the Anglo-Arab committee held in London in February 1939 to consider the correspondence, it was noted that the late Sir Gilbert Clayton, who was on McMahon's staff in 1915 and 1916, confirmed McMahon's claims. In 1923, Clayton said:

I was in daily touch with Sir Henry McMahon throughout the negotiations with King Hussein, and made the preliminary drafts of all· the letters. I can bear out the statement that it was never the intention that Palestine should be included in the general pledge given to the Sharif; the introductory words of Sir Henry's letter were thought at that time—perhaps erroneously—clearly to cover that point. It was, I think, obvious that the peculiar interests involved in Palestine precluded any definite pledges in regard to its future at so early a stage.[50]

Significantly, the Arabs did not dispute what McMahon claimed, but countered:

The proper basis for a judgment on the whole question is primarily the text of the Correspondence itself. The fact that, in a letter published in *The Times*...Sir Henry McMahon declared it as having been his intention to exclude Palestine from the area of Arab independence ought not to be given more weight than it deserves...That which Sir Henry said he intended to mean is of no consequence whatever, for it was not he who was giving the pledge but His Majesty's Government, whose instrument he was. That which matters is what Sir Henry McMahon actually said, not what he may have intended, nor what Sir Gilbert Clayton may have thought he intended.[51]

Legally this might have had some justification, but McMahon had exceeded his authority by obligating the British government to policies it did not sanction. Therefore, McMahon was in position to know precisely what he meant, and when he mentioned the four towns he knew they constituted all the territory of the Arab empire in Syria—and nothing else.[52]

The British Lord Chancellor also responded to the Arab arguments made at the London conference, noting that the British would not have included Palestine in any agreement for a number of reasons. First, there was concern with respect to "French interests" which were "meant to apply to all territory, including what is now called Palestine, to which the claims of France extended at the time." The

British were bound by Article LXII of the Treaty of Berlin to ensure that "the rights of France were expressly reserved."[53]

Britain also "was not free to make promises about Palestine in the autumn of 1915," because interest in Palestine played an important part in "almost all the countries in the world," and these concerns…

> …had to be taken into account…Palestine was in a very special position at the time of the Correspondence having in view its position as the Holy Land of three great religions, the interest which it held for Christians, as well as for Moslems and Jews, all over the world, the large number of religious and other buildings and institutions belonging to non-Arab persons, and the obvious practical interests of Great Britain in a territory so close to Egypt and the Suez Canal. The United Kingdom representatives also contend that Palestine was not a purely Arab country.[54]

The Lord Chancellor further pointed out that he did not wish to suggest, "that Palestine was excluded from the area of Arab independence merely because it was not mentioned," in the Hussein-McMahon correspondence, even though this argument was not advanced "either before the Royal Commission or anywhere else." A "fair construction of the Correspondence which takes into account the circumstances in which its language was used Palestine was in fact excluded," he said, "even though it was not mentioned." In other words, he maintained, "that the Correspondence as a whole and particularly the reservation in respect of French interests in Sir Henry McMahon's letter of the 24th October, 1915, not only did exclude Palestine, but should have been understood to do so, having in view the unique position of Palestine."[55]

With regard to the referenced Holy Places, the Lord Chancellor maintained,

...that the phrase 'Holy Places' as used in the Correspondence meant and was taken to mean the Holy Places of Mecca and Medina. But assuming that the phrase covered Jerusalem and the other Holy Places of Palestine, the fact that Great Britain might have been willing to protect the Holy Places of Palestine against external aggression did not mean or contain an implication that she or other Christian peoples thereby acquired any rights in regard to those Holy Places. It is exceedingly improbable, to say the least, that Great Britain would have accepted this liability without a clear understanding as to these rights.[56]

This view was "forcibly stated in a speech" in the House of Lords on June 27, 1923 by Lord Alfred Milner, a self-declared, ardent supporter of pro-Arab policy and of Arab independence, who thought the Arabs were making a "fatal mistake" in claiming Palestine as part of the Arab Federation. In 1923, Milner said that:

Palestine can never be regarded as a country on the same footing as the other Arab countries. You cannot ignore all history and tradition in the matter. You cannot ignore the fact that this is the cradle of two of the great religions of the world. It is a sacred land to the Arabs, but it is also a sacred land to the Jews and the Christian; and the future of Palestine cannot possibly be left to be determined by the temporary impressions and feelings of the Arab majority in the country of the present day.

At the same time, he also opposed complete control of the area by the Jews.[57]

The Lord Chancellor said that with regard to...

...the term *Syria* [which] in those days was generally used to denote the whole of geographical and historic Syria, that is to say the whole of the country lying between the Taurus Mountains and the Sinai Peninsula, which was made up of part of the *Vilayet* of Aleppo, the *Vilayet* of Bairut, the *Vilayet* of Syria, the *Sanjaq* of the Lebanon, and the *Sanjaq* of Jerusalem. It included that part of the country which was afterwards detached from it to form the mandated territory of Palestine.[58]

Even though the British understood that Syria was a "French preserve," some British officials discussed the possibility that if the Ottoman Empire collapsed, an attempt should be made to separate "southern Syria as far north as Haifa and Acre to form a separate entity and to fall under British influence." Lord Kitchener became a strong proponent of this view and promoted it among British officials before the First World War. In 1913, he "instigated" a military survey of the Sinai Peninsula that confirmed his belief "that southern Syria up to Haifa and Acre and down to the Gulf of Aqaba would be, on political and strategic grounds, an indispensable asset to the British Empire in the event of a break-up of the Ottoman Empire."[59]

According to the Lord Chancellor, when Hussein sent his first note to McMahon in July 1915, the British Government had already received the recommendations of the committee about the advisability of distinguishing between northern Syria and southern Syria with regard to French claims to the whole country. "The reservations" expressed by McMahon in his note of October, 24, 1915, must, therefore, be seen in view of the prevalent attitude in Whitehall at that time.

Throughout the correspondence McMahon is at pains to explain to the Sharif that the only portions of Syria which Great Britain wished to exclude from the area of Arab independence were those portions in which Great Britain felt that she was not free to act "without detriment to the interests of her ally, France."

This same qualification is expressed in different wording by Sir Henry McMahon in his note of the 14th December 1915, when he says that…

...with regard to the *Vilayet*s of Aleppo and Bairut, the Government of Great Britain have taken careful note of your observations, but, as the interests of our ally, France, are involved, the question will require careful consideration and a further communication on the subject will be addressed to you in due course.

Similarly, the Sharif, throughout the Correspondence, is clearly under the impression that the only portions of Syria in question are those of the northern coastal regions of Syria, meaning Lebanon and its seaboard, which he understands Great Britain to wish to reserve solely because of French claims. Southern Syria (i.e., Palestine) could not have formed part of the reserved territories because Great Britain, far from wishing it to be included in the area of French influence, wanted it to be included in the area of Arab independence, that is to say, within the sphere of future British influence.[60]

The assurances given by General Sir Edmund Allenby to Amir Faisal ibn Husseini, the Sharif's son, should also be clarified. On October 19, 1918, the general reported to His Majesty's Government a communication that he made to the Amir Faisal:

I gave the Amir Faisal an official assurance that whatever measures might be taken during the period of military administration they were purely provisional and could not be allowed to prejudice the final settlement by the peace conference, at which no doubt the Arabs would have a representative. I added that the instructions to the military governors would preclude their mixing in political affairs, and that I should remove them if I found any of them contravening these orders. I reminded the Amir Faisal that the Allies were in honour bound to endeavour to reach a settlement in accordance with the wishes of the peoples concerned and urged him to place his trust whole-heartedly in their good faith.[61]

Had British officials taken Allenby's approach, a number of misunderstandings might have been avoided. Their "reckless proclamations," were made because they did not believe their expressions would be taken literally, but "were at best only a kind of metaphor." An undated note by Ronald Storrs to McMahon attached to a telegram of May 14, 1915 probably in response to an Arabic leaflet received in Cairo illustrates this point:

> The expression 'Arab Empire,' 'Government,' 'Possessions,' etc., is used throughout the Sherifial correspondence, on both sides, in a general and undefined sense and is variously rendered by the words Hukuma (Government) Mamlaka (Possessions) and Dawla (Power, Dynasty, Kingdom). Neither from these terms, nor from any phrase employed by H.M.G. throughout the negotiations, is it possible to elaborate any theory as to the precise nature of this vaguely adumbrated body.[62]

Inexplicably, they did not consider how their words might be interpreted, the effect they might have, or that they could be accepted literally.[63]

BRITISH SUPPORT FOR A JEWISH HOMELAND

Why did the British support the establishment of a Jewish state? In 1908, Winston Churchill, then Colonial Under-Secretary, concluded:

> The establishment of a strong, free Jewish State astride the bridge between Europe and Africa, flanking the land roads to the East, would not only be an immense advantage to the British Empire, but a notable step towards a harmonious disposition of the world among its peoples.[64]

Support for Zionism provided the British with a legitimate and respectable justification to be in Palestine where they could pursue their interests in the Middle East. Unquestionably, sympathy toward Zionism was consistent with British compassion for subjugated and oppressed peoples, but the official records show that emotion did not dictate state policy. Had the British Foreign Office and the War Cabinet determined that the Balfour Declaration would not serve British interests, it never would have been promulgated. A confluence of reasons led to the decision, the most important of which was the desire to enlist the support of the world Jewish community— especially Russian and American Jews—toward Britain and the Allies during World War I.[65]

At the beginning of 1917, the British were faced with a number of urgent military concerns. General Archibald Murray's advance into Gaza was halted, heavy losses were sustained at the Western Front, the French military had mutinied, Russian Tsar Nicholas II had abdicated, and the Allies sustained heavy shipping loses in the Atlantic as a result of U-boat attacks. The British hoped their backing might accelerate America's entry into the war and delay Russia's departure. Furthermore, Jewish intelligence services in Palestine might be enlisted to assist General Allenby in resisting the Turks.[66]

British determination to secure Jewish support through the Balfour Declaration was also based on the belief that Jews were basically unified, yielded power, were pro-German, and a major influence in pacifist and revolutionary circles in Russia.[67] On October 31, 1917, Balfour concluded that:

> [F]rom a purely diplomatic and political point of view, it was desirable that some declaration favourable to the aspirations of the Jewish nationalists should now be made. The vast majority of Jews in Russia and America, as indeed, all over the world, now appeared to be favourable to Zionism. If we could make a

declaration favourable to such an ideal, we should be able to carry on extremely useful propaganda both in Russia and America.[68]

Winston Churchill, then Colonial Secretary and cabinet minister responsible for Palestine, reiterated this point in responding to attacks against the Balfour Declaration in the House of Commons on July 4, 1922. He acknowledged that the "pledges and promises" made during the War had been given "because it was considered that the support which Jews could give us all over the world, and particularly in the United States, and also in Russia, would be a definite palpable advantage."[69]

After 1917, Balfour often spoke about Zionism publicly. Sometimes he attributed a religious motivation to his decision to support the declaration, but never emphasized it. He expected the movement to solve the problems causing antisemitism. As he noted on September 20, 1918…

> "Zionism differs in kind from ordinary philanthropic efforts and it appeals to different motives. If it succeeds, it will do a great spiritual and material work for the Jews, but not for them alone… It is among other things, a serious endeavor to mitigate the age-long miseries created for Western civilization by the presence in its midst of a Body which is too long regarded as alien and even hostile, but which it was equally unable to expel or absorb."[70]

At a private luncheon on February 7, 1918, Colonel Richard Meinertzhagen asked Balfour whether the Declaration was given as "reward or bribe to the Jews for past services and given in the hope of full support during the war." Balfour responded, "Certainly not; both the Prime Minister [Lloyd George] and myself have been influenced by a desire to give the Jews their rightful place in the world; a great nation without a home is not right."

Was this then a "charter for ultimate Jewish sovereignty in Palestine or are you trying to graft a Jewish population on to an Arab Palestine," Meinertzhagen asked. After reflecting for a while, Balfour replied, "My personal hope is that the Jews will make good in Palestine and eventually found a Jewish State. It is up to them now; we have given them their great opportunity."[71]

In mid-July 1917, Balfour was prepared to inform the Zionists that he would designate Palestine as "the national home of the Jewish people," except that leading British Jews, particularly Edwin Montagu, then Secretary of State for India, feared this might endanger the position of the Jews in England. It would harm Britain's relationship with other religious and nationalist groups, especially the Arabs. This angst caused a delay in the decision throughout August and September.[72]

Leopold Amery, a Conservative MP, who was Prime Minister Lloyd George's political appointee to the War Cabinet secretariat and a dedicated Zionist, rejected Jewish concerns. Once there is a national home, he asserted, English Jews would have nothing more to fear:

> The Jews alone can build up a strong civilization in Palestine which could help that country to hold its own against German-Turkish oppression; and by enlisting their interest on our side in this country, we will gain a great deal. It would be a fatal thing if after the war, the interest of the Jews throughout the world were enlisted on the side of the Germans, and they looked to Berlin as their spiritual home.[73]

"The ultimate end," of British support, as Amery noted in his diary on July 26, 1928...

> ...is to make Palestine the centre of a western influence, using Jews as we have used the Scots, to carry English ideal through the Middle East and not merely to make an artificial oriental Hebrew enclave in oriental country. Secondly that we meant Palestine

in some way or other to remain within the framework of the British Empire...[74]

To those who claim that the authors of the Balfour Declaration were oblivious to the hundreds of thousands of Arabs living in Palestine, Amery countered that the historic document "was not issued in haste or lightheartedly. It was not a sudden happy thought, a piece of propaganda, meant to win the support of American or Russian Jewry; still less was it issued in ignorance of the facts of the case in Palestine." All pertinent information and issues that might or would arise "from the natural reaction of a primitive population in contact with a new element, separated from it even more by centuries of development than by race and religion—all those aspects were canvassed for many months and were fully understood."

Authors of the Balfour Declaration viewed the looming dissolution of the Ottoman Empire as a singular opportunity "which could never recur for contributing to the solution of that baffling and tragic problem," the fate of the Jewish people.[75]

SELF-DETERMINATION

In a letter of February 19, 1919, to Prime Minister Lloyd George, Balfour acknowledged Britain's "weak position" with regard to the issue of self-determination for Palestine, but justified the policy because Palestine was "absolutely exceptional," and considered the "question of the Jews outside Palestine as one of world importance." The British also considered the Jews "to have an historic claim to a home in their ancient land; provided that home can be given them without either dispossessing or oppressing the present inhabitants."[76]

On July 30, 1919, Balfour explained to Colonel Meinertzhagen that it might appear difficult to reconcile Zionism with the principle of self-rule, but suggested that "the creed of self-determination...could not be indiscriminately applied to the whole world, and Palestine was a case in point and a most exceptional one." In any plebiscite on Palestine, the issue would be discussed with world Jewry. Balfour was convinced that "an overwhelming majority would declare for Zionism under a British Mandate." Once the Arabs understood the British were determined that "Palestine be the National Home of the Jews...Arab opposition would therefore be futile and would not be tolerated."[77]

In a speech in Parliament on November 17, 1919, Balfour made it clear that the Jews had the better claim to Palestine:

> The four great powers are committed to Zionism. And Zionism, be it right or wrong, good or bad, is rooted in age-long traditions, in present needs, in future hopes, of far profounder import than the desires and prejudices of the 700,000 Arabs who now inhabit that ancient land...[78]

Arnold Toynbee argued that the principle of self-determination was not relevant in this case and also in Armenia, since there would be a mixed population with the Jews being one group that "for special reasons, will be entitled to a position more than mathematically proportionate to its numbers at the start." For this and a number of other reasons, "the desires of inhabitants, or of the several sections of them, will have to some extent, to take second place."[79]

In addition to an indisputable historical claim to the land, Churchill underscored the presence of Jews in Palestine before "the great hordes of Islam" invaded the area and "broke it all up, smashed it all up." The hills that were once cultivated, now languished under Arab rule and reverted back to a desert. For 1,200 years, Palestine remained a wasteland where Arabs "lived fairly easily in a flat squalor typical of pre-war Turkish Empire provinces." For having failed to advance human civilization in the area, the Arabs had forfeited their right to rule the land.[80]

He emphasized this point again in the House of Commons after being criticized for granting Jewish engineer Pinhas Rutenberg the concession to harness the waters of the Jordan and Auja rivers for electrical power. His critics claimed that the Arab majority had the responsibility to produce economic prosperity in Palestine. He replied:

> I am told that the Arabs would have done it themselves. Who is going to believe that? Left to themselves, the Arabs of Palestine would not in a thousand years have taken the effective steps towards the irrigation of and electrification of Palestine. They would have been quite content to dwell—a handful of philosophic people—in the wasted sun-scorched plains, letting the waters of the Jordan continue to flow unbridled and unharnessed into the Dead Sea.[81]

Philip Graves questioned whether the agreement with Rutenberg should have be made without putting it up for public bidding, but dismissed the notion that Arabs had the "capital and the brains for such an [ambitious] undertaking." Had the Arabs "possessed ability of this sort," he said, "they would long have been the independent masters of the Near East." Without Jewish support "can the Arabs play any worthy part in the modern world?"[82]

The British had the authority to determine the future of the region, Churchill asserted, for the British army had liberated the Arabs from the Turks. "The position of Great Britain in Palestine is one of trust, but it is also one of right," Churchill said. "...Supreme sacrifices were made by all these soldiers in the British empire, who gave up their lives and blood." Their graveyards were scattered throughout the land. More than 2,000 were buried in one graveyard on the road to Government House in Jerusalem.[83] Meinertzhagen added that by the end of the Second World War, all of Asia and Europe including Britain, had sacrificed considerably, while the Arabs had not. During both World Wars, the Arabs had "gained everything and contributed nothing..." "Why," he asked, "should not the Arabs give up something to suffering humanity? Palestine is but a small part of the Arab countries. On the other hand the Jews have contributed a great deal during both wars and have suffered more than any other nation. It is gross injustice that they should be refused a home which once was theirs. This simple act of justice is held up for fear of the Arabs and hatred of the Jews. A policy of fear leads nowhere; it is no policy."[84] [By the end of August 1944, there were 25,825 Jewish volunteers from Palestine in the British defense forces, including 4,000 women, while there were only 9,200 Arabs.[85]]

To those who suggested that Jews immigrate to countries other than Palestine, Churchill responded: "Zionism without Zion is nothing at all. The Jews want a Home, not an Apartment."[86]

CHAPTER 3

Arabs Resort to Violence

ARAB PROTESTS AGAINST THE BALFOUR DECLARATION AND JEWISH IMMIGRATION

When Arabs protested against the Balfour Declaration in 1921, Sir Herbert Samuel responded that Jews were expected to immigrate to Palestine within certain fixed limits "to help with their resources and efforts to develop the country, to the advantage of all its inhabitants."[1]

Jewish immigration, Winston Churchill assured them, was being monitored with regard to the numbers and character of the people. The country was "greatly under-populated," which allowed for more people to build a life there. The work already accomplished by the Jews during the last 20 to 30 years could not be "brutally and rudely overturned by fanatical attacks of the Arab population" launched against Jews in Jaffa, Rehovot, Petach Tikva and other Jewish areas in May 1921.[2]

Despite its initial pro-Zionist orientation, the British government gradually "whittled down" the Balfour Declaration, reflecting the hostility towards Zionism of many in the government. By 1921, immigration had practically ceased, the "bulk" of the British officers in Palestine were not sympathetic to Zionism, and the Zionists were not receiving the concessions needed to establish a national Jewish homeland. Public hostility in Britain, Meinertzhagen thought, was a result of the failure to understand the purpose of Zionism, fear of its potential financial cost, and a general antisemitic British temperament that quickly translated into anti-Zionism.[3]

In order to pressure the British to end Jewish immigration, anti-Zionist riots broke out in Palestine in 1920-1921, killing a number of Jews. In April 1920, during a religious festival (al-Nebi Musa) in Jerusalem, a large number of Arabs, led by the Mufti, attacked Jews in the Old City. On May 1, 1921, there was a riot in Jaffa, after which the Arabs attacked Jews in Petah Tikvah and Hadera, pillaging and destroying a significant amount of property. The disturbances, which shocked the Jews and the British, lasted several days and demonstrated the Arabs' fierce opposition to continued Jewish immigration into the country,[4] and their insistence on remaining part of Syria.[5]

In view of the intensity of the attacks during which 88 people were killed and 238 injured, Sir Herbert Samuel, the Jewish first High Commissioner in Palestine,[6] brought in the army to quell the disturbances. Many were arrested and heavy fines were levied against Arab villages involved in the riots. However, he also sought to ease Arab hostility and insisted that the Zionists demonstrate no ill-will toward the Arabs. This had to be done through economic development and by making conciliatory declarations that would assuage Arab fears of Jewish immigration and Jewish political dominance. "Unless there [was] very careful steering, it [was] upon the Arab rock that the Zionist ship may be wrecked," Samuel concluded.[7]

Another response to the riot was a meeting at the Colonial Office in London on November 29, 1921, arranged between Dr. Chaim Weizmann and members of the Arab Delegation from Palestine. This meeting, and others, ended in failure as the two groups were unable to reconcile their differences about the proposed Mandate and the future structure of Palestine.[8]

Jews saw Samuel's capitulation to violence as appeasement and proof that their criticism of the British administration in Palestine and their disillusionment with the British were justified. Samuel further alienated the Jews of Palestine on June 3, 1921, in his first major address after the riots. Samuel tried to assure the Muslim and Christian inhabitants that he would implement whatever measures required to prove that their rights were "really safe." The British Government, he said, which is the "trustee under the Mandate for the happiness of the people of Palestine, would never impose on them a policy which that people had reason to think was contrary to their religious, their political, and their economic interests."[9]

Chaim Weizmann had no illusions about Samuel. "He is meek and mild and timid. Still he is, with all that, the best we can have in the circumstances."[10]

The Jewish press, however, reflected the community's anger toward the British, and their profound concern that these riots were similar to the ones they had experienced in Russia. Berl Katznelson, a leading figure of the Zionist labor movement, declared, "The pogrom against Israel in Eretz Israel is still continuing." Ben-Gurion concurred: "We who experienced the pogroms knew quite well that without the wish of the authorities and their open or clandestine backing, actively or passively, the task of the pogrom cannot succeed."[11]

When the riots occurred in 1921, Samuel held the Jews responsible and brought them to trial. The British claimed this was a clash between communist and anti-communist Jewish demonstrators on May Day, which the Jews dismissed as absurd.

The British also sought to obscure the fact that the Arabs had been the sole aggressors. Arab policemen involved in the riots were not punished, while Jews attempting to defend themselves were arrested when they harmed their assailants. Stolen property was not returned, and those who killed Jews were not tried. Jewish immigration was halted, and those caught trying to enter the country were sent back to their ports of origin. This was another example of where the British encouraged the oppressors, rewarded violence and penalized the victims.[12]

British reaction reminded Jews of the Russian government's response to pogroms. First, the British took their time in responding to the al-Nebi Musa riots, and behaved with a combination of apathy and "criminal neglect." Then they arrested Ze'ev Jabotinsky, the Zionist activist, and his men who were attempting to organize their own self-defense in Jerusalem. Jabotinsky had established the Jewish Legion under British auspices during World War I. At the end of the riots, the British tried to reduce tensions by prohibiting the Jews from holding a public funeral for the victims. Most of the rioters were not tried, whereas when Jews were apprehended with weapons they were given substantial sentences. Eventually, the convictions were rescinded, but in the context of a general amnesty for the rioters and the Jews. This prompted Berl Katznelson to refer to the Jewish victims by the ancient Hebrew idiom *harugei malkhut* (those slain by the government), a term used for the Ten Martyrs who were tortured and executed by the Romans.[13]

ARABS TAKE THEIR CASE TO THE BRITISH IN LONDON

While Arab leaders fomented attacks in Palestine against the Zionists, other leaders went to London to protest the Balfour Declaration. On August 12, 1921, the Palestinian Arab Deputation, a delegation of Palestinian Arabs, met with the top officials in the British government to protest against the Balfour Declaration and issued the Colonial Office a memorandum listing their demands. Their first was to establish a National Government, accountable to a Parliament elected by those living in Palestine before World War I. Their second was for the British to renounce the idea of a homeland for the Jewish people in Palestine, since this would endanger their survival as a nation. Their third goal was to end Jewish immigration until after a National Government was established. Their other demands included abolishing all laws enacted by the British and for Palestine to become part of the other Arab states in the region under "one confederated government."[14]

Three days after receiving the memorandum, Winston Churchill, then Colonial Secretary and cabinet minister responsible for Palestine, met with members of the delegation. The Arabs vehemently protested against the Balfour Declaration, were disturbed that Jews were being employed in the British administration in Palestine, and angry that Hebrew was one of the three official languages sanctioned by the Mandatory authorities. Churchill responded that the Jews "are to be encouraged to go to Palestine and found there a home for themselves...in proportion as there is room, and there is good livelihood, provided of course they develop the resources of the country."[15]

On August 22, 1921, the Arab Deputation again met Churchill where he reassured them that the Jews would not be allowed to...

> ...take any man's lands. They cannot dispossess any man of his rights or his property or interfere with him in any way. If they like to buy people's land, and people like to sell it to them, and if they like to develop and cultivate regions now barren and make them fertile, then they have the right, and we are obliged to secure their right to come into the country and to settle.[16]

The British Government, he continued, "wants to see Jews developing and fertilizing the country and increasing population of Palestine." It was "a pity" so few people lived in Palestine, since once it had been "three or four times" more populated. Churchill wanted to see an increase in prosperity in Palestine "instead of it being occupied by a few people who were not making great use of it." The British were determined to allow more Jews to enter, and expected the Arabs to accept this fact.[17]

Before the end of the meeting Churchill asked why couldn't they live together in peace and develop the country in harmony since there was room for all. "The Jews," he said "are a very numerous people and they are scattered all over the world. This is a country where they have historic traditions, and you cannot brush that aside as though it were absolutely nothing. They were there many hundreds of years ago. They have always tried to be there. They have done a great deal for the country..." He then pointed out that this is "a sacred place..." for Jews. Many "go there to be buried in the city which they regard as sacred—as you regard it as sacred."[18] If the Jews had come after the land had been developed and an infrastructure had been in place, the Arabs "would have reason to complain..." but this was not the case. "Give the Jews their chance," he urged.[19]

In a letter of June 22, 1922, the British government provided further clarification regarding their position on the Jewish community in Palestine:

> When it is asked what is meant by the development of the Jewish National Home in Palestine, it may be answered that it is not the imposition of a Jewish nationality upon the inhabitants as a whole, but further development of the existing Jewish community; with the assistance of Jews in other parts of the world, in order that it may become a centre in which the Jewish people as a whole may take, on grounds of religion and race, an interest and a pride. But in order that this community should have the best prospect of free development and provide a full opportunity for the Jewish people to display its capacities, it is essential that it should know that it is in Palestine as of right and not on sufferance. That is the

reason why it is necessary that the existence of a Jewish National Home in Palestine should be internationally guaranteed, and that it should be formally recognized to rest upon ancient historic connection.

...For the fulfillment of this policy it is necessary that the Jewish community in Palestine should be able to increase its numbers by immigration. The number of immigrants should not exceed the economic capacity of the country. No section of the population should be deprived of employment.[20]

Churchill was disappointed with the Delegation for not wanting to discuss the provision in the draft constitution that would have established "some permanent machinery" to preserve the rights and interests of the non-Jewish population.[21]

The Arabs replied that increased tensions were warranted because...

...immigrants being dumped upon the country from different parts of the world are ignorant of the language, customs, and character of the Arabs, and enter Palestine by the might of England against the will of the people who are convinced that these have come to strangle them. Nature does not allow the creation of a spirit of co-operation between peoples so different, and it is not to be expected that the Arabs would bow to such a great injustice, or that the Zionists would so easily succeed in realising their dreams.[22]

In a cabinet memorandum in March 1928, Balfour stated that the British had a strategic and political interest in being in Palestine—to protect the security of the Suez Canal, "the jugular vein of the British Empire"—and guarantee access to the East. The British wanted to remain in Palestine and have a presence in Egypt, which it occupied in 1882, in order to thwart French designs in Syria and Lebanon, and prevent them from moving south and establishing a "land bridge" to the oil fields in Iraq. Egypt was declared a British protectorate on December 18, 1914.[23]

Arthur Ruppin, a German-Jewish lawyer and sociologist who had been sent by the Jewish Agency to Palestine in 1907 to evaluate the feasibility of Zionist settlement in the country had serious reservations about the compatibility of the Arabs and Jews. Ruppin eventually became head of the newly created Palestine Zionist Organization. He wrote in his diary of December 31, 1924:

> What continually worries me is the relationship between the Jews and the Arabs in Palestine. Superficially, it has improved, inasmuch as there is no danger of pogroms, but the two peoples have become more estranged in their thinking. Neither has any understanding of the other, and yet I have no doubt whatsoever that Zionism will end in a catastrophe if we do not succeed in finding a common platform.[24]

RESORT TO FORCE

By resorting to force, the Arabs had hoped to influence British policy "by making that policy impossible," observed Meinertzhagen.[25] The Arabs were determined to stop Jewish immigration, and used the anti-Jewish riots in Jaffa of May 1, 1921 to "demonstrate the futility and unfairness" of the Zionist movement and its "inevitable" demise. After the riots, Sir Herbert Samuel seemed "hypnotized by the danger and everything was done to placate the Arab. Immigration was stopped, elective assemblies were discussed, whereas what the Arab wanted was a good sound punishment for breaking the peace and killing Jews." This appeasement did not go unnoticed: "The Arab is fast learning that he can intimidate a British Administration. Samuel has not been able to stand up to the solid block of anti-Zionist feeling among his military advisers and civil subordinates."[26]

According to Meinertzhagen, Muslims had been warned in mid-April 1920 not to introduce politics into religious rituals and ceremonies,[27] but instead they exploited the religious emotions of the general population to incite riots, domestic dissension, and protests—all simple to orchestrate. The Mufti exacerbated the religious tensions when he warned that the Jews posed a serious threat to the Muslim Holy Places, especially the Haram-el-Sherif—The Temple Mount—on Mount Moriah. The ultimate aim of the Zionists, he claimed, was for the Jews to gain control over the entire Temple compound and other Muslim Holy places, and expel the Arabs from Palestine. The Jews would then be the sole power in the country.[28]

In 1922, there had been considerable controversy among Jews and Arabs about whether benches were permitted to accommodate Jews at the Western Wall in Jerusalem, which was Muslim Wakf (endowments) property. In 1918, the Zionists had tried to buy the property, causing "much unrest and resentment" among the Muslims. In an effort to raise funds for the *Yishuv*, the Zionist Commission issued a number of stamps, including one that had a picture of the Wall and surrounding area on it, with the implication that this would be the first property to be "reoccupied" by Jews. During the Turkish regime, benches and seats were officially forbidden to prevent Jews from establishing any right to the area, but the prohibition was ignored. Even before the British arrived, Jews began paying the neighboring Muslims a fee to allow benches to be set up in the area. Resolving the question of the benches was important, the British believed, because it was "apt to raise passions to a dangerous height." Strident articles in the Arab and *Yishuv* press showed how volatile the issue had become.[29]

As the British noted, "The initial difficulty" was "that for centuries past Jews had carried on the practice of praying at this place which, from the point of view of ownership, belonged to Moslems, not to private Moslem owners but to Moslem ecclesiastical or pious foundations."[30]

On October 8, 1928, the Mufti sent a memorandum to the Palestine Government accusing the Jews of trying to "take control of the Mosque of Al-Aqsa, called Al-Burak or to raise claims over that place." When the Jews erected a canvas screen at the Western Wall on September 28 on the eve of Yom Kippur (the Day of Atonement) to separate men from the women during prayers, the Mufti claimed the Jews were trying to "take possession of the Mosque of Al-Aqsa gradually." Keith-Roach, the District Commissioner for Jerusalem, personally went to the Wall to order the screen removed and gave the Jews overnight to comply. He then went to the Churva Synagogue in Jerusalem's Old City to confer with Norman Bentwich, the first Attorney-General of Mandatory Palestine (1918-1929).[31]

Despite pleas from Bentwich that night, and a rabbinical delegation the next morning, that nothing be done until after the fast, Keith-Roach ordered a British police officer to forcibly remove the screen, which he did during *Neilah*, the final service of Yom Kippur.[32]

Jews in Palestine and throughout the world were incensed with this attempt to interfere with their right to pray at the Wall. At the 16th Zionist Congress, held in Zurich from July 28th to August 11th 1929, delegates passed a resolution describing this intrusion as "an indignity" and "a sacrilege."[33] In its petition to the League of Nations, the Zionist Organization renounced the malicious rumors that Jews were trying to take control of the Wall. They pointed out that the Muslims were permitted to station the muezzin in the area to call their people to prayer five times a day, to play music, construct new buildings, re-establish the Zikr religious ceremony and wander around the Wall with their domestic animals while Jews were praying. The disturbances were seen as a deliberate attempt to annoy the Jews and stir "up enmity and dispute between two sister nations. This can only bring misfortune upon both sides, and can profit neither."[34]

After his assistant inspected the Wall, Ronald Storrs, the Military Governor of Jerusalem, concluded that the repairs to the *Waqf* buildings and the wall below were imperative, but that when done during the hours of prayer, fragments would drop on the heads of the worshippers below. He ordered that no work be permitted on Friday and Saturday, and limited the *Waqf* to repairing only the upper portion of the Wall, which provoked an angry protest from the Mufti.[35]

The *Vaad Leumi* (General Council of the *Yishuv*) reiterated Jewish outrage at the false charges made against the community and publicly declared "emphatically and sincerely" that Jews would not think of "encroaching upon the rights of Moslems over their Holy Places." At the same time, the Arabs should recognize "the rights of Jews" with regard to places "holy to them." The *Vaad* asked that "the poisonous clouds of the false rumors" be "dispersed," and urged that a climate of "constructive cooperation" be created instead.[36] Lt. Colonel Frederick H. Kisch, a member of the Palestine Zionist executive and director of the Political Department, remarked, "If there was a spark of real religious feeling among the Moslem leaders they would not object to seats being provided for the old people who constitute most of the worshippers."[37]

Rather than accept this conciliatory offer of the *Vaad Leumi*, Arab leaders tried to exacerbate the tensions. At the General Muslim Conference on November 1, 1928, held under the presidency of the Mufti of Jerusalem, the Mufti urged limits be placed on Jewish worship at the Wall. In a resolution, a copy of which was sent to the League of Nations, the Conference strongly "protested any actions or attempt which aims at the establishment of any right to the Jews in the Holy Burak area and to deprecate any such action or attempt." They asked the British...

...to immediately and perpetually to prevent the Jews from placing under any circumstances whether temporary or permanent any objects in the area, such as seats, lamps, objects of worship or reading, and to prevent them also from raising their voices or making any speeches, in such a manner as would not compel the Moslems to take such measures themselves, in order to defend at any cost this holy Moslem place and to safeguard their established rights...[38]

On August 14, 1929, the eve of Tisha B'Av, the day Jews commemorate the destruction of the First and Second Temples, 6,000 members of the Haganah and Betar (Ze'ev Jabotinsky's Revisionist Jewish defense forces) demonstrated in Tel-Aviv. At the rally, a resolution was passed condemning the "Wailing Wall outrage," demanding the dismissal of officials of the Palestine Administration who wanted to thwart the creation of the Jewish state, and insisting that the British Government "restore to us our full rights on the Wall." At the end of the rally, Jewish flags covered with black ribbons were displayed.[39]

The next day, about 300 demonstrators marched to the Wall, passing through the Muslim quarters of the Old City. Upon arrival at the Western Wall, they unfurled the Zionist flag, read a political speech, had two-minutes of silence and sang *Hatikva*, the Jewish national anthem. Individuals who joined the demonstration shouted, "The Wall is ours," "Shame on the Government," and "Shame on those who profane our Holy Places." The procession occurred without incident.[40]

Having technically violated rules set forth by the British concerning the unfurling of flags and marching in military formation, the Jews had opened themselves to attack. Muslim leaders exploited the peaceful demonstration by claiming it was an affront to the Muslims, and organized a counter-protest for the following day. In the early afternoon on August 16, "a crowd of some two thousand fanatical

Moslems rushing down a narrow lane into the narrow passage before the Wall," almost reached their destination, but stayed within the prescribed area. There were agitated cries of "there is no God, but God, the religion of Mohammed came with the sword."[41]

At the Wall, Hassan Abou Seoud, one of the Sheikhs of the Mosque of Aqsa, delivered...

> ...an inflammatory speech, a table belonging to the Shammas or Jewish beadle was upset and broken, petitions which had been placed in the crevices of the Wailing Wall by Jewish worshippers were taken out and burnt by the crowd, as were also some prayer books and prayer-sheets. The Shammas, who was said to have been the only Jew at the Wall, was hustled and his clothes were torn.[42]

After this disturbance, the British took a number of precautionary measures to prevent and be better prepared for further episodes. The Jews were asked to refrain from publishing articles in the Hebrew Press about the incident that might provoke Jewish public opinion. On August 18 the British installed a telephone not far from the Wall, so the police could be alerted to any imminent strife. Arabs were instructed to lock the door between the house that had been converted into the *Zawiyah* (literally, sacred corner), and the pavement allowing access from the Haram-el-Sherif to the Wall.[43]

Tensions remained high. On August 17, a Jewish boy was stabbed after he retrieved an errant ball in an Arab garden. A melee ensued, wounding 15 Arabs and 11 Jews. Within the next four days there were 12 attacks on Arabs and seven on Jews in the Jerusalem district alone. Additional assaults were reported within Jerusalem and outside the city.[44]

The young boy's funeral became a massive protest against Arab violence and British rule. On Friday August 23, 1929, the Arabs began what the Shaw Commission—the British Commission sent to investigate these disturbances—called a "ferocious attack," in Jerusalem, ostensibly over Jews worshipping at the Wall. To disperse the many "fanatical" Arab crowds—who were wielding clubs, sticks and some even swords—the police "opened fire for the first time," employed armored cars, and arranged for a number of British aircraft to fly over Jerusalem as a show of force. British naval assistance and troop reinforcements were requested after the police advised they were no longer able to ensure public security.[45]

When reports about the riots reached Hebron, angry Arab crowds gathered to vent their anger. The major assault on Hebron began at approximately 9 a.m. on August 24th. Eight American Jews were killed and 15 wounded from the Slobodka Yeshiva.[46]

In Nablus, the police thwarted an attack on their headquarters by a menacing crowd in search of weapons with which to attack Jews. Jews were assaulted in Beisan, in Jaffa, on Har HaCarmel, the Jewish suburb of Haifa, and in a number of Jewish colonies including Motza, where "the horrors of Hebron were repeated on a smaller scale."[47]

An attack on Safed, an isolated town in the Upper Galilee, began at 5:15 p.m. on August 29th, two hours before British troops managed to arrive. Forty-five Jews were either murdered or wounded, and a number of Jewish homes and businesses were torched. Arab mobs engaged in "wanton destruction."[48]

The massacre at Safed marked the end to major assaults against the Jews at this point. Isolated incidents occurred, but the situation continued to improve. Altogether, 133 Jews were murdered and 339 were wounded while 87 Arabs were killed, many as a result of police fire.[49] Significantly, these attacks were directed at the long-established Jewish communities, not the new Jewish settlements.

Three weeks after the massacres, a reporter who had witnessed the slaughter in Hebron described the horrors in a private communication: "Even to one who went through war as a combatant [the scene of the Hebron bloodbath] is still an appalling sight. It is perfectly clear that...the Arabs who took part...behaved liked like the wildest of savages untouched by the hand of civilization."[50]

Students were killed while seeking refuge at the home of Rabbi Jacob Slonim. The rabbi sought protection from the British, but his pleas were either ignored or rebuffed. An American woman who survived the attack, wrote about what she saw:

> With me in Rabbi Slonim's house were about 40 people, mostly the students of the Jewish Theological Seminary of Hebron, among them many Americans. The reason we were congregated in Rabbi Slonim's house was the fact that Rabbi Slonim enjoyed a great deal of popularity among the Arabs and we felt surer in his home than in any one else's. All of a sudden we heard a rattle at the outer gate which was closed. A few minutes later a crowd of savage Arabs burst through the door. The rabbi, together with all those present, rushed to a corner of the room where we awaited the attack. The first to get killed was the rabbi. After him came the young men who, unarmed and unable to protect themselves, recited the prayer for the dead. I saw some of my dearest friends killed right in front of my eyes. Presently I was hit, too, and I fell unconscious. I was buried under a load of dead bodies which covered me and which accounts for my being saved.[51]

Reporters and survivors described in detail the murders and mutilation that took place. In other cities where rioting occurred, American witnesses accused the British police of standing idly by or not being present. When Jews attempted to defend themselves, the British incarcerated them.[52]

Americans were outraged by the attack on American citizens and demanded that the U.S. State Department protect its people. The Jewish War Veterans and the American veterans of the Jewish Legion even wanted American Jews to enlist for military duty in Palestine. A British account of a meeting of American Jewish leaders in November 1929 provided an astute observation concerning the American Jewish community and the American Zionist movement. "The American Jews are" he warned, "generally very well disposed towards Great Britain. But anything which affects the Holy Land touches in them…something inborn and stronger than themselves, and any cause for a grievance, real or imaginary, would…be quickly and actively resented."[53]

The Jewish press in Palestine provided extensive coverage of the riots and assaults. Words like "slaughter" and "butchery" were used to describe the events along with pictures of those murdered. *Haaretz*, a liberal *Yishuv* newspaper, admonished the students for not trying to defend themselves from their attackers—a moral failing in the eyes of the Zionists. Jews should be prepared to risk their lives rather than act like "sheep to slaughter." One writer complained that their inability to kill even one of their killers was "immoral."[54]

The Government initially did not want to provide rations to the 400 remaining survivors from Hebron, according to Helen Bentwich, the Attorney-General's wife, who was a member of a country-wide relief committee under the direction of Hadassah Medical Organization. The Jews who had fled the Old City were living in "any odd hole" they could scrounge outside the walls. After the Government agreed to assist the approximately 2,000 Jews displaced in the massacres, rations were supplied and housing was offered in vacant school buildings.[55]

At the hospitals, Bentwich discovered that the majority "of the children had fractured skulls from being beaten with clubs and other ghastly wounds." When a woman whose husband had been murdered "put her arm round her children to protect them" the Arabs "deliberately slashed each child's head and cut her so badly that she died. Another woman, whose fingers were cut off, lay so long under a pile of dead bodies with her baby that she has since gone out of her mind." Bentwich took some comfort in that "many Jew were saved by their Arab neighbors, even in Hebron."[56]

In Safed, she found the plight of the Jews quite "sad." The Jews had no confidence in the Government, while the Arabs were in "open contempt" of the administration. Arabs in the police force, who had refrained from intervening during the "horrible atrocities," had not been removed. Only the efforts of a doctor from Hadassah prevented an epidemic from erupting in the city.[57]

When Bentwich, accompanied by a few refugees and a police escort, visited the Jewish Quarter in Hebron to help the Jews find some of their effects, she was amazed to find Arabs asking the Jews to return home: "Arabs came up to the men with me, threw their arms round them, and begged them to come back again. It's as if they had been mad, and were now sane again. But the Jews will never go back."[58]

Bentwich was particularly critical of the Government's unwillingness to arm Jews to defend themselves.[59] On August 24 representatives of the Palestine Zionist Executive asked (Sir) Harry Luke, Deputy Commissioner for Jerusalem, to enlist and arm 500 Jewish youths to defend remote Jewish colonies.[60]

Luke denied this request after speaking to the Group Captain in charge of the Royal Air Force, who assured him adequate troops were on the way. Luke and his civil advisors also alleged that arming the Jews would aggravate the already volatile atmosphere, and jeopardize the safety of a significantly larger number of Jews than could be protected by arming these young Jews. Brigadier General

William Dobbie, who was in command of the military and security forces in Palestine, told Luke that Jews should not "be armed or employed as special constables" to reassure the Moslem Council, who had asked the British to remain "impartial." Luke then disarmed and disbanded the few Jewish constables and replaced them with other British nationals.[61]

On September 1, 1929, Sir John Chancellor, then the High Commissioner for Palestine, issued a Proclamation in which he deplored the horrible violence and...

> ...atrocious acts committed by bodies of ruthless and blood-thirsty evil doers, of savage murders perpetrated upon defenceless members of the Jewish population regardless of age or sex, accompanied , as in Hebron, by acts of savagery, of burning farms and houses in town and country and the looting and destruction of property.[62]

The Arabs resented these accusations and even tried to fault the Jews for what transpired. The British established a Commission to examine the rights and claims regarding the Wall. The Commission found that while Muslims were the sole proprietors of the Western Wall and the pavement in front of it, they were "not permitted to do any construction or repair that would impair Jewish access to the Wall or disturb their services if it could be avoided. Jews were permitted to pray at the Wall and bring the Ark with the Torah scrolls on the Sabbath, fast days and government-recognized holy days. Benches, carpets, chairs, curtains, screens could not be brought to the Wall. Prayer mats were allowed during Rosh Hashanah and Yom Kippur, but they could "not obstruct the right of passage along the Pavement." No animals were permitted to be driven along the Pavement during hours of prayer, but Muslims could walk along the Pavement "in an ordinary way," during this time. The place in front of the Wall could not be used for political activities, demonstrations, rallies or speeches.[63]

The violence had not been anticipated by the *Yishuv* or its leaders, forcing them to reconsider their belief that a Zionist entity could be established in Palestine before Arab nationalism became a potent force. The disturbances in 1920 and 1921 were seen by many as isolated events, and not an organized effort directed by Arab leaders. In 1929, however, Jews throughout the country were again attacked, this time threatening the future of their community.[64]

After eight years of calm beginning in 1921, the Jews and the British had falsely assumed that riots were a thing of the past.[65] Provocative Arab slogans added to the Jews' fears about the Arabs' ultimate goal: "The law of Muhammad is being implemented by the sword", "Palestine is our land and the Jews our dogs," and "We are well armed and shall slaughter you by the sword." Under these conditions, Ben-Gurion wondered if Jews could live securely as a minority in Palestine. The Labor parties and others believed that the Arabs wanted to eliminate all the Jews in Palestine.[66]

For two years after the disturbances, the Arab question and its significance were key issues in the *Yishuv*. Rather than seeing this as an expression of Arab refusal to accept Jewish settlement in Palestine, some Zionists sought to explain the violence as a result of provocations by the Mufti and the Jews who marched at the Western Wall.[67]

The riots had not resulted in any modification in Zionist or British policy, but reinforced in the Jews the self-image of the victim, an innocent bystander assaulted by ruthless killers. Nevertheless, the average Jew did not forget the August civil disobediences. They remained apprehensive and skeptical of the Arabs. The world, and especially the British, saw the position of the Jew differently. The violence raised anew the wisdom of the Balfour Declaration, the British Mandate and the entire question of Palestine. Instead of condemning the riots, the British accused the Jews of creating the hostile environment that encouraged this response by seeking to transform the economic and social dynamics in Palestine. As a result, the British suggested the need to limit future immigration and restrict the amount of land Jews could purchase.[68]

Meinertzhagen suggested that Herbert Samuel should have been given explicit instructions to arrest and, if needed, to deport those who promoted violence. This radical approach "will not fail to appeal to a race who are by nature cowards, and who have from time immemorial been accustomed to strength and dictation." Half-measures merely "weaken" the British position, "increase Arab contempt" for them, and "destroy Jewish confidence. If the mandate is a live charter let us act on it. Else let us tear it up."[69]

In a speech to the Royal Institute of International Affairs on December 9, 1930, Arnold Toynbee analyzed the reasons for Arab anger and expressed his own frustration with Arab negativism and "non-cooperation." He said the British, "have made a number of quite sincere and serious attempts [to solve the Arab-Zionist conflict], but the intransigence of the Arabs, in their opposition to the establishment of a Jewish national home, has proved an insuperable stumbling block every time."[70]

After every negative encounter with the Arabs, the British established a Committee of Inquiry that brought the Arab case to the attention of the world, often prompting changes in British policies.[71] The recommendations of the Shaw Commission, and one by Sir John Hope-Simpson, never went far enough for the Arabs, who wanted a complete cessation of Jewish immigration. Attacks against public buildings and the police during the last week of October 1933 in Jaffa,

Nablus and Jerusalem were meant to force the British to accede to their demands.[72]

ARAB REBELLION

The first battle in the fierce clash between the Arabs and the Jews for control of Palestine began on April 19, 1936. Known as the Arab Rebellion, the passion, intensity and the political response it precipitated far surpassed previous violent encounters between these two peoples, forcing the Jews to reassess their belief that Zionist goals could be achieved through peaceful means.[73]

On April 15, 1936, the Arabs initiated a general strike for six months to protest any further immigration. On May 7, Arab leaders met in Jerusalem and demanded an end to immigration, a prohibition against any more land sales to Jews and the establishment of a government with an Arab majority. The strike would end once the demands had been met.[74]

Initially, the Arab Rebellion did not appear to be different from prior violent Arab episodes. After hearing fallacious reports that Arabs had been attacked in Tel-Aviv, Arabs began assaulting Jews in the street. On April 19, "Bloody Sunday," nine Jews were killed and ten were injured.[75] Throughout Palestine, Jewish homes and farms were ransacked and burned, while Jews were attacked on public buses. In one month, 21 men, women and children were killed. By October 1936 the number had risen to 80, yet the Jewish Agency advised restraint, and the Jews did not retaliate.[76]

Arab leaders responded to the strife initiated spontaneously by young Arab radicals, and supported by large sections of the community, by establishing the Arab Higher Committee. The conflict had been transformed from "a violent protest movement to an organized rebellion."

The Arab economy paid dearly for the strike. The Arabs did not go to work in the Jewish settlements, stopped selling their produce to Jews, and Arab businesses were closed. Jews avoided the Jaffa port out of fear of being killed or injured. Without access to fresh fruit and vegetables, the Jews had to develop and manage their own agricultural facilities. Many Jews saw this development as justification for their insistence on "Jewish labor" and "Jewish produce," which had been the subject of much controversy in the early 1930s.[77]

The violence accelerated the separation of Jews from the Arabs, a process begun in the aftermath of the 1929 riots. Fearing for their lives, Jews living in mixed Arab-Jewish neighborhoods, now called "frontier neighborhoods," abandoned their homes and escaped to all-Jewish areas.[78]

Unlike the previous clashes, the Arab Revolt signified a marked increase in Arab participation, organization, and sophistication. Arabs were willing to sacrifice their economic livelihoods, and often their lives, to fight the Jews. Over the years, increased Jewish immigration followed by economic growth in Palestine had caused anxiety among the Arabs that they could no longer contain the Jewish presence peacefully. A number of groups began to believe that violence was the only way to prevent more Jews from entering the country, and beginning in the early 1930s gangs of Arab terrorists started killing Jews indiscriminately.[79]

This popular national uprising was an organized political operation under a central command in which the Arabs remained disciplined. The failure of the British to accede to the three prerequisites for ending the strike did not affect the reputation of the Arab leaders. Arab kings had asked that the strike end in order to allow the British royal commission to investigate the fundamental causes for the revolt. The Peel Commission was appointed in August 1936. In July 1937, the Commission presented its findings to Parliament, which concluded that partition of Palestine offered "a chance of ultimate peace. No other plan does."[80]

The Arab rebellion revived the question in the *Yishuv* as to whether this was a pogrom or the manifestation of an Arab national movement. Ben-Gurion interpreted the attacks as "a bloody war against the [British] government and against us."[81] Others were not as convinced. Whatever the reasons for the disturbances, there was a realization that hostilities between the Jews and Arabs would continue until the Arabs accepted the permanent presence of the Jews in Palestine.[82]

The brutal nature of the assaults against unarmed and defenseless civilians reinforced the image of the Arabs as bloodthirsty, "hungry for spoil" and devoid of all moral inhibitions. Arabs frequently set fires to Jewish property and fields just to destroy years of Jewish labor. When they chopped down thousands of trees that Jews had planted, they attacked one of the most visible symbols of the *Yishuv*. After graves in Safed were desecrated, Beryl Katznelson remarked that "human life is more precious than plant life and stone graves in a cemetery…but the destruction of plant life and stone is instructive regarding the nature of the destroyer and his dark urges; it teaches us [about] more than bloodshed."[83]

Daily interaction between Arabs and Jews was profoundly affected by the revolt. Old friendships were replaced by mutual suspicions, absence of trust, and apprehension about engaging in any out-of-the-ordinary activities. Arabs could walk freely in Jewish sections, but Jews risked being killed if they were found in Arab areas.[84]

For the Arabs, all Jews were the enemy simply because they were Jews. This was an all-out war against the Jews in Palestine that they were determined to win. Arab terrorists were lauded for their exploits, and no Arab leaders denounced these vicious acts and killings. When Jews engaged in brutal actions against Arabs, the *Yishuv* responded with outrage, alarm, and severe doubts. Ben-Gurion claimed that Arab terror influenced the British, but that it was destructive for the Jews: "Terror brings advantages to the Arabs; but terror will destroy Zionism and the Jewish community in Palestine."[85]

The rise of fascism in Germany and Italy struck a responsive chord among the Arabs in Palestine, causing concern among members of the *Yishuv*. The Arab Higher Committee received funds directly from Italy that were used to finance the rebellion. Arab shop windows were adorned with portraits of Hitler and swastikas appeared in towns. Some Jews saw events in Palestine as part of Nazi terror.[86]

The need to respond offensively to Arab aggression encouraged the *Yishuv* to establish an autonomous Jewish fighting force to confront the Arabs or at least fill in the vacuum left by the British. The possibility of establishing a Jewish state added urgency to providing security for the nation, as did the growing interest of the Arab states in the future of Palestine. After the Arab Kings called a halt to the Arab strike, they began to evince interest in the fate of the area, leading to fears that they might intercede in any conflict between the Jews and Arabs.[87]

BLUDAN CONFERENCE

Following the publication of the Peel Commission report, which called for the partition of Palestine, nearly 500 Arab representatives gathered at a Pan-Arab Congress in the Syrian resort of Bludan on September 8, 1937. The presiding officer called Zionism "a cancer which ought to be removed from the body politic."[88]

The Arab nation and the Muslim people, the representatives declared, would continue the fight to free Palestine and establish an Arab government.[89] The presence of a number of Christian Arab activists and an anti-Zionist speech by the Greek Orthodox Bishop of Hama, suggested that Muslims and Christian Arabs had common political goals.[90] This was the first time the Arab world became involved in Palestine's affairs, and set the pattern for their continuing to do so in the years ahead.[91]

The Bludan Conference authorized the maximum financial support to the Palestinian Arabs and the establishment of a center to promote Arab propaganda, with branches in leading Arab countries. Another resolution urged that a rigorous boycott of Jewish products be initiated, which would be expanded to British goods should the English continue what they perceived as anti-Arab policies.[92]

Shortly after the conference, demonstrations and strikes were held in Arab capitals to protest the impending partition. In Palestine, the revolt against partition by the Arabs began in October 1937 after the murder of Lewis Andrews, Acting District Commissioner for the Galilee, who had organized in-country travel arrangements of the Peel Commission. By mid-October there were renewed attacks against Jews and British officials and property. Many Arab moderates who did not support the Mufti's policies were killed. This led Arab leaders at Tulkarm to formally request the District Commissioner's permission to obtain arms to protect themselves against Arab extremists.[93]

Palestinian Arabs living in Damascus, recruited known criminals, including murderers, from Syrian slums to create chaos in Palestine. Some bands infiltrated into Palestine from Lebanon. Anti-Jewish Arab peasants were enlisted and paid for their services. They spent their days blowing up trains, destroying the oil pipeline, harassing and killing officials, soldiers, policemen and civilians, sniping at Jewish buses and trucks, extorting money at gunpoint from Arabs and Christians, cutting phone lines, and engaging in a myriad of disruptive and murderous activities.[94]

In response to these unprovoked attacks, members of the Jewish underground killed 25 Arabs in Haifa on July 6, 1938. After other Jews were murdered, they retaliated by exploding a bomb in the melon market in Haifa killing 39 Arabs on July 24. These reprisals were widely condemned by the Jewish establishment. British officials claimed that there had been no pleas for restraint from moderate Arab leaders, although they opposed the killings, as did the majority of the Arab public. Fear of the terrorists prevented them from speaking out against them.[95]

William Ormsby Gore, the British Colonial Secretary, believed that Arab opposition to partition would not impede its implementation since the Arabs in Palestine had never "regarded themselves as 'Palestinians,' but as part of the Arab world."[96]

However true this might have been, it was no longer accurate. In addition, the neighboring Arab countries were beginning to assume a more active role with regards to Palestine. They adamantly opposed the Mandate and were resolute in the need to establish an independent Arab state. The lack of unity among the Palestinian Arab leaders, the termination of the Arab Higher Committee in September 1937, and the increase of unity among the Arab nations created the opportunity for Arab leaders to begin coordinating their activities concerning Palestine.[97]

In the spring of 1939, representatives of Arab states, in addition to those from Palestine and from the Jewish Agency, were invited to London to discuss the current conditions of the Mandate. Despite the Arabs' refusal to meet with their Jewish counterparts, Great Britain issued the MacDonald White Paper on May 17, 1939.[98]

The White Paper contained most of the Arab demands, but this still did not satisfy the Mufti and the Arab Higher Committee. The White Paper restricted the number of Jews allowed into the country over five years to 75,000 beginning in April 1939. At the end of that period, the extent of Jewish immigration was contingent upon Arab approval.[99] On February 27, 1940, the land law was promulgated, forbidding Jews from buying land in new areas, while permitting them to do so in areas where they already owned property.[100]

In the debate on the White Paper in the House of Commons on May 22, MP Amery accused the government of having enacted the policy to "appease the Arabs," which was nothing more than "a direct invitation to the Arabs to continue to make trouble."[101]

In his House of Commons speech, Winston Churchill addressed the matter of Jewish and Arab immigration to Palestine since the establishment of the Mandate. The Peel Commission had reported that Arab migration to Palestine had increased as Palestine became a center of economic activity. The Palestine census of 1931 revealed that many Arabs living in Palestine were born in Algeria, Tripoli, Yemen and Morocco. Churchill was so struck by this fact that he remarked: "So far from being persecuted, the Arabs have crowded into the country and multiplied till their population has increased more than even all world Jewry could lift up the Jewish population."[102]

In a debate in the House of Commons on August 1, 1946, Churchill noted the extensive progress made in land reclamation, cultivation, and trade in Palestine which benefited Arabs and Jews.[103] Three years later he observed that in the 27 years since the White Paper of 1922, the Jewish population "doubled or more than doubled, but so did the Arab population of the same areas of Palestine." The notion "that only a limited number of people can live in a country is a profound illusion," he concluded. "There are more people today living twenty storeys above the ground in New York than there were living on the ground in New York a hundred years ago. There is no limit to the ingenuity of man if it is properly and vigorously applied under conditions of peace and justice."[104]

He rejected Arab allegations that Britain had not been their friend:

> The House of Hussein reins in Iraq. [Emir] Feisal was placed
> on the throne, his grandson is there today. The Emir Abdullah,
> whom I remember appointing at Jerusalem, in 1921 to be in
> charge of Transjordania, is there today…Syria and Lebanon owe
> their independence to the great exertions made by the British
> Government to make sure that the pledges made by them…were
> honoured.[105]

CHAPTER 4

Arab Activities During World War II

While the British maintained that they were operating in good faith toward the Arabs, the same could not be said for Arab actions. Haj Amin el-Husseini, the Grand Mufti of Jerusalem, was the titular head of the Muslim community in Palestine, a position that bestowed upon him considerable stature.[1] Since January 1922, his role as president of the Supreme Muslim Council also provided him with an extensive economic, organizational and political network. The Council controlled the Muslim religious *Waqf*s, with substantial endowments and annual budgets, and selected and appointed imams for the mosques, and judges *(Qadis)* for the *Shari'a* religious courts formally administered by the Ottoman government. The Council also had the authority to dismiss all Shari'a and *Waqf* officials employed by Muslim institutions that received *Waqf* funds.[2]

The 1937 Peel Commission concluded that the Mufti was "the most influential Arab in Palestine," and that he could be "truthfully described as the head of yet a third parallel government."[3]

ARAB-NAZI SYMMETRIES

The Mufti's prime objective was to stop all Jewish immigration to Palestine, and nowhere else in the world were his antisemitic views shared more equally than by Nazi Germany. It would not be long before the Mufti would join with the Nazis in their plans for the Jews, that were congruent with his desire to ignite a pan-Islamic Holy War to solve the Jewish Question once and for all.[4]

The summer of 1933 appears to mark the first effort to establish an Arab Nazi organization. The Jaffa correspondent of *Al-Ahram,* a widely read Cairo daily, approached the German consul for help. Although the request was denied mostly for "strategic considerations," Nazi ideology found fertile ground in Palestine. This can clearly be seen in the autobiographical memoir of Syrian Sami al-Jundi, a founder of the Ba'ath Party: "We were racists, admiring Nazism." He and his colleagues read Nazi literature and the works of German philosophers Friedrich Nietzsche, Johann Gottlieb Fichte and Houston Stewart Chamberlain's *Foundations of the Nineteenth Century,* which served as the source of Nazi ideology. They were the first to suggest translating *Mein Kampf* into Arabic.[5] Anyone living in Damascus in the 1930's, al-Jundi said, would understand Arab proclivity to Nazi ideology. "Nazism was the power which could serve as its champion and he who is defeated will by nature love the victor."[6]

For a while, the Mufti's youth organization was called the Nazi Scouts and members wore Hitler youth style shorts and leather belts. After the Nazis passed the Nuremberg racial laws in September 1935, Hitler received congratulatory telegrams from Arabs and Muslims throughout the Islamic world, but especially "from Palestine, where German propaganda had been most active."[7]

The Mufti was not alone in his sympathy for the Axis Powers. The masses were impressed by German propaganda and military victories, and were sure the Germans would ultimately triumph. Public demonstrations of support followed every German approach to British-held Egyptian territory. British soldiers in Egypt were in danger of being assaulted and killed, making sections of Cairo off limits to the British military.[8]

The Germans and Italians succeeded in mobilizing these groups after years of having cultivated relationships with Arab groups within the Axis Powers. They arranged for Arab students to travel to their countries, and German politicians and agents visited Arab lands. Arabic radio broadcasts and Arabic newspapers from Germany and Italy were sent to Arab states along with money to create a relationship that was exploited during the war.[9]

There were also long standing connections between various Syrian leaders and Axis States. There were significant Arab-Nazi organizations in Syria and Lebanon: the "Iron Shirts" led by members of the Syrian Parliament; the League of National Activity; the An-Nadi al-Arabi" (Club of Damascus); "the Councils for the Defence of Arab Palestine;" "The National Bloc," the main party in Syria; the "Istiklal" group led by the President of the Syrian Republic, an openly pro-Nazi faction. Baldur von Schirach, leader of the Hitlerjugend, visited Syria before the war to develop a close relationship with these organizations and with Arab youth groups.[10]

During the 1936-1939 Arab Revolt, the swastika was used liberally on pamphlets and graffiti, Arab children greeted each other with the Nazi salutes, and major events, including Mohammed's birthday, were adorned with large numbers of Nazi flags and pictures of Hitler. Those driving through areas affected by the revolt affixed a swastika on their vehicles to avoid being targeted by Arab snipers.[11]

Nazi ideology found fertile ground in Arab lands in part because the Arabs and Nazis were both fighting common enemies: France and England. The victors in World War I, both countries were seasoned and confident geopolitical imperialists, fulfilling their "national and territorial aspirations" through the occupation of nation-states. Although Arab nationhood itself was well-established, it was expressed through culture and language, not through any singular state. Notions of nationalism and patriotism were foreign to them.[12]

Thus the Arabs did not have one nation-state, but were separated into many different states, practically all of which were in one way or another under foreign domination.

Arab identification with the Nazis was more in keeping with their own history. The Nazis defined their identity through language, culture, history, and blood rather than by borders and political sovereignty, akin to the Islamic concept of *Ummah* (community, nation). The ethnic ambiguity and political divisions in the Middle East bore similarity to that in German lands, where areas had been divided into many separate states and principalities, some of which even integrated non-German entities. Arabs therefore found German nationalism more comparable to their own situation and, hence, more attractive.[13]

In a speech on January 21, 1944, el-Husseini proclaimed, "National-Socialist Germany is fighting against world Jewry. The Koran says: 'You will find that the Jews are the worst enemies of the Moslems.'" He added, "There are also considerable similarities between Islamic principles and those of National-Socialism...All this brings our ideologies close together and facilitates cooperation."[14] On March 1, 1944 he said, "Kill the Jews wherever you find them. This pleases God, history and religion."[15]

The growth of a Jewish National Home in Palestine and the possible establishment of a Jewish state became another reason for the Arabs to embrace Nazi dogma. Hatred of Jews was emphasized in German propaganda aimed at the Arabs, and conversely, in Arab appeals to Germans.[16] In 1921, Alfred Rosenberg, a leading Nazi racial theorist, published *Der staatsfeindliche Zionismus* (Zionism, Enemy of the State), in which he claimed that Jews were forcing the indigenous population of Palestine out of their land through legal subterfuge. In their place, they would establish a Jewish base to advance their sweeping "oriental policy" objectives.[17]

Hitler expanded on this theme in 1925 in Mein Kampf when he said the Jews did not want to merely a Jewish state in Palestine, but a base "for their international world-swindling" complete with "its own states rights...free from other states, a place of refuge for convicted scoundrels and a university for up and coming swindlers."[18]

In the spring of 1933, the Grand Mufti assured Dr. Heinrich Wolff, the German consul in Jerusalem, that "the Muslims inside and outside Palestine welcome the new regime of Germany and hope for the extension of the fascist, anti-democratic governmental system to other countries."[19] When Wolff informed Berlin of the offer, he suggested that Germany reject or at least ignore it. At that point, the Germans had hoped to recruit the British as an ally. Establishing a relationship with an anti-British movement would only have alienated them. Hitler abandoned the idea of enlisting the British after the Munich Agreements in 1938, when the British, French and Italians agreed to let the Germans annex the Czechoslovakian Sudetenland. The Germans were then amenable to developing a connection with the Mufti.[20]

The Arabs warned Winston Churchill that "Zionists are ambitious. If to-day they accept the mandate of England they may not to-morrow. Their aim is to establish a Jewish kingdom, bring back the glory of Israel in the 'Land of Promise' and gradually control the world..."[21]

FROM ADMIRATION TO COLLABORATION

The Nazis did not publicly identify with the pan-Arab goals of the Mufti until the final stages of the conflict, but they did agree to annul the Balfour Declaration and abolish the Jewish National Home. Until the summer of 1937, when the Anglo-Nazi relationship became strained, the Nazis wanted to retain the goodwill of Great Britain. British friendship, they believed at that time, was critical in achieving Nazi diplomatic aims in Europe. At the same time, the Nazis were willing to disturb the British in the Middle East as long as it was done surreptitiously.[22]

The Mufti based Arab support for the Nazis on the need to defeat their common enemies and their shared long-term ideological objectives. "The Jews were the bitterest enemies of the Muslims. They had always expressed their antagonism with cunning and deception," he declared in a speech on December 18, 1942. According to the Mufti, from Islam's inception, the Jews had directed their "hatred" and "intrigues" against Muslims. They came to Palestine to create "a base from which to extend their power over neighboring Islamic countries." Their "essence" is to foster instability in the world by fomenting wars and wreaking havoc between nations. Jews are nothing more than "a destructive force on earth."[23]

In 1936, Admiral Wilhelm Canaris, head of the Abwehr, the German military's counter-intelligence organization, secretly provided financial aid to assist the Arabs rioting against the Jews and the British. Heralded as protests against increased Jewish immigration to Palestine and loss of their land to the Jews, the Mufti admitted that without German funds he could not have initiated and sustained the uprising.[24] However, after the Arab gangs failed to achieve their objectives, the funding was stopped. On the other hand, Hitler was pleased that Jews were immigrating to Palestine because he expected their presence to antagonize the Arabs against the British, and force the British to divert their attention and resources to areas outside Europe.[25]

The German Propaganda Ministry, the Deutsche Nachrich tenbüro (German News Agency-DNB), established an Arab service in 1936 to incite the Arabs against the British and Jews by secretly funding Arab newspapers, especially the *Difa* in Jaffa, whose editor was a Gestapo informer.[26] In a letter written while on a tour of Palestine in 1937, Schwarz van Berk, the editor of the Berlin newspaper *Der Angriff*,

(The Attack) founded by Joseph Goebbels in 1927, explained why the Jews should be permitted to immigrate to Palestine, "…it is good that the Jews from Germany come to Palestine…They will not take root here, their fortunes will be spent and the Arabs will liquidate them… the Jews in Palestine are doomed, their end will be to leap from the frying pan into the fire."[27]

After the Peel Commission recommended that Palestine be partitioned into separate Arab and Jewish states in June 1937, German Foreign Minister Konstantin von Neurath feared the Jewish state would enable international Jewry to establish an additional power base from which to operate.[28] To counter this threat, the Germans decided to strengthen the Arabs in a number of ways. Scholarships were offered to Arab students for study in Germany, German companies provided apprenticeships, political officials were hosted at the Nuremberg party rallies, and military leaders were invited to watch German military exercises. In Berlin, an "Arab Club" became the center for Arabic-language broadcasts and anti-British activities in Palestine.[29]

The Deutsche Nachrichtenbüro used its Jerusalem regional office to increase its activities by bribing journalists and luring dissident Arab newspapers back by buying expensive advertisements in their papers.[30]

In September 1937, Adolph Eichmann spent several weeks touring the Middle East followed by extensive visits from Baldur von Schirach, the leader of Hitler Youth in Germany, and Wilhelm Canaris. Von Schirach provided funds to establish an "Arab Club" in Damascus, Syria where Germans prepared "recruits for the Mufti's insurgents." Canaris created a spy network throughout the area.[31]

THE MUFTI-FUHRER PARTNERSHIP

After fomenting the 1936 riots in Palestine in which many Jews and British were killed, the Mufti escaped to Lebanon in 1938, and then to

Iraq with the aid of the French. In April 1941, Arab nationalist Rashid Ali al-Kailani led a pro-Nazi military rebellion in Iraq. The Germans provided limited air support in early May.

On May 9, 1941 the Mufti broadcasted over Iraqi and Axis radio "a *fatwa* announcing a *jihad* against Britain", and appealed to all Muslims to defend Islam and "her lands" against its "greatest foe..."[32] Earlier, he had gone to Baghdad with Jamal el Husseini, his cousin and right hand, who later became head of the Arab Higher Committee (AHC). Also accompanying the ex-Mufti, was Musa Bey Alami, his legal advisor and manager of the anti-British propaganda campaign in Iraq. He later became head of Arab propaganda in London. In addition, there were Emil Ghori, his media spokesperson in Baghdad and secretary of the Palestine Arab Party, and Fawzi el-Kawukji, the ex-Mufti's military adviser and later commander of the Arab Liberation Army that fought against partition.[33]

When the British forces overwhelmed the rebels in late May, the Mufti fled Baghdad for Tehran. From Iran he escaped to Italy, arriving in Rome on October 11, where he represented himself to the Italian Military Intelligence, who hosted him, as the "head of the secret organization, 'The Arab Nation,'" with branches throughout the Middle East.[34]

On October 13, 1941, the Mufti submitted a comprehensive plan offering to join forces with the Axis Powers "on the sole condition that they recognize the unity and sovereignty of an Arab state of a Fascist nature, including Iraq, Syria, Palestine and Transjordan." No other areas outside the Middle East were included to avoid a conflict with the Axis territorial and colonialist objectives. North African countries such as Libya and Tunisia were never even alluded to since they were vital to the Italians. At a meeting on October 27, 1941 with Italy's Benito Mussolini, the Mufti reported that Mussolini agreed that the Arabs were entitled to realize their own independence, and that a public declaration by the Axis Powers be made to acknowledge Arab aspirations.[35]

The Mufti drafted a copy of the joint declaration on November 3, which was approved by Mussolini and then sent to the German Embassy in Rome on November 6, 1941, the same day the Mufti arrived in Berlin. By November 21, the details of the declaration had been agreed upon and prepared for publication pending the Mufti's meeting with Hitler.[36]

At a meeting on November 28, 1941, Hitler informed el-Husseini, "The foundations of the difficult struggle [I am] waging are clear. [I am] waging an uncompromising struggle against the Jews. It pertains to the struggle against the Jewish home in Palestine, since the Jews wish to use it to create a national centre for their pernicious actions in other countries. . . A decision has been made to solve the Jewish problem step by step and to demand that other peoples, including non-European peoples, do the same."[37]

Hitler assured the Mufti that after the Germans broke through the Caucasus into the Middle East, "Germany's objective would then be solely the destruction of the Jewish element residing in the Arab sphere under the protection of the British power." At that point, Hitler would publicly explain his intentions to the Arab world, and the Mufti, who "would be the most authoritative spokesman for the Arab world," would then "set off the Arab operations which he had secretly prepared," in the Middle East to help the Germans defeat the British.[38]

Hitler viewed the Mufti as a "sly old fox," and ascribed his "quite exceptional wisdom" to the likelihood of "Aryan" blood. "With his blond hair and blue eyes," Hitler speculated, "he gives the impression that he is, in spite of his sharp and mouse-like countenance, a man with more than one Aryan among his ancestors and one who may well be descended from the best Roman stock."[39]

A marked transformation in Nazi propaganda occurred in January 1942, when the Nazis began directing appeals to Muslims and Arabs in the Middle East and North Africa. The Office of Anti-Semitic Action in Propaganda was changed to the Office of Anti-Jewish Action by the German Propaganda Ministry to preclude Arabs from being insulted by use of the term "anti-Semitic."[40] The Germans established a special office for the Mufti in Berlin, with branches in Germany, Greece, Japan and Italy. Arabic-language broadcasts were transmitted to Turks, Arabs, Persians, and Indians from Zeesen, a village south of Berlin. The Oriental Service, with a staff of 80, including announcers and translators, had "absolute priority" over all other foreign language service broadcasts. From 1939 to 1945, when most of the Arab world listened to radio broadcasts in cafes and pubic arenas, the Zeesen service was the most popular. Antisemitic propaganda was cleverly mixed with Arab music and passages from the Koran, all supervised by the Mufti.[41]

In the Mufti's radio broadcast to the people of Egypt on July 2, 1942, he said that the initial successes in North Africa of German Field Marshal Erwin Rommel, commander of the Deutsches Afrika Korps, "filled all Arabs in the whole Orient with joy." The English and the Jews were "common enemies" of the Arabs and Axis powers, who were now waging a war against the Bolsheviks. With the possibility of Germany occupying Egypt, the Mufti saw a parallel between Egypt's attempt to free itself from British imperialistic domination with the struggle of the Palestinian Arabs against the "concentrated British power and its alliance with the Jews."[42]

Following the American landings in North Africa in November 1942, the Mufti assailed the United States in a broadcast in Arabic to North Africa on November 26, 1942. The speech is a remarkable example of how the Nazis adapted their propaganda to Arab and Muslim audiences. He accused the "Jews and capitalists" of pressuring the U. S. to expand the war in order to increase their own influence and wealth from energy resources in newly acquired territories. The North Africans, he said,

>...know very well what unhappiness the Jews have brought them. They know that the Jews are the vanguard fighters of imperialism that mistreated North Africa for so long. They [North Africans] also know the extent to which the Jews served the imperialist as spies and agents and how they seek the energy resources of North Africa to expand their wealth...The American intervention in North Africa strengthens the power of the Jews, increases their influence, and doubles their misdeeds. America is the greatest agent of the Jews, and the Jews are rulers in America.[43]

The Mufti urged Arabs and Muslims throughout the world, including those living in the United States, to become a fifth column and carry out acts of sabotage against the Allies and kill Jews.[44] He claimed helping the Axis powers was imperative for the Arabs, even if it meant martyrdom. If they were willing to demonstrate adequate sacrifice, God would ensure their success.[45] Should England prevail, "Israel would rule the whole world, the Arabian fatherland would suffer an unholy blow, and the Arab countries would be torn apart and turned into Jewish colonies." Only when England and her allies were vanquished, would "the Jewish danger" to the Arabs be swept away.[46]

ENLISTING ARABS FOR THE NAZI CAUSE

From 1941-1945 about 5,000 Arab and Indian Muslims volunteered to serve in the German armed forces, hardly sufficient to constitute an army of liberation. Their worth as a military force was negligible compared with units created with Muslims in the Balkans and the

USSR. Though the Germans failed to conquer the region, the units did have propaganda value which the Nazis exploited.[47]

The Germans viewed Muslim volunteers, who numbered approximately 510,000 men from the Balkans, Russia, Kazakhstan, Central Asia, Northern Caucasus and from the Volga and Crimean Tartars (about one third of the foreign volunteers in the German military), as a vehicle to spread dissension in Europe, particularly among the English, French, and the Muslim countries. They also used the enmity between the Orthodox Serbs and Muslims in the Balkans. In the USSR, Muslim units were active at the front, with the advancing Nazi forces, and in the rear, where they tracked down partisans and conducted harsh reprisals against the local civilian population. The campaign to establish Arab units dissipated by the spring of 1943, after German defeats on the Eastern and North African fronts.[48]

A number of Palestinian Arabs, who enlisted with the British forces, were taken prisoner by German forces and subsequently joined Arab units in the German army at the Mufti's request. Jews from Palestine encountered a substantial number of them when they were taken prisoner again, this time by British troops. Instead of being repatriated to Palestine as German prisoners-of-war, the British sent them back as though they were British prisoners-of-war.[49]

The Mufti also helped establish espionage networks to provide information about British troop movements. His news transmissions to the Middle East reported acts of sabotage that would normally have been censored. His agents, who infiltrated the Middle East by land or by air, cut pipe and telephone lines in Palestine and Transjordan and destroyed bridges and railways in Iraq.[50]

He also organized an Axis-Arab Legion known as the *Arabisches Freiheitskorps*, that wore German uniforms with "Free Arabia" patches. As part of the German Army, the unit guarded communications facilities in Macedonia and hunted down American and British paratroopers who jumped into Yugoslavia and were hiding among the local population. The legion also fought on the Russian front. Another major success was el-Husseini's recruitment of tens of thousands of Balkan Muslims into the *Wehrmacht*.[51] On a visit to Bosnia in 1943, the Mufti appealed to local Muslims to join the Moslem Waffen-SS Units and met with the units that were already operational.[52]

In addition, Haj Amin used his contacts with Muslim leaders in North Africa to urge them to obstruct the Allied advance in every way possible. After Allied troops invaded North Africa in November 1942, Vichy officers in Tunisia established the Phalange Africaine, also called the *Légion des Volontaires Française de Tunisie*. There were 400 men in the unit, approximately one-third Arab and the rest a mélange of European pro-Fascists. The German Army assumed command of the *Phalange* in February 1943, fighting the British and the Free French for most of 1944. In 1944, a French military court convicted the unit's commander, Pierre Simon Cristofini, of treason and executed him.[53]

A second all-Arab unit under German command, known as the *Brigade Nord Africaine*, was established by Mohamed el-Maadi, a former French officer and antisemite whose nickname was "SS Mohamed." They fought the partisans, a group of resistance fighters, in the Dordogne region in South-West France.[54]

In July 1944, the Mufti broadcasted appeals to French Moslems urging them not to join General de Gaulle's army because by fighting the Nazis, de Gaulle was aiding the Jews. Haj Amin's many Japanese broadcasts also helped the Japanese in their propaganda campaigns in India and Asia. In one program on September 20, 1944, he said: "...We desire victory for Germany and Japan because the interest of the Arab and the Moslem can never be fulfilled except through close cooperation with them under all circumstances. We can expect nothing from the Allies who are controlled by world Jewry."[55]

In keeping with this religious imperative, el-Husseini had asked the German Foreign Minister on May 13, 1943 "to do his utmost" to prohibit further departures of Jews from Romania, Bulgaria and Hungary to Palestine. Four thousand Jewish children, accompanied by 500 adults, had recently arrived in Palestine, prompting the Mufti to urge that the escape routes be terminated. When the International Red Cross asked Romanian Prime Minister Marshal Antonescu, two weeks later, to allow Jewish emigration to Palestine on Red Cross ships, the German Foreign Office refused, asserting that Palestine was an Arab country.[56]

In 1943, when Himmler suggested that 20,000 German prisoners in Allied hands be released in return for allowing Jewish 5,000 children to leave the Third Reich, the Mufti allegedly said he would rather have all the Jews be killed. When the plan failed to materialize, the Mufti got his wish.[57]

On July 27, 1944, he wrote to Himmler to ask that Jews be prevented from entering Palestine. In acceding to the Mufti's request, Himmler would thus demonstrate Germany's "friendly attitude" to Arabs and Muslims.[58]

THE MUFTI AND THE SHOAH

At the post-war Nuremberg Trials, Dieter Wisliceny, an aide to Adolf Eichmann, confirmed that the Mufti had secretly accompanied Eichmann to observe the gas chamber at Auschwitz, and that he was an "initiator" of the policy to exterminate the Jews. Eichmann and the Mufti denied the accusations in 1961. Historian Bernard Lewis found no corroborating testimony about either statement, but the Germans hardly required any encouragement from anyone to annihilate the Jewish people.[59] Gerhard Höpp, an Arabist and Islam scholar, posits that the Mufti may have visited Auschwitz, but rejects the probability of him having visited Majdanek, Treblinka and Mauthausen.[60]

Others claim he did tour these camps.[61] An associate of the Mufti and three associates of the former Iraqi prime minister Rashid al-Kailani did go to the Sachsenhausen concentration camp near Oranienburg, Germany for a two-hour visit in July 1942. It is also known that the Mufti had a cordial relationship with Himmler, whom he often met for tea. In his memoirs, the Mufti records that in the summer of 1943 Himmler informed him that "up to now we have exterminated [abadna] around three million of them."[62]

Even if the Mufti never actually visited the German death camps, he labored diligently to ensure the destruction of the Jews of Europe. He even urged the Germans to bomb Jerusalem and Tel-Aviv.[63] In 1943 the Mufti began asking the German Air Force Command to bomb the headquarters of the Jewish Agency in Jerusalem and to launch an air assault on Tel Aviv on November 2, the anniversary of the Balfour Declaration. The appeal was refused as was the one he made on April 1, 1944.[64]

THE MUFTI: A VIOLENT NATIONALIST

As early as 1918, Haj Amin demonstrated that he was a zealous nationalist who hated the British and the Jews. I.A. Abbady, a Jew who worked with him for five months, to translate Reuters' press releases at the office of the military governor of Jerusalem, was continually warned about the dangers awaiting the Jews. "Remember, Abbady," he would say, " this was and will remain an Arab land. We do not mind you [Jewish] natives of the country, but those alien invaders, the Zionists, will be massacred to the last man. We want no progress, no prosperity [deriving from Jewish immigration]. Nothing but the sword will decide the future of this country."[65]

General Sir John Glubb, commander of the Arab Legion between 1939 and 1956, loathed the Mufti for being a "fanatical politician." He believed there was considerable justice with the Mufti's aim of "resistance to the armed suppression of the people of Palestine, who objected to the mass immigration of Jews against the will of the majority of the inhabitants." He believed that the "Mufti's methods were both unwise and immoral—utter intransigence, a complete refusal to compromise and terrorist murders of Palestinians who differed from him."[66]

ARAB APOLOGISTS AND EUROPEAN APPEASEMENT

In return for having organized the SS division of Muslim soldiers in Bosnia-Herzegovina, which was responsible for the deaths of thousands of Croatians and Serbs, Yugoslavia put the Mufti on its war criminals list. After the British asked the French to extradite him in 1945, the Muslim Brotherhood, who regarded the Mufti as the only representative of the Arabs in Palestine, sent a telegram to the British ambassador in Cairo asking that the Mufti not be exposed to any danger. His close alliance with the Nazis was cause to celebrate as a badge of honor and pride.[67]

When Washington agreed with Britain's request for the Mufti's expulsion from France, Hassan al-Banna, founder of the Muslim Brotherhood, warned the U.S. to cease its "unjust Zionist policy." He assured the Americans that the members of the Brotherhood were always prepared "to sacrifice" themselves to rescue their men. The Arab League supported the Brotherhood, which prompted Britain, France and the U.S. to acquiesce to their demand not to extradite the Mufti, rather than provoke the Arab world. Under the circumstances, Yugoslavia also capitulated.[68]

On May 8, 1945, he, his 16–person staff, and Günter Obenhoff, an officer appointed by the Gestapo, escaped to Switzerland. After being denied asylum, he was extradited by the French in late May 1945 and arrived in Paris with 12 colleagues. On May 11, the French Ministry of the Interior informed the French ministry of Foreign Affairs that the Mufti was viewed as "the brains of German espionage in all Muslim countries."[69]

While concurring with this assessment, the French embassy in Cairo acknowledged that the Mufti had "betrayed" the Allies, especially the British, but had not hurt the French directly. French officials saw no point in confronting him since this might adversely affect their relations with the Arab countries. They also believed that Haj Amin would play a pivotal role in the future of Palestine, which remained undecided.[70]

During his stay in France, Haj Amin lived in the Villa Les Roses in the Paris suburb of Louvecienne with a chauffeur, two body guards and his secretary provided by the Paris mosque. He denied any knowledge of the extermination camps or of ever hearing of Adolf Eichmann.[71]

On June 10, 1946 he left France, after the French announced that they would not prevent him from immigrating to an Arab country. When he arrived in Egypt, he received a hero's welcome. Several thousand Nazi war criminals fled to Egypt due to the country's growing pro-German sympathies and the rise of antisemitism. In his role as the Chairman of the Arab Higher Committee in Palestine, he re-established al-Futwwa, his paramilitary youth organization. To guarantee that the Arabs did not accept the partition of Palestine, he regularly consulted with the Arab League. Since he was prohibited from leaving Egypt, the Mufti became the "symbolic" President of the Muslim Brothers in Palestine and al-Banna's deputy.[72]

THE AFTERMATH OF PARTITION PLAN APPROVAL

The Mufti's influence in Palestine continued during his Egypt years even after the demise of Nazi Germany. On November 29, 1947, two-

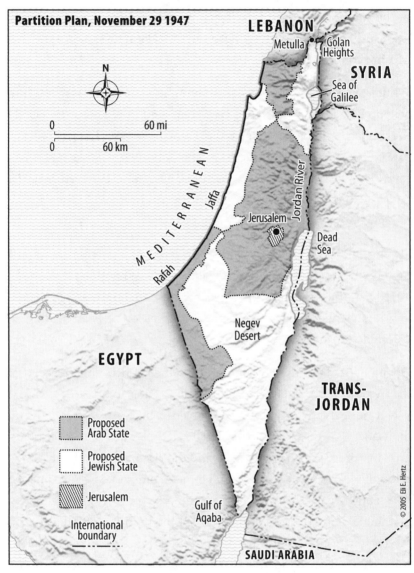

Partition Plan, November 29 1947

Courtesy of Eli Hertz

thirds of the members of the U.N. voted for partition of Palestine into two independent states—one Arab and one Jewish—marking the first agreement between Washington and Moscow at the new international body.[73] Just before the resolution passed, the Mufti declared, "We would rather die than accept minority rights in a prospective Jewish state."[74]

As soon as the resolution passed, the Arab U.N. delegates denounced the legitimacy of the resolution, refused to be bound by its recommendations, and reserved the right to take whatever action they saw appropriate, within what the Saudi Arabian delegate called the "principles of right and justice."[75] Thus partition was never consummated and never approved by the Arabs.

In accordance with decisions ratified at a meeting of Arab Premiers in Cairo from December 12-17, 1947, the Arab leaders vowed "to arm Palestine Arabs, reinforce them with volunteers and collect funds to finance an all out fight in Palestine." They were determined to thwart the establishment of a Jewish state and were committed to maintaining the country "Arabic, independent and united."[76]

DECLARING WAR ON A U.N. RESOLUTION

A major concern of the Arab Higher Committee (AHC), established on April 25, 1936 as the Arab authority in Palestine, was to organize the Arab nationalist groups and clans dominated by the Mufti, and to create a united, rejectionist front against the Zionists.[77] Differences between the AHC and the Arab League (AL), the organization of independent Arab states, over Palestinian representation and voting rights in the AL reached a point at the end of 1947 where the AL sought to control the AHC and assume more of its responsibilities. All primary matters regarding the military or political domain were under the control of the AL.[78]

The Arab premiers agreed that the Mufti would not be permitted to direct policy in Palestine in any manner, despite his concerted efforts to do so from Cairo. He could not be ostracized completely because "his name and prestige" were important to the masses.[79]

In keeping with their pledge to resist partition, Arab leaders collected 10,000 rifles and other small arms and ammunition, enlisted 3,000 volunteers, and set up a Technical Military Committee connected with the AL to train the volunteers. Significantly, there were no serious discussions about direct military intervention by Arab states in Palestine at this point. Their armed forces would invade Palestine only if all other avenues failed, asserted Jamil Mardam Bey, the Syrian Prime Minister.[80]

Emboldened by this support, the AHC refused to appoint a representative to the U.N. Special Committee on Palestine (UNSCOP) about implementing partition. To do so would have recognized its legitimacy. Any attempt to establish a Jewish state in "Arab territory" would be viewed as an aggressive act.[81]

To ensure there would be no conciliation with the Zionists, the AHC began carrying out the threat made by Jamal El Husseini, acting president of the AHC and the Mufti's cousin, that "the partition line shall be nothing but a line of fire and blood."[82] Islamic religious leaders of the Cairo University of al-Azhar decreed a *jihad* in Palestine,[83] a three-day protest strike was declared by the AHC "to allow the people to relieve their feelings." In Nablus, Tiberias and Beisan there were demonstrations, representing a new phase in Arab-Jewish relations.[84] This was followed by a protest on Friday, December 5 after the mid-day prayers.[85]

The Jewish Agency reported daily attacks "with varying intensity" against Jews and their property. Hundreds of Jews were killed, and the material losses were estimated to run "into many hundreds of thousands of pounds." In many parts of the country, vehicular traffic had become extremely vulnerable to attack. Development projects were suspended until order could be restored.[86]

Meanwhile, Jews across the Arab world were being persecuted and murdered: Jews were attacked and killed in Aden and Kuwait. In Aleppo, Syria, Jews were murdered, and synagogues, schools, homes and shops were destroyed. The priceless Aleppo Codex, the oldest complete text of the Bible, was significantly damaged.[87]

An anonymous bulletin, sent to "all news agencies", reported that a proposal had been submitted to the Arab League advocating that Jewish citizens living in Arab countries be considered citizens of the Jewish State, and thus enemies of Arab States. Jews would be incarcerated as political prisoners, unless they enlisted in the struggle against the Zionists, and their bank accounts would be frozen. An outbreak of cholera in southern Syria was ascribed to "Zionist biological warfare."[88]

Disputes intensified when the Arab states failed to abide by their commitments to provide the Palestinians with arms and funds. Interaction between the local Arabs and the Arabs from surrounding countries also created hostility. AL officers accused the Palestinians of being spineless, land speculators and spies. The Palestinians saw the AL as mercenaries and interlopers. Two days before his death in Jerusalem on April 9, 1948, Abd al-Qader al-Husseini, a local Palestinian commander, blamed the AL for losing Palestine.[89]

Because of traditional fractionalism, the AHC did not eliminate the struggles over personal status and factional power that prevented the creation of a national leadership. Tribal interests prevailed over national interests, in large part due to the Husseini family, who were the established leaders of Palestine. They refused to allow the formation of any national structure where they did not dominate, a demand other parties refused to accept. Jamal el-Husseini assumed control of the AHC in February 1946, guaranteeing that its non-Husseini members were neutralized. The el-Husseinis did not permit criticism or disagreement, and would use violence to silence their opponents.[90]

Jamal also gained control of existing Palestinian economic organizations and took over the *Najada* and *Futuwa*, forcing it to incorporate into the Arab Youth Organization (Munazamat al-Shabab al-'Arabi). The AHC also attempted to establish *al-Jihad al Muqaddas* (the Sacred Jihad), a military structure with a mobile strike force whose objectives were to attack Jewish lines of communication.[91]

Within a short time, the spontaneous acts of violence were being controlled by organized gangs led by Hasan Salama, infamous for his "gangster and extortionist methods during the Arab Rebellion," and Abd al-Qader el-Husseini, cousin of the Mufti.[92] The British called them "low grade thugs with no interest in the maintenance of peace."[93] The Jews responded to the attacks with "punitive actions," resulting in counter-reprisals leading to a rapidly deteriorating situation.[94]

In desperation, the British High Commissioner appealed to the Mufti and the Higher Arab Executive (HAE) to stop the bloodshed, assuming that the HAE and the Mufti did not want the conflict to escalate uncontrollably. In the meantime, because of this lack of effective national leadership, local leaders in Jaffa and Gaza established Watch Committees to maintain law and order and protect Arab businesses.[95]

Once again the British misunderstood relations in the Arab hierarchy. In mid-December 1947, the British military reported that the HAE was repeatedly demanding that the Mufti and his followers supply them with arms, funds and men to continue the riots. Previously, the requests were made formally to the authorities in Lebanon. Arms arriving from Transjordan were received, stored and distributed by the HAE until the responsibility was transferred to the Jerusalem office of the "Boycott Committee" (of Jewish goods from Palestine), under Tewfik el-Husseini, Jamal el-Husseini's brother and Deputy Chairman of the Arab Party.[96]

While the British attempted to placate these separate factions, what they failed to understand was that the Mufti and the Arab League were at odds with each other. The Mufti wanted to establish an Arab Government in Palestine, which he would head. The League opposed the move. They alleged that instead of organizing for the defense of Palestine while he was in Egypt for a year and a half, the Mufti had used the time to enrich himself. They also disagreed about who should command the Arab forces. The Mufti believed a committee should be in charge since a single leader might be killed. His opponents feared the Mufti would consolidate the operation under the el-Husseini clan.[97]

Participation in the rioting varied. Arabs in Hebron were criticized by the HAE for not taking a sufficiently active part, while towns and villages—especially Haifa and Jaffa—asked for an increased infusion of men, money and arms to continue the rioting. The HAE had an extensive plan, outside the regular campaign to boycott Jewish products that started before the riots, to "starve out" the Jews of Jerusalem. Arab merchants were instructed to refuse to sell eggs, vegetables and any other food to Jews. If they refused to comply, hooligans would be dispatched to enforce the rule.[98]

When UNSCOP sought to implement the General Assembly's Resolution establishing an independent Arab State and an independent Jewish State in Palestine not later than October 1, 1948, the AHC refused to cooperate and, organized a general strike and a boycott of the UNSCOP Committee when they came to Palestine.[99] On February 6, Jamal el-Husseini, representing the AHC, wrote to Secretary-General Trygve Lie that, "The Arabs of Palestine...will never submit or yield to any Power going to Palestine to enforce partition. The only way to establish partition is first to wipe them out—man, woman and child."[100]

Ben-Gurion had hoped that a war could be averted, but by December 1947 he noted that the "Arab world is beginning to fight the Jewish state, this war has already begun." Intelligence reports confirmed that the Mufti had acquired control over the Arabs in Palestine, and that there was talk among the Arabs of a "total war." Ben-Gurion responded with a strategy of "self-restraint," rather than going on the attack, to avert serious clashes. Reflecting this decision, by mid-December 1947 he initiated a limited call-up of only 6,700 new Haganah recruits. However, following the siege of Jewish Jerusalem in April 1948, in which the city was nearly overrun by the Arab Legion, Ben-Gurion had the Haganah shift to attack mode.[101]

On March 10, 1948, a British intelligence report analyzed the objectives of these assaults on the Jews. In an interview with the Mufti in a Jaffa weekly Al Sarikh, the Arab leader said that the defeat of the partition plan would not satisfy the Arabs. They would not stop fighting until all the Zionists were killed and Palestine became a completely Arab State. Nothing could divert them from this solution.[102] In the March 9, 1948 issue of al-Difa, (a local Arab newspaper of the pan-Arab *Istiqlal* or Independence Party), Ahmed al-Sharabati, the Syrian Defense Minister, said that the British would not be attacked because they opposed partition, and had agreed to leave the country. He said that critical fighting would begin after May 15, and until then the Jews would be attacked in every area the British had evacuated. By May 15, the Arabs would have all the equipment and supplies they needed.[103]

Similar belligerent statements were made by other leading Arab statesmen, and many articles in the Arab press showed that Syria, Lebanon, Egypt and Iraq shared the Mufti's goal of exterminating the Jews of Palestine and eliminating them once and for all.[104]

Radio broadcasts from Arab countries reinforced the view that the Arabs would succeed in this mission, while warning of the dangers the Zionists would bring to the region. For example, on January 10, 1948, Jerusalem Radio, an Arab radio station, informed its listeners that 600 fighters from Syria had entered Palestine. After infiltrating Jewish settlements they returned to Syria without fear of being pursued by the Haganah. Had the Jews followed them across the border, they would have been charged with aggression. The Haganah would also encounter Arab armies, which Radio Cairo said were charged with creating an impassable barrier around Palestine.[105]

Contempt for the Jews was also evident in the manner in which Arab fighters treated captured Jewish prisoners. In the markets of Jerusalem, Arab fighters sold pictures of 16 Jews who had been killed in a battle between Ramallah and Jerusalem, "showing their naked bodies with Arab swords stuck through their backs and stomach, and Arabs kicking their heads." In its daily and weekly bulletins, the Propaganda and Information Office of the HAE encouraged the murder of Jews, and "any outrage" Arabs committed was seen as "a national victory."[106]

Significantly, at the end of the Second World War, the American Jewish community was not eager for mass trials of Nazi war criminals. In all the discussions of the American Jewish Conference, established in August 1943 to unite American Jews, only the Mufti's name was suggested for prosecution.[107] Political analyst David Pryce-Jones observed that the Mufti's violent campaign against the emerging Jewish state "extended the ruin" of the Arabs in Palestine and has plagued the region ever since. He was the link between two attempts to annihilate the Jewish people—by the Nazis and the Arabs.[108]

Efforts by the British to accommodate Arab political demands were perceived as a serious weakness on the part of the British. Arab power politics necessitated a tougher stance. When the British sought to expose Nazi atrocities, the horrific accounts reinforced Arab confidence in Germany's power and the astuteness of their decision to side with them. Pro-British Arab leaders generally feared revealing their views lest they lose the support of their followers.[109]

Syria, Saudi Arabia, Lebanon, and Egypt did not declare war on Germany until February 1945, when the war was almost over and the Allied victory practically assured. Iraq declared war in January 1943, only after the Allied victory at Al-Alamein that led to the retreat of the Afrika Korps. These declarations of war were mere formalities, since none of the Arab States were directly involved in combat, and were made with an eye towards obtaining seats at the U.N. Transjordan declared war on Germany in 1939, but the principality was under the British Mandate and was not an independent country. It relied primarily on aid provided by the British, which also supported the Arab Legion, Transjordan's military.[110]

The Allies spent enormous sums of money in the Arab States during the war. Tens of thousands of Arab workers were employed at unusually high wages to build roads, airfields, railroads and a variety of buildings. Foodstuffs and commodities were provided to the Arabs at a time when Europe and England were under harsh restrictions themselves. Direct subsidies to the Arab States between 1943/1944 reached enormous proportions. The British even compensated Saudi Arabia for the loss of income sustained by the suspension of the Muslim pilgrimages to Mecca. Most of the support the British received in return from the Arabs was the result of how far British "forces could compel" them to cooperate or what their funds could buy.[111]

After the defeat of Germany, the Arabs remained so firmly pro-German that no one even tried to hide their strong feelings toward the Nazi movement or their Nazi past. The Nasser regime did not conceal its sympathies for the Nazis either, especially since it was competing with South Africa, Spain and South America in offering a refuge for Nazi war criminals to hide and continue their war against the Jews. Those who chose Egypt were afforded a very hospitable and supportive environment in which to pursue their mission.[112]

CHAPTER 5

The Jewish Contribution to the Allied Cause During WWI and WWII

In sharp contrast to the Arabs, the Jewish community of Palestine actively supported the Allied cause in both World War I and World War II. The *Yishuv* provided technical assistance, established espionage networks, assembled military production lines, and even volunteered to fight in Europe. Future Israeli Defense and Foreign Minister Moshe Dayan lost his eye while fighting Vichy forces in Syria. While much of the Arab world either fought with or cheered for the demise of the British and French, and the ascendancy of the Ottomans and the Nazis, Palestinian Jewry remained committed to the Allied cause.

NILI SPY RING

After Turkey joined the Central Powers during the First World War, the Jews in Palestine realized that a German victory, with its designs on the Far East, might preclude the restoration of a Jewish commonwealth in Palestine. This prompted the founding of NILI, a pro-British spy ring that provided critical intelligence about the state of the Turkish military, and the internal conditions in the region. By late 1915, NILI members exposed the low morale and the rampant illness in the military forces of Djemal Pasha on the Palestine Front, where he also served as military governor of Turkish Syria.[1]

In mid-1917, NILI gave the British the Turkish order of battle, an analysis of their organization, and unit configuration, including the number of forces assigned to Mesopotamia. A report on the availability of water in the Sinai desert was invaluable to General Allenby, since almost half of his soldiers were cavalry and mounted infantry. Knowing where to find water allowed Allenby to assemble his cavalry, infantry and transportation at Beersheba, a town at the eastern edge of Turkish defenses, which was not as securely protected as Gaza. After Allenby captured Beersheba, he attacked from the east and outflanked Gaza. Two previous attempts to capture Gaza by Allenby's predecessor, Sir Archibald Murray in March-April 1917, had failed.[2]

NILI was led by Aaron Aaronsohn, a world renowned scientist, who directed the Jewish Agricultural Experiment Station at Atlit, approximately 12 miles south of Haifa, his brother Alexander, who attained a level of prominence as an writer in the U.S., and Absalom Feinberg, an accomplished poet who was secretary of the Experiment Station.[3]

Aaronsohn was aided by 23 active members who traveled throughout Palestine collecting information and transmitting it to EMSIB (Eastern Mediterranean Special Bureau in Egypt), with the aid of trawlers that went from Palestine to Port Said in Egypt, and by 12 individuals who took a less active day role. Aaronsohn was in regular communication with, among others, General Gilbert Clayton, chief political officer to General Allenby, and with Colonel Wyndham Deeds, of British intelligence service.[4]

After arriving in London in October 1916, Aaronsohn met with Sir Mark Sykes, a Conservative Member of Parliament, to explain the pre-war accomplishments of the Jews in Palestine. Consequently, and in large part because of these conversations, the British government sent a note to the Italian government, with whom they were in discussions, asking them to grant the British railway rights in the impending Baghdad-Haifa railway, and to "generally respect the civic and colonizing rights of the Jews in Palestine.[5]

During his second premiership (1951-1955), Winston Churchill praised the Jewish contribution in both World Wars, especially Chaim Weizmann's development of a new way to manufacture acetone, used in explosives vital to winning the war, and Albert Einstein's generation of the physics of the atomic bomb with which "we were able to put the seal" on World War II.[6]

JEWISH MILITARY ASSISTANCE

In September 1940, the British established a Palestinian battalion attached to the East Kent Regiment, but the Jews wanted to fight under their own Jewish flag. The British wanted the battalion to be composed of equal numbers of Jews and Arabs, but this was unrealistic due to the large number of Jews who volunteered and the "greater proneness to desertion of the Arabs."[7]

By the end of war, there were more than 26,000 Jewish men and women from Palestine serving in the British Air Force, Navy, and Army. After six years of protracted wrangling by the leaders of the Jewish Agency, the British allowed the formation of the Jewish Brigade in September 1944. The Brigade fought in Italy in the last battles of the war.[8]

Jewish efforts on behalf of the British amounted to little more than a moral victory, as they had little effect on changing British policy. The importance of the Brigade became apparent at the end of the war when the soldiers aided Jews in the Displaced Persons (DP) camps, assisting them to immigrate illegally to Palestine and to acquire arms.[9]

In the spring of 1940, the Haganah, the *Yishuv*'s underground military organization, secretly offered to provide the British with

Romanian-speaking agents to help incapacitate Romanian oil fields, but this turned out to be too ambitious a task. The contacts did lead the British military to training members of the Haganah in fighting behind enemy lines.

In May 1941, after the British defeated Greece but had not yet subdued Crete, members of the Haganah, under the command of a British officer, tragically failed to destroy the oil fields in Tripoli, Libya. Also in May, members of IZL (Menachem Begin's Irgun Zeva'i Le'umi, National Military Organization) were involved in trying to kidnap the Mufti in Baghdad, where he was inciting rebellion.[10]

On July 15, 1940, the Royal Air Force established the Haifa Investigation Bureau, an interrogation office headed by Immanuel Yalan and staffed by Jews, to interview escaped British prisoners who had found their way to the Middle East. Later on, the escapees were mostly Jews. The bureau's objective was to obtain information about Germany's military aims, any economic and industrial secrets as well as the temperament of the people under enemy control. By the time it closed in November 1944, 4,400 people had been interviewed. A similar bureau was established in 1943 in Istanbul to interrogate refugees coming from the Balkans.[11]

During 1941, the Haganah was in Syria and Lebanon, sometimes under British command, to gather intelligence and initiate clandestine propaganda campaigns. Free French radio broadcasts in Arabic and French, Bulgarian and Hungarian originated from the home of David Hacohen, director of the Histadrut Construction Company Solel Boneh, and continued until Syria was occupied. In June 1941, two Jewish saboteurs were sent to Aleppo, where they destroyed the railroad station and an army camp. Toward the end of 1940, the Vichy secret police in Syria captured 12 members of the unit and put them in prison where they were tortured, ending this chapter of their activities. When the British entered Syria and Lebanon in July 1941, a platoon of Haganah scouts guided them and acted as saboteurs.[12]

When it appeared that the Germans would be advancing towards the Middle East, Professor Yohanan Rattner, head of the National Command of the Haganah, who was a staff officer in the Russian army during World War I, was recruited to help the British in determining the vulnerable points along the possible route the Germans might take. Rattner targeted railroad tunnels in the Taurus Mountains and other strategic transport links in Turkey, Iraq and Syria. By the summer of 1941, the plans were complete.[13]

JEWISH PARACHUTING

Jews were also parachuted behind enemy lines in Europe, after being trained by the British. In May 1943, Peretz Rosenberg, a radio operator, was parachuted into Montenegro with the first British mission to the headquarters of Josip Broz Tito, the leader of Yugoslavia. For several months, Rosenberg was the only link to the outside world. In October 1943, he was sent to Italy.[14]

Two parachutists were dropped into Romania on October 1, 1943. In January 1944, Rehaveam Amir, another radio operator, was dropped onto the island of Vis to work at Tito's headquarters until April. In May, he parachuted into Slovenia to establish radio contact between the Yugoslavs and the British in Italy. He returned to Bari, Italy in August where he was given equipment and dropped back again to Slovenia. After teaching a group of Yugoslav fighters how to transmit, he went back to Italy in September 1944.[15]

In March 1944, four Jews were dropped into Slovenia. Two were on their way to Hungary. Hannah Senesh, a young poet, was betrayed to the Hungarian authorities, and was arrested in June once she crossed the Hungarian border. After she was tortured and given a show trial, the fascist Szalasi government executed her on November 7, 1944. In

May, two additional men were sent to Slovenia en route to Hungary. The Germans murdered one; the other escaped and found refuge in Budapest.[16]

Ten parachutists were scheduled to go to Romania. One group of Communist Yugoslav partisans refused to help one of them to reach her destination, forcing her to return home. Two were mistakenly dropped where they were immediately apprehended by the Romanian secret police. Two more were caught before they reached Romania. Four arrived in late July and early August 1944, but by that time the Romanian king had already changed allegiances and began fighting the Germans. They helped an entire prisoner camp of American and British pilots escape Romanian captivity.[17]

In September 1944, five parachutists were dropped into an area liberated by the Slovak National Rising. When the Germans occupied the town of Banská Bystrica on October 28, the commandos organized a group of Jews and fled to the mountains to fight as partisans. Two days later, Russians collaborating with the Nazis arrested four out of the five, and executed them. The fifth joined a Soviet partisan group until the Red Army freed the territory.[18]

For the most part, the project did not succeed as planned by the British. Most of the parachutists were apprehended. Seven were killed. Many did not engage the enemy in combat until the Russian Army liberated an area, and sometimes even later. Yet a number of military operations in Austria, Romania and Yugoslavia, and to some degree in Slovakia were successful. They were also able to help Jews immigrate, particularly from Romania and Bulgaria. After the war, they helped re-establish Jewish life and Zionist activities in these countries.

The Jews had hoped to organize an anti-Nazi Jewish underground, thwart the destruction of European Jewry and actively fight the

Germans, but the restrictions imposed by the British precluded this from happening. From a symbolic perspective, the operation demonstrated that the *Yishuv* had not abandoned the Jews of Europe, and encouraged the yearning for Jewish sovereignty.[19]

A JEWISH-ARAB COMPARISON

The contrast between the two communities could not be clearer. While Palestinian Jewry actively aided the Allies to defeat Hitler at all costs, the Palestinian Arabs not only supported the Nazis, they energetically engaged in their own campaign to rid the world of the Jews. As has been noted, Haj Amin el-Husseini shared Hitler's and Eichmann's goal of annihilating the Jewish people and even organized a Muslim SS unit in Yugoslavia to accomplish this task. Following the defeat of Germany, the Mufti and other Arab leaders continued to harbor pro-German sympathies and sought to finish the sacred mission Hitler began by trying to destroy the fledgling Jewish state. Having sided with the defeated powers in Europe in ideology and practice, the Palestinian Arabs had lost an opportunity to establish their own state.

To compare, Jewish leaders vigorously supported the British, despite British limits on Jewish emigration to Palestine, restrictions on Jewish land purchases, and uncertainty about the extent of British commitment to establishing a Jewish state. Their zealous volunteerism, knowledge of the Middle East, and energetic commitment to the defense of Palestine demonstrated enormous goodwill.

"AS MUCH AS WE COULD DO"

While many Arabs were working with the Nazis to defeat the British, the Jews in Palestine volunteered to protect the British position in the Mediterranean. The precarious nature of the situation was described by David Horowitz, an ardent Zionist and a U.N. correspondent:

The Middle East has been completely isolated from the West and the Mediterranean line of communication cut. Civilian and military supplies have arrived in Palestine via the Cape of Good Hope and Port Said. Thus there was no way of escaping an effort to turn the Middle East into an almost self-sufficient economic unit.[20]

Despite Britain's limiting Jewish immigration to Palestine, restrictions on their land purchases, and vagueness about recommitting itself to the Balfour Declaration, members of the *Yishuv* knew they had to join forces with the British to fight their mutual adversary. David Ben-Gurion, Chairman of the Zionist Executive, expressed this commitment clearly: "We shall fight with Great Britain in this war as if there was no White Paper, and fight the White Paper as if there were no war."[21]

Following a Jewish Agency appeal for mobilization on September 3, 1939, out of a population of approximately 600,000, 130,000 men and women enlisted for duty, including 400 physicians. In an effort to preserve a judicious "balance" between the Jews and the Arabs, the British Mandatory Government declined the offer. However, the exigencies of war forced the British army to circumvent political considerations and contact the staff of the Hebrew University through personal relationships and connections to ask for their help.[22]

JEWISH TECHNICAL AND PROFESSIONAL HELP

When the British army encountered considerable difficulty with maps needing immediate modification, it approached Professor Ernst Rosenthal to manufacture compasses. After the success of this manufacturing venture, the British requested the repair of 500 watt radio tubes that were a meter long and 30 centimeters in diameter. There was only one radio station in the Middle East broadcasting messages to submarines, which were the only means to prevent supplies from reaching Rommel. The station had two transmitters installed with these tubes. Since they could not obtain new transmitters during the war, the British had to close down the transmitters while the tubes were being repaired. After finding the 500-watt tubes too difficult to repair, the British brought five kilowatt tubes, which were ten times more powerful. Repairing tubes was arduous and complicated requiring master-craftsmanship.[23]

Manufacturing airplane transmitter panels used in stabilizing transmission frequencies posed another challenge because a quartz panel in an electronic circuit helped it achieve maximum accuracy. Adjusting the thickness of the quartz panels enabled the transmission codes to be changed. Codes had to be replaced repeatedly to preclude the enemy from discovering them. Until the staff of the Hebrew University's Physics Department was asked to cut the crystals and ground them, only two facilities—one in the United States and the other in England—had the needed expertise.[24]

During the war, Palestinian Jewish scientists were the primary source of bromide, a chemical used in manufacturing a fuel additive that increases octane levels, and found in large quantity in the Dead Sea. British aircraft, with piston-propelled engines, required high-octane fuel to operate.

After the process of converting bromide to calcium bromide in solid form was developed by the Department of Physical Chemistry under Professor Ladislau Farkas at Hebrew University, the results were sent to the Dead Sea Works, where they extended the process. In this way, they were able to ship regular supplies to England without any danger.[25]

The Department also formulated means to camouflage the camps, storage facilities, tents and equipment of the British units based in the Western Desert opposite Rommel. Eight different types of paint were

developed for use by soldiers. The university staff devised methods
to insulate British tanks from the desert heat, prepared a process
for delivering Vitamin C to British soldiers fighting in the desert,
produced methyl chloride for refrigerators in ships (because unlike
other gases it did not explode even when sustaining a direct hit), and
developed an unconventional process to cut iron underwater to clear
ships sunk by the Italians so that vital supplies could be transported
to the region.[26]

When physicians in the Australian army arrived in Palestine with
Allied forces, they approached the Mandatory Government about
repairing their X-ray equipment, and were assured that no such
resource existed. A number of the scientists who knew about the
Hebrew University went directly to the staff, who agreed to help
repair the machines. They soon learned that university scientists were
able to assist them in other areas through their scientific discoveries.[27]

Some of the information the Allied physicians received was in the
form of courses focusing on relevant civilian medicine and issues they
might encounter in the Middle East and the Near and Far East. They
were allowed to attend lectures and staff meetings given by Hebrew
University's Pre-Faculty of Medicine and by physicians at Jerusalem's
Hadassah Hospital. Among the most discussed topics at these
sessions was viral hepatitis (then known as jaundice), a ubiquitous
disease found in the military. Medical officers were especially worried
about the disease since the chance of soldiers becoming infected
increased significantly in their very cramped living space. There were
also courses on malaria, disease-carrying insects, worms, snakes
and dysentery.[28]

Despite volunteering in large numbers, Jewish doctors, except for
malariologists, were not eagerly welcomed by the British Army
because of a purported British desire to balance the number of Arab
and Jewish physicians in their service. However, given the small

number of Arab physicians in Palestine, the British more likely feared that Jews of German and Austrian descent would not be loyal to the Allied cause, prompting the withdrawal of many doctors' applications. Other problems included differences in medical training, languages, communication skills and an aversion to foreigners. Some British even questioned the wisdom of having any doctors from Palestine serve with the army. Out of the 400 physicians who answered the appeal by the Jewish Agency and the Medical Association to enlist in the British army, 200 were accepted. They served in various British military units in Ethiopia, Iraq, Egypt, Transjordan, India, Italy, Greece, Iran, Austria, Palestine, Malta, Libya and Tunisia.[29]

Malaria specialists, however, were quickly inducted since malaria was considered the primary threat. Anti-malaria units accompanied troops wherever they went. They evaluated the danger of malaria from local populations to determine the most secure route for the troops to traverse past towns and villages. The specialists performed a defensive role by providing drugs, eradicating mosquitoes, and supplying mosquito netting and repellent creams.[30]

The initial ten anti-malaria units in the British army, four of which were commanded by Jewish malariologists from Palestine, were sent as out as "vanguards" and served in Egypt, Libya, Tunisia Lebanon, Syria, Iraq and Palestine. They forged the way by using D.D.T. against mosquitoes and managed the anti-malaria operation in the Burma jungles. Protecting soldiers on the battlefield in Greece, Italy, North Africa and other Far Eastern countries with mosquito repellant ointment was of paramount concern.[31]

Jewish factories and farms were mobilized to provide supplies to the Allies in the Middle East. All the land mines used against Rommel's forces were produced by Jewish factories in Palestine, as were all the silk parachutes.[32] Optical instruments for the Royal Air Force and Navy, for example, were manufactured and repaired by a Russian Jew

who had been the former technical director of the Zeiss Works at Jena.
Other items produced by the *Yishuv* included medical and electric
instruments, geodetic instruments, hospital equipment, cables, wires,
ambulances and army field kitchens.[33]

Jewish factories also produced anti-tank components, three million
mines, machine gun parts, propellers for ships, six million two-
gallon containers and accumulators for tanks and the British Air
Force, several hundreds of tons of cast-iron shrapnel balls and
port installations for the British Army in Alexandretta on the
Mediterranean coast of Turkey. They repaired guns, ships, and
machinery, and built small naval boats and two minesweepers.[34]

Jews assisted the war effort additionally by providing fresh milk,
vegetables, citrus fruits, bread, cigarettes, beer and wine to the British
military across the Middle East and North Africa. Significant amounts
of wheat were milled for the British and cold-storage facilities
were made accessible to them. By increasing production of Jewish
agriculture by 70 percent during the war, precious shipping space
was freed up for more vital military requirements.[35]

Considerable contributions were made from the textile industry
including military and hospital tents, camouflage nets, uniforms,
underwear, socks, knitted items, ropes, furs for the pilots, fur gloves,
flying vests, rubber boots and life-saving items. More than 1,000,000
boots and shoes were produced, as were large numbers of books
and pamphlets.[36]

Ether, a highly flammable anesthetic, was manufactured in a factory
near Tel Aviv. This factory became the single source of that product
for all the military hospitals in the region. Other chemical products
produced were dry ice, fertilizers, acetone, pharmaceutical bromides
and methyl bromides used as a fire extinguisher on aircraft.[37]

Jewish engineers, building contractors, architects and laborers reconstructed airport runways, built bridges, harbor installations and airfields throughout the Middle East as far as Iran and Bahrain. During the El Alamein campaign, which led to the retreat of the German Afrika Korps and an Allied victory 150 miles west of Cairo, they built sea and land fortifications.[38]

Hadassah Medical Center gave courses for military officers on dysentery, malaria, typhoid, typhus and other tropical diseases. A procedure to hasten the healing process of wounds was developed and shared with the medical personnel of the U.N. British army scientists and doctors had use of the laboratories to pursue their own research. British military hospitals used the laboratory of Pathological Physiology for blood examinations and to test the vitamin content of food for the troops. The Polish Government awarded the head of the Hadassah Bacteriology Department the Golden Cross of Merit for developing anti-typhus vaccine used by Polish troops and refugees. Dysentery vaccines were prepared for Polish troops and refugees in the Middle East and Russia.[39]

The Electrotechnical Laboratory developed an electro-magnetic mine detector. The Institute's workshops assembled emergency generators, produced special frames for guns, tank parts, 96 types of tools to assemble and dismantle aircraft, and a wide variety of measuring instruments and machines. The metallographic laboratory examined large amounts of materials to determine their strength, inner structure, chemical reactions and other potential issues.[40]

CHAPTER 6

Israel's Right to Exist

ASSAULT ON ISRAEL'S RIGHT TO EXIST

Questioning Israel's right to exist is now widely accepted as a legitimate undertaking, engaged in by both Arabs and American Jews who have widely divergent motives. A close examination of the historical records makes it clear that the Arabs have never accepted the right of Jewish self-determination in the Middle East.[1] In fact, denying Israel's historical and spiritual connection to the Land of Israel is an official policy of the Palestinian Authority (PA) that is expressed in formal and informal educational settings. In textbooks and educational media broadcasts, PA leaders and educators seek to expunge any vestige of the Jewish presence in all of Israel, especially Jerusalem, with the intent to undermine the rationale of Israel's right to exist.[2]

For some American Jewish intellectuals, Israel's existence is a reminder of the enduring distinctiveness of the Jewish people, which draws attention to themselves as Jews. Israel thus becomes "an ethnic embarrassment" and "a source of continuing personal resentment." Others see Israel as "retrograde," and ideologically incompatible with their political philosophy. They support Palestinian Arab nationalism, but Jewish nationalism makes them uncomfortable, especially when the Jewish state exercises its right of self-defense. Even when justified in criticizing a particular policy or action, their frustration often suggests something deeper than political differences.

Perhaps they have a need for greater social acceptance, and a means to demonstrate their "progressive" credentials. Anti-Zionism and anti-Americanism are now "the new litmus test of progressive politics... If one is not at least a serious doubter of the legitimacy of Israel... one runs the risk of being excluded...from the left." The fact that anti-Zionism—the denial to Jews of a national homeland in the land of Israel—is basically a form of antisemitism either escapes or does not appreciably concern Jews in these groups.[3]

These assaults fail to recognize a number of key issues. In the last century, Israel is the only state established whose legitimacy was acknowledged by the League of Nations and the United Nations. Significantly, the League of Nations did not establish the legitimate rights of the Jewish people to a national home in Palestine but recognized a "pre-existing right." The connection of the Jews to their ancient homeland was acknowledged by world leaders such as President John Adams, Napoleon Bonaparte, President Woodrow Wilson, and British Foreign Secretary Lord Palmerston. Within the Judeo-Christian tradition it was considered self-evident.[4]

For Muslims, there is a religious imperative to destroy the Jewish state. As Bat Yeor, a pioneer in the study of the legal and social status of Jews and Christians living under Islamic rule observed, due to the inferior status of Jews in Islam, and because divine will dooms Jews to wandering and misery, the Jewish state appears to Muslims as an unbearable affront and a sin against Allah. Therefore it must be destroyed by Jihad.

Here the Pan-Arab and anti-Western theses that consider Israel as an advanced instrument of the West in the Islamic world, come to reinforce religious anti-Judaism. The religious and political fuse in a purely Islamic context onto which are grafted foreign elements. If, on the doctrinal level, Nazi influence is secondary to the Islamic base, the technique with which the Antisemitic material has been reworked, and the political purposes being pursued, present striking similarities with Hitler's Germany.[5]

Andrew Bostom, pre-eminent scholar on Islam, has pointed out that Hamas' view on the jihad against Israel and Islamic hatred of Jews are completely in accord with those of Al Azhar University in Cairo, Egypt, the most authoritative and respected religious educational institution in Sunni Islam:[6]

> In April 1948, the Grand Mufti of Egypt, Sheikh Muhammad Mahawif, issued a fatwa declaring jihad in Palestine obligatory for all Muslims. The Jews, he claimed, planned to take over...all the lands of Islam...Eight years later, a fatwa written January 5, 1956 by then Grand Mufti of Egypt, Sheikh Hasan Mamoun, and signed by the leading members of the Fatwa Committee of Al Azhar, and the major representatives of all four Islamic schools of jurisprudence, declared:[7]

> The question put to us reveals that the land of Palestine has been conquered by the Muslims [by Jihad, in the 7th century] who have lived there for a long time, and has become part of the Muslim territory where minorities of other religions dwell. Accordingly, Palestine has become a territory under the jurisdiction of Islam and governed by Islamic laws. The question further reveals that Jews have taken a part of Palestine and there established their non-Islamic government and have also evacuated from that part most of its Muslim inhabitants

> In this case the Jihad is the duty of all Muslims, not just those who can undertake it. And since all Islamic countries constitute the abode of every Muslim, the Jihad is imperative for both the Muslims inhabiting the territory attacked and Muslims everywhere else because even though some sections have not been attacked directly, the attack nevertheless took place on a

part of the Muslim territory which is a legitimate residence for any Muslim.

Muslims cannot conclude peace with those Jews who have usurped the territory of Palestine and attacked its people and their property in any manner which allows the Jews to continue as a state in that sacred Muslim territory. Muslims should cooperate regardless of differences in language, color, or race to restore the country to its people

Everyone knows that from the early days of Islam to the present day the Jews have been plotting against Islam and Muslims and the Islamic homeland. They do not propose to be content with the attack they made on Palestine and Al Aqsa Mosque, but they plan for the possession of all Islamic territories from the Nile to the Euphrates.[8]

Bostom concludes with the warning that the *jihad* against the Jews is but one aspect albeit primal of the *jihad* to establish global Islamic hegemony.[9]

DENYING THE JEWISH PAST

In order to delegitimize the Jewish state, Arabs often deny the Jewish historical connection to the land, especially the city of Jerusalem.[10]

Yasser Arafat, former chairman of the PA, claimed that in all the archeological excavations conducted during 34 years near the Western Wall, they "found not a single stone that the Temple of Solomon was there, because historically the Temple was not in Palestine [at all]. They found only remnants of a shrine of the Roman Herod."[11] At the 2000 Camp David summit, Yasser Arafat alleged that "Solomon's Temple was not in Jerusalem, but Nablus."[12] Dennis Ross, the chief U.S. peace negotiator, understood that in making this outrageous charge, Arafat "was challenging the core of Jewish faith, and seeking to deny Israel any claim in the Old City."[13] Mahmoud Abbas (Abu Mazen), Arafat's successor, also impugns Israel's "claim that 2000 years ago they had a temple. I challenge that this is so."[14]

"The first connection of the Jews to this site [the Western Wall] began in the 16th Century…The Jewish connection to this site is a recent connection, not ancient…like the roots of the Islamic connection…The Jewish connection to this site is a fabricated connection, a coincidental connection," asserted Dr. Hassan Khader, founder of the *Al Quds Encyclopedia* on PA TV.[15]

Sheik Raed Salah, who directs the northern faction of the Islamic Movement in Israel, also denied the Temple ever existed, insisting that, "the claims of the Jews are big lies and they have no right to any speck of dust here."[16]

In addition, some members of the Arab academic community have gone so far as to deny Israel's legitimacy by portraying the Jewish state as a product of colonialism and that Jews have a tenuous claim to the land at best. Among the most recent purveyors of this view is Nadia Abu El-Haj, a professor of anthropology at Barnard College. She argues that Israeli archeologists use their craft to substantiate Israel's right to establish a Jewish national homeland in a land where Jews never lived. "There never was an actual metropole [mother city] for Jewish settlers in Palestine…the projects of settlement and of nation-building developed at one and the same time on a single colonial terrain."[17] In the process, the Israelis have "erased other geographies. Most centrally, it effaced Arab/Palestinian claims to and presences within the very same place."[18]

Given Israel's alleged attempts to erase the Arab/Muslim presence, Abu El-Haj believes that one can understand the behavior of an Arab mob that set fire to Torah scrolls, prayer books and other religious objects at Joseph's Tomb on October 7, 2000. They used hammers, crowbars and pickaxes to destroy the stone building and the Od Yosef Chai Yeshiva located at the site, and brutally murdered Rabbi Hillel Lieberman, the American-born head of the yeshiva. They then turned the tomb into a mosque.[19]

"In destroying the tomb, Palestinian demonstrators eradicated one 'fact on the ground,'" Abu El-Haj concludes. "Archeology remains salient in this world of ongoing contestation. It is a sign of colonial presence and national rights, of secularism and science as various groups in Palestine and Israel engage in struggles to (re)configure the Israeli state and polity to determine its territorial limits."[20]

The problem with Israeli archeology, she says, is the pervasive belief within the Palestinian Arab community that Israeli archeologists tend "to systematically erase evidence of other (non-Jewish) pasts in the country's history in efforts to legitimize Jewish presence in this land."[21] This is accomplished by using bulldozers, considered "the ultimate sign of 'bad science' and of nationalist politics guiding research agendas."[22]

Using mechanical earthmoving equipment, however, has become an established technique since the 1960's, asserts historian Ralph Harrington. Abu El-Haj distorts the Israeli use of bulldozers not out of confusion about the technical operation of this machinery, but because she is "ideologically-motivated." Her target is not the alleged transgressions of Israeli archeologists, but the very "existence of Israel."[23]

In contrast with her reaction to the wanton and gratuitous destruction of Joseph's Tomb in October 2000, which she excuses, Abu El-Haj neglects to discuss the ongoing efforts of the Arabs to destroy Temple Mount antiquities, the attempt since 1997 in Nazareth to build a huge mosque to dwarf the Christian Basilica of the Annunciation, and the repeated Arab sniping on Rachel's tomb, Judaism's third holiest site.[24]

The damage to the antiquities on the Temple Mount is designed to change the 36-acre compound into an exclusive Muslim preserve by obliterating any remains or trace of the Jewish past. Muslims even assert that the area is the site of an ancient mosque from the era of Adam and Eve. As such, in 1996 the Western Hulda Gate passageway and Solomon's Stables, two ancient underground Second Temple buildings, were converted into mosques able to accommodate 10,000 people.[25]

After September 2000, the Muslim *Waqf* prohibited the Israel Antiquities Authority from having any archeological oversight of the Temple Mount and even banned them from entering the area. In the process of completing underground mosques, 13,000 tons of rubble was removed from the Temple Mount, including relics from the First and Second Temple periods. In February and March 2001, an arched structure was demolished by bulldozers.[26]

ESTABLISHING THE HISTORIC JEWISH PRESENCE

Archeologists have been using the evidence found in archeological excavations as another means to validate Israel's claim to a Jewish presence in the land from the time of Joshua bin-Nun (1354 BCE-1244 BCE) to the Arab conquest in the 7th century.[27] For Abu El-Haj, this undertaking is essentially an attempt to establish "material signs of an ancient and supposedly uninterrupted occupancy of the Jewish national home and nation..."[28] Keith W. Whitelam, a professor of religious studies, claims that "Western scholarship...invented ancient Israel and silenced Palestinian history."[29]

During the British Mandate (1920-1948), the Zionists wanted to increase "national consciousness and strengthen Israeli ties to the land they were settling."[30] As Norman Bentwich, the first Attorney-General of Mandatory Palestine, observed, "Wherever you plant your foot in that land you tread on history. A hundred years ago Palestine was largely deserted and derelict." Aside from the holy cities of Jerusalem, Hebron, Bethlehem, Nazareth and Tiberias, which were visited by pilgrims, and except for a number of Biblical sites such as Gaza, Ascalon, Jericho, Shiloh, and the graves of the righteous, most of the locations referred to in the Torah were not identified.[31]

Hani Nur el-Din, a professor of archeology at Al Quds University in Jerusalem, and his colleagues aver that biblical archeology is an attempt by Israelis "to fit historical evidence into a biblical context." He added, "The link between the historical evidence and the biblical narration, written much later, is largely missing. There's a kind of fiction about the 10th century. They try to link whatever they find to the biblical narration. They have a button, and they want to make a suit out of it."[32]

This "nationalistic agenda" has shaped Israeli archeology and infused Israeli culture with archeology's importance. The acquisition of territory through continuous wars, the construction of new settlements, especially in areas of Jewish historical importance, and the plethora of new archeological discoveries has exposed Israeli archeology to "sectarian bias," and "tendentious arguments."[33] One possible answer to critics of Israeli archeology is offered by Shalom Paul, a Biblical scholar and William G. Dever, a leading archeologist. In analyzing the role of archeology, it is essential, they assert, to understand that the connection between archeology and the Bible is frequently misconstrued. "The most dangerous error" is to assume that the role of archeology is "to prove the Bible." Faith in the Bible is founded on history, but fundamentally "biblical faith is beyond history: it is a way of viewing the result of God's action in history which interprets events through the 'eyes of the faith.'" With regard to the Land of Israel, the Bible's "claim is not that Israel took the Land, but that God *gave* the Land to Israel." This declaration is not open for investigation, since this is a matter of faith which archeology cannot prove or disprove. Archeology increases our ability to study the Bible in the context of contemporaneous events, and becomes a valuable tool to understand the life of the Jews who lived in the land of Israel.[34]

Beginning in 2004, Israeli archeologists examined the ruins the *Waqf* deposited in the Kidron Valley eight years ago. Among the rubble, they found remnants from the late period of the kings of Judea (8th and 7th centuries BCE) including a seal of impression in ancient Hebrew script of the last days of the First Temple.[35]

In the summer of 2007, a ditch of 350 meters was dug to replace power lines, causing significant destruction of pottery shards that were found broken in their original position *(in situ)*, where they had been since the days of the First Temple.[36]

GREEK AND ROMAN SOURCES

Ancient Greek and Roman writers, dating from the 3rd century BCE to the 3rd century CE, are often overlooked as sources to refute false claims about Jerusalem, contends historian Rivka Fishman-Duker. Writers such as Egyptian priest Manetho (mid-3rd century BCE), Apion, a Greek grammarian and intellectual who lived in Alexandria in the mid-1st century CE, Roman historian Tacitus (56-117 CE) and Roman satirist Juvenal (66-130 CE), all described the Jewish identity of Jerusalem, even while expressing negative and historically false statements about Jews. There was also resentment that Jews sent substantial amounts of money, gold and silver annually to the Temple. Lucius Valerius Flaccus, Roman governor of the province of Asia, was even accused of having stolen gold destined for Jerusalem.[37]

There is "unanimous agreement" among these men that Jerusalem was Jewish because it was established by Jews, its residents were Jewish, and that the Temple, situated in Jerusalem, was the center of Jewish religious life. Aside from describing the physical features of the Temple and its location in the center of the city, Greek historian Hecataeus of Abdera (300BCE) explained the role of the priests in the Temple, a religious service and the animal sacrifices that were offered. Writing in the first century, Roman historian Titus Livius (Livy – 59BCE-17CE) said that the Jews did not indicate "to which deity pertains the temple at Jerusalem, nor is an image found there, since they do not think the God partakes of any figure."[38]

Around 110CE, Tacitus wrote in his *Histories* that Jerusalem is "the capital of the Jews." In other words, by the early 2nd century BCE, Greeks and Romans routinely wrote about Jerusalem, which they acknowledged was founded by Jews and was the center of their lives.[39]

Historian Joel Fishman notes that no matter how absurd or historically inaccurate the accusations might be, Israel's adversaries have elevated this issue to legitimate discourse by inverting the truth and reality, a propaganda technique honed by the Nazis.[40]

Fishman sees Arab attempts to deny the Jewish past not only as a problem for Jews, but for the West as well:

> Beyond the specific circumstances, inversion of truth constitutes an assault on the foundations of modern culture which is based on empirical and rational thought. If this assault succeeds, there is a danger that language will be debased and society will regress to a condition of *anomie*. There is, therefore, an urgent need to expose the lies which have become part of the media war and to discredit those who spread them.[41]

THE JEWS ARE NOT A PEOPLE

The charge that Jews are not a people or a religious community because they do not have a common language, history or ancestry is a further attempt to deny them the right to self-determination and their own state. Professor George Scelle, an international jurist and member of the U.N. International Commission, defined what constitutes a people in his lectures at the Hague Academy of International Law: "It is commonly accepted today that every collective, united by links of conscious solidarity—of which the members thereof, themselves, are the judges—should be regarded as a 'people.'"[42] A number of years earlier, he said that there "can be no doubt that the whole body of Jewish communities together can be considered one nation or one people." The situation of the Jews was "exceptional," he noted, due to their dispersion. Although "they lack some of the elements of solidarity" found in other groups living closer together, "their traditions, customs, the persecutions they have endured, their religious practices and mystic aspirations are so firmly integrated— certainly far more so than in the case of other people—for the very reason that they have not assimilated with the political groups in whose midst they have lived or settled."[43]

The French jurist, Paul Fauchille, regarded Jews in the same way. When discussing the Balfour Declaration and other Allied and Associated Powers declarations about Zionism, he said: "The Great War of 1914-1919 brought with it official recognition of the nationhood of yet another persecuted people: namely the Jewish people."[44]

The Council of the League of Nations recognized the existence of the Jewish people and its historical connection to Palestine on July 24, 1922 when it defined the Palestine Mandate. The Mandate also recognized the Zionist Organization as the representative of the Jewish people in dealing with the establishment of the national home.

The judges at the International Tribunal in Nuremberg found that "atrocities against the Jewish people were committed." On practically every subsequent page of their ruling, mention is made of the murder of "the Jews" in countries throughout Europe, which means members of the Jewish people. Nathan Feinberg, a professor at the Hebrew University, notes that the judges meant in the "ethnic, not the religious sense;" because during the Holocaust even Jews who had converted to other faiths were murdered.[45]

JEWISH NATIONALISM

The Ottoman Empire ruled Palestine from 1517 until WWI, relinquishing the sovereignty of the territory to the Allies in the Treaty of Sevres. This enabled the Jews to pursue their historic claim to Palestine.[46] The British did not give Palestine to the Jews; "it was a *de jure* recognition of a situation that existed *de facto*." They assumed that the Arabs and Jews would be able to live together in harmony and that the Arabs would profit from this arrangement. But the British acknowledged an overriding issue: The Jews had the more compelling and credible case, and that this was *sui generis*.[47]

The Jews are the only people in the world who insisted they could not live without their land, even though they had not lived there for 2,000 years, noted former Israeli Ambassador Yaacov Herzog. In a debate with British historian Arnold Toynbee, Herzog asserted that the normal laws of history do not apply in this case, "so long as the world agrees that there is something unique about the Jews in the history of mankind, it cannot deny the right of the Jews to this land."

In describing the Children of Israel 3,000 years ago, Balaam the Prophet referred to them as "a people that dwells alone." This is how the Jews are perceived today. Whether this concept suggests privilege with a unique responsibility or an anomaly, which must be refuted and rejected, is "*the* question of Jewish history."[48]

Attacks on Israel's distinctive Jewish character also fail to take into account the many new states established in the last half of the 20th century that do not have deeply rooted identities, such as Syria, Iraq, and many Eastern European states. Jewish nationhood, on the other hand, has existed thousands of years before the creation of most modern nation states.[49]

THE RIGHT TO RE-ESTABLISH SOVEREIGNTY

On the most fundamental level, the conflict remains unresolved because the Arabs have never accepted the historic right of the Jewish people to re-establish their sovereignty in their ancestral homeland—a homeland that was never regarded as a national homeland by any other people; a homeland that the Jewish people continually inhabited for the last four millennia.[50]

The Arab claim to the land is founded on having lived there for a thousand years; the Jews' is based on their historical connection to the land, present bond and religious faith.[51]

When the Jews began immigrating in increasing numbers beginning in 1882, they were returning to their ancient homeland, fleeing persecution and rebuilding their lives in a land that generations of Jews had "immortalized...in its previous era of independence." Here they were to be safe and able to defend themselves against physical annihilation and spiritual assimilation.[52]

When other civilizations and cultures were destroyed, their identities discarded or lost, they vanished into oblivion. The Jews refused to abandon their religious and spiritual connection to Jerusalem and attachment to their land. They never stopped affirming their right to the land of Israel. "This continuous, uninterrupted insistence, an intimate ingredient of Jewish consciousness is at the core of Jewish history, a vital element of Jewish faith."[53]

The concept of exile and return to Zion dominates *halakhah* (Jewish law). A man was forbidden to coerce his wife to leave Palestine, but could divorce her if she refused to go with him to the land of Israel. An individual purchasing property in Palestine could complete the transaction even on the Sabbath. This is why British Prime Minister Benjamin Disraeli could say, "The vineyards of Israel have ceased to exist, but the eternal law enjoins the children of Israel still to celebrate the vintage. A race that persists in celebrating their vintage, although they have no fruits to gather, will regain their vineyards."[54]

Jewish law asserts that if a person loses an item through an act of aggression and never gives up hope of recovering it, neither he nor the one who stole the article can consecrate it for religious use: the one who pilfered the item because it is not his; the owner because he does not have it in his possession. Since the Jewish people were stripped of their land by violence, they never gave up hope of reclaiming it. Foreign occupation was deemed a transitory phenomenon, while the Jewish people had an eternal link to the land.[55]

Zionism was thus "born out of memory, out of ritual and prayer, out of faith in the promise, out of loyalty to the biblical command, never to forget our origin, our link, never to relinquish hope for Zion and Jerusalem."[56]

"The return to Zion," observed Rabbi Abraham Joshua Heschel, "is an unprecedented drama, an event *sui generis* for which there is no model, no analogy." Never before in history "has a nation been restored to its ancient hearth after a lapse of 1,897 years." For Jews this resurrection was "an accord of a divine promise and a human achievement."[57] Rabbi Joseph B. Soloveitchik, the spiritual leader of Modern Orthodoxy, saw the rebirth of the State of Israel "in a political sense," as an "almost a supernatural occurrence."[58]

A team of experts from the Royal Institute of International Affairs, headed by British historian Edward Hallett Carr concluded in 1939 that, "Jewish national feeling [in the Diaspora] could never have remained so strong if Jerusalem had been blotted out and the place of it forgotten...."[59]

Five years before Israel's War of Independence, theologian Eliezer Berkovits said, "The creation of an autonomous Jewish body corporate is the *sine qua non* for the regeneration of Jewish religion and culture. Without it, further development of Judaism is impossible; without it Judaism can hardly be saved in the present."[60]

ONGOING NECESSITY TO PROTECT THE JEWISH PEOPLE

The need for a homeland where Jews could protect themselves was another factor in establishing the Jewish state. After personally experiencing antisemitism, Theodore Herzl, the founder of modern political Zionism, wrote in his diary in June 1895 that he "recognized the emptiness and futility of efforts to 'combat anti-Semitism'" in Europe. "Declamations made in writing or in closed circles do no good whatever; they even have a comical effect." At one point he thought the press could be mobilized to fight antisemitism, but soon realized this idea to be a "feeble, foolish gesture. Anti-semitism has grown and continues to grow—and so do I." The only solution was for the Jews in the Diaspora to found a Jewish state.[61]

Moses Hess, a Zionist theorist, independently concluded that nothing the Jews would do could change the views of antisemitic Europeans. "For despite the fact that the Jewish people has been living together with these nations for two thousand years, it can never be organically united with them." Europeans "have considered the existence of the Jews in their midst as nothing other than an anomaly." Jews "will always remain strangers among the nations which might well emancipate us out of humanitarianism and a feeling of justice but will never, never respect us…"[62]

Antisemitism had taken its toll on the Jews of Europe and Russia, as Victor Jacobson, a member of the Russian-Jewish Scientific Society in Berlin and later a Zionist leader explained in 1883: "The consistent humiliation and slander of the Jews has led us to begin believing these lies."[63]

Nothing less than "a return to the land of their forefathers," would be conceivable, insisted Asher Ginzberg (Ahad Ha'am), a leading ideologue of secular cultural Zionism. This "historic bond between the people and the land" meant that "allocating them the most magnificent expanses of farm land in Canada or Argentina will not enhance the strength of the wandering Jew as much as settling on the lowly plain through which the Jordan flows and upon which the Lebanon looks out."[64]

When a portion of modern Kenya was proposed and debated between 1903 and 1905 as a place to settle the Jews as an alternative to the Land of Israel, a firestorm developed against the idea, ending its feasibility. Without any religious, spiritual or historic ties to eastern Africa, the Jews would not have been motivated to emigrate there.[65]

The systematic destruction of six million Jews by Germany during World War II demonstrated the extent to which Jews were not accepted in their respective countries. They were killed simply because they were Jews. Whether Western civilization would continue to accept the right of Jews and other minorities residing in its midst as distinctive entities with their own group consciousness is a question the Holocaust raised, and one that remains unanswered. Antisemitism and racism are still part of Western culture, and will be so for the foreseeable future.[66]

During the Holocaust, not one state in Western Europe offered to help the Jewish people "defend its interests or even its existence" against the Nazis and their collaborators, declared Andrei Gromyko, the Soviet Ambassador at the U.N. The same can be said for the behavior of the nations in the East. The inability to protect the Jews' fundamental rights or compensate them for their suffering emphasized the necessity to establish a separate state.[67]

The hundreds of thousands of homeless Jewish displaced persons (DPs) wandering in Europe seeking sanctuary and a means to earn a living added urgency to finding a solution. Speaking for the Jewish Agency for Palestine at the U.N., David Ben-Gurion summed up their predicament when he said there exist "large numbers of homeless Jews for whom there is no other salvation in the future except in their own national home."[68]

When the issue of allowing the DPs into Palestine was broached, the Arab states argued that they should not be held accountable for the persecution of the Jews in Europe or compelled to alleviate their plight. No one assumed the Arabs would be responsible for solving the problem of the DPs or that Arab countries would be expected to absorb them, Ben-Gurion argued. Homeless and persecuted Jews were being brought to "our own country," where they would be settled in the Jewish towns and villages of Petach Tikva, Tel-Aviv, Haifa, Rishon le Zion, Jerusalem, Degania, and the Negev. Moshe Shertok (Sharett), another spokesman for the Jewish Agency, added that the Jews were not coming "as guests of anyone." Every acre of land they would farm had been paid for and "had to be wrested from wilderness and desolation."[69]

THE RIGHT OF A STATE TO EXIST

For many years there appeared to be little need to justify Israel's right to exist as a Jewish state. The League of Nations had acknowledged the country's legitimacy and the United Nations conferred a recognized juridical reality on the nation. A member of the U.N. is acknowledged by other nations as having 'sovereign equality' with all others. From May 11, 1949, when Israel was admitted as a member of the U.N., the question of whether Israel was a state was legally irrelevant. Until 1973, when the U.N. passed the Zionism equals Racism resolution, only the Arab states and a few countries with large Moslem populations denied Israel's legitimacy, while the Soviets and their proxies attacked Israel within the confines of the U.N.[70]

The Mandate for Palestine announced by the League of Nations Council on July 24, 1922, and signed by 52 member states, is of even greater importance to Jewish claims. When the Council of the League of Nations was asked to verify the wording of the Palestine Mandate, it was keenly aware of the Arab legal case, yet the Council rejected their arguments.[71]

Issued by the Allies following the conquest of Palestine and the defeat of the Ottoman Empire, and after the Arabs fought on the side of the Turks, the Mandate explicitly affirms that "recognition has thereby been given to the historical connection of the Jewish people with Palestine and to the grounds for reconstituting their national home in that country."[72] The Permanent Mandates Commission, which from 1924-1939 was charged with supervising the Mandates, discussed the issues involved in the Palestine Mandate each year, and was also well informed of Arab legal claims, which they dismissed.[73]

Despite having fought against the Allies, the Arabs expected to be rewarded with conquered Ottoman territory. Sol Linowitz, an American businessman who served as President Jimmy Carter's personal representative to the Middle East peace negotiations,

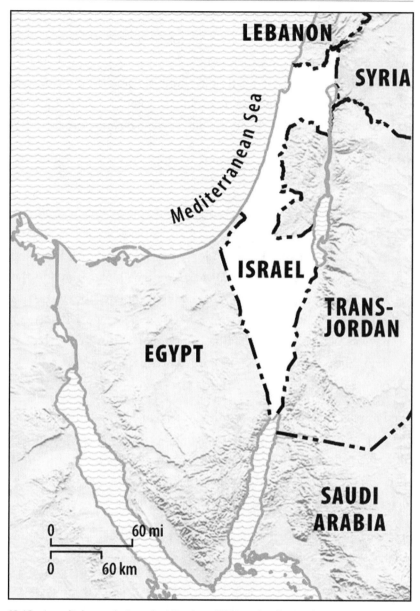

1949—Israel's boundaries after the Israeli War of Independence.
Courtesy of Eli Hertz

suggested that the Arabs should protest against the Allies, not the Jews, "who in solemn proclamation recognized prior Jewish rights to Palestine."[74] In other words, "Jewish and Arab claims in the vast area of the former Ottoman Empire came to the forum of liberation together, and not (as is usually implied) by way of Jewish encroachment on an already vested and exclusive Arab domain."[75]

Monsieur Pierre Orts, Chairman of the Permanent Mandates Commission, reiterated the sentiment:

> Was not consent to the establishment of a Jewish National Home in Palestine the price—and a relatively small one –which the Arabs paid for the liberation of lands extending from the Red Sea to the borders of Cilicia on the one hand, Iran and the Mediterranean on the other, for the independence they were not winning or had already won, none of which they would ever have gained on their own efforts, and for all of which they had to thank the Allied Powers and particularly the British forces in the Near East?[76]

The Permanent Mandates Commission recognized the unique plight of the Jews. "It should be remembered," a report states, "that the collective sufferings of Arabs and Jews are not comparable, since vast spaces in the Near East...are open to the former, whereas the world is increasingly being closed to settlement by the latter."[77]

Speaking in 1947 to the U.N. Special Committee on Palestine (UNSCOP), David Ben-Gurion added:

The Arabs own 94% of the land, the Jews only 6%. The Arabs have seven States, the Jews none. The Arabs have vast underdeveloped territories—Iraq alone is three times as large as England with less than four million people—the Jews have only a tiny beginning of a national home. The most glaring disparity perhaps is that the Arabs have no problem of homelessness and immigration, while for the Jews homelessness is the root cause of all their sufferings for centuries past.

Furthermore, when the Arabs were liberated from the Ottoman Empire, they realized their political aspirations "in an area of 1,250,000 square miles, 125 times as large as the area of Western Palestine with a population of some 15 to 16 million Arabs—about the number of Jews living then in the world.[78]

When the Arabs brought their case before UNSCOP, the committee concluded, "There would seem to be no grounds for questioning the validity of the Mandate for the reason advanced by the Arab States." Though the Arabs viewed themselves as having a "natural" right to Palestine, the UNSCOP report further asserted that the "Arabs have never established a government there and…that not since 63 B.C., when Pompey stormed Jerusalem, has Palestine been an independent State."[79]

Legally, the U.N. General Assembly could not alter this commitment in any manner. In Article 16 of the 1923 Treaty of Lausanne, Turkey relinquished all rights and title with regards to Palestine, "the future of these territories…being settled or to be settled by the parties concerned." This means that the establishment of Israel did not legally depend on the U.N. partition resolution. Furthermore, as Sir Elihu Lauterpacht, the eminent international jurist noted, the right of a State to exist is determined by "its factual existence—especially when that existence is prolonged, shows every sign of continuance and is recognized by the generality of nations."[80] The Jews argued that the colonialists in America and the British settlers who colonized Australia and Canada had irrevocably changed an existing way of life.

[H]istory does not invalidate their intrusion, since it applauds the results. Posterity, with these results before it, declares them to be "natural" and bears no retrospective rancor for those who brought them to pass. The Palestine transformation...need not be regarded solely in the light of present disharmonies and dislocations. Statesmanship must regard it *sub specie aeternitatis* [objectively] and anticipate what history will pronounce."[81]

NO ABSOLUTE JUSTICE

In testimony before the Anglo-American Committee of Inquiry on Palestine in 1946, Chaim Weizmann observed, "...There is no absolute justice in this world...and what we are all trying to do in our small way, is just rough human justice...Injustice there is going to be." Nevertheless, the Arabs emerged from World War II with at least two kingdoms, four republics, six seats in the U.N. and one in the Security Council. Weizmann questioned whether this was commensurate with what the Arabs contributed during the war. How many fatalities did they sustain? To what degree did they suffer?[82]

If you compare the Arab experiences with the suffering, casualties and the Jewish contribution to the war effort, then "there may be some slight injustice politically if Palestine is made a Jewish State, but individually the Arabs will not suffer. They have not suffered hitherto. On the contrary, economically, culturally, religiously, the Arabs will not be affected."[83]

Weizmann urged the U.N. to tell the Arabs: "Gentleman, whatever you have got out of the last war, you owe to our arms and to our sacrifices; whatever you have got out of this war, you equally owe to us. It would have been otherwise if Hitler had won the war!" In particular, Weizmann felt the Arabs were indebted to the Allied powers in both World Wars. "Surely to goodness," he said, "if the Allied Powers found it just to give what Mr. Balfour called this 'little notch' for the Jews to live there as a nation, they have a right to expect the Arabs to accept it?" Weizmann had asked Franklin Roosevelt and

Winston Churchill to make this point so that Arabs and Jews would be spared a "great deal of trouble." Like the U.N., however, they chose not to articulate a "firm and definite policy."[84]

Rabbi Abba Hillel Silver, a leading American Zionist leader, told the U.N. General Assembly that the Jews had earned the right to their own state because...

...they were your allies in the war, and joined their sacrifices to yours to achieve a common victory. The representatives of the Jewish people of Palestine should sit in your midst. We hope that the representatives of the people which gave to mankind spiritual and ethical values, inspiring human personalities and sacred texts which are your treasured possessions, and which is now rebuilding its national life in its ancient homeland, will be welcomed before long by you to this noble fellowship of the United Nations.[85]

Father Benjamin Nunez, the Costa Rican ambassador to the U.N., a Catholic priest and a self-described leftist who argued the cases for the independence of Algeria, Indonesia, New Guinea and Cyprus at the U.N., did not like what the official representative of the P.L.O. described as the legitimate rights of the Palestinian people at the U.N. On November 5, Nunez said, "The crux of the problem is the liberation of *geographic* [author's emphasis] Palestine now totally under Israeli occupation."[86]

The ambassador suggested opening any history book to see that the area held by Israel is "an infinitesimal part of historic Palestine." The territory allotted Israel under the terms of the British Mandate was originally 120,466 square kilometers. From this, the British took 92,300 square kilometers to create the sovereign state of Trans-Jordan, which left 28,166 square kilometers west of the Jordan. In 1947, this was to be divided again by the U.N. to establish separate Jewish and

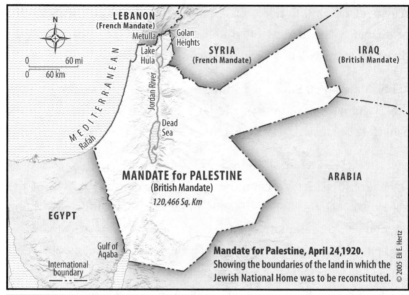

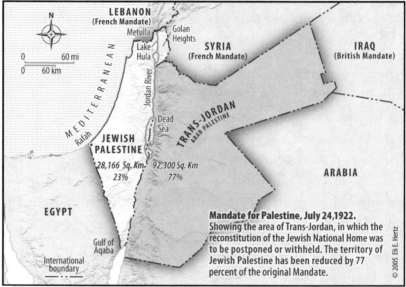

Courtesy of Eli Hertz

Arab states. The P.L.O., he explained, maintains that peace will reign once Israel relinquishes the land it captured in the June 1967 war, and when the legitimate rights of the Palestinian people are recognized.[87]

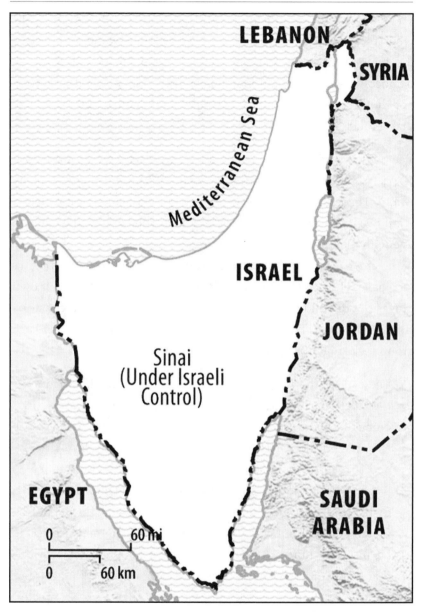

1967—Israel's boundaries following the Six-Day War. Egypt, Jordan, and Syria in a war of aggression lose the territories of the Sinai Peninsula, the West Bank, and the Golan Heights. For the first time, Israel is in control of Jewish Mandated Palestine. Courtesy of Eli Hertz

The fallacy of this argument, he said, was proven on May 14, 1948, when the State of Israel was declared. The Arabs wanted to destroy the infant state then and are still unwilling "to accept a Jewish democratic state as an autonomous entity." The Arab refugees were not the "cause for the attacks" by the Arab states, but a result of that conflict.[88]

The tragic paradox Nunez talked about, was that both groups spoke of peace, but if that was true, he asked, "Why are there so many wars?" The Israelis, he knew, wanted to build a democratic state that would be "a beacon for their people" and anyone else who wanted to live with them in peace. Arab extremists "want for Israel...the peace of the graveyard, and they have come up against a generation of Jews who have returned to the land of their forefathers not to dig their own graves but to build roads of peace, to plant trees of life and construct cities of progress. That is the difference between the peace that each group seeks in the Middle East."[89] He continued:

> The call for the extermination of the State of Israel, which in its formulation constitutes one of the greatest and most serious crimes in history, would appear not to be enough for the Arab leaders and the Palestine Liberation Organization. Euphorically, and supported by an overwhelming majority, the Committee on Social, Humanitarian and Cultural Affairs (Third Committee) of the UN adopted the most aberrant decision that could be imagined, a blasphemy against truth and common sense and an insult to human decency; they have adopted the principle that Zionism is racism and racial discrimination. What a tragic paradox; that the Jewish people, with its ideal of Zion, the greatest victim of racism and racial persecution throughout history, is now, by virtue of a resolution of the 'petro-majority', a racist people and movement. That truth is that, rather than reality, it seems like a Dantean nightmare. That same majority could have voted

for a resolution stating…we, the majority of the United Nations, decide that as from today, there is no God.[90]

According to Biblical scholar Robert Alter, some Jews justify the establishment of the state in moral terms—as a choice between "two alternatives neither of which absolutely satisfies all moral requirements but one of which will be a lesser violation of morality than the other." After the Holocaust, the choices are whether

> the Jews should have a place they can call their own at the cost of uprooting several hundred thousand Palestinians from their lands and resettling them in another part of the *same* Palestine, or that the Arabs should continue to occupy their own lands while the survivors of the Holocaust have no place to go—then…the establishment of the State has a justification.[91]

Before the establishment of the state, Reinhold Niebuhr, Professor of Practical Theology at Union Theological Seminary in New York and one of the greatest Protestant theologians of the 20th century, said there couldn't be "a just solution of this conflict—any more than there can in any other similar conflict—of competing claims." Instead of trying to find a conventional solution, he urged that the Jewish claim—at least to a large part of Palestine—be granted, and that the Arabs be compensated elsewhere in the Near East. Even though the Arabs had not played a role in the defeating the Axis powers, Niebuhr thought it best for the Arabs to become federated to strengthen their unity and independence.[92]

There were numerous sources for Arab enmity, including Israel's democracy and its technological advances, which were a threat to the feudal and rich rulers of "desperately poor peasants." There were so many causes for Arab enmity in fact, that no amount of economic development could have placated the region. Given the "depth and the breath of the Arab spirit of vengeance," he wondered whether the West should have allowed the Jews to return, especially since the biblical right of the Jews to Palestine had "evaporated some thousands of years ago." Yet a "confluence of historical forces," made the establishment of the state "unavoidable." These doubts are now "irrelevant, for it is not possible to roll back history, and it has been proved that we cannot wean the Arabs from their passions by equivocation in regard to Israel."[93]

What was needed, Niebuhr believed, was resolve by the West in dealing with the Arabs that will not allow "any nation so conceived and so dedicated to perish from the earth." He recognized,

> The simple fact is that all schemes for political appeasement and economic co-operation must fail unless there is an unequivocal voice from us that we will not allow the state to be annihilated and that we will not judge its desperate efforts to gain some strategic security...as an illegitimate use of force.[94]

WITHOUT A JEWISH STATE

Without a Jewish state, asserts Ruth Gavison, professor of Human Rights at the Faculty of Law at the Hebrew University in Jerusalem, the Jews would become a cultural minority again, which would most likely involve living in continuous fear of antisemitism, persecution and genocide. Relinquishing a state would be similar to "national suicide." Jews have endured for two millennia without a homeland, but at times at great personal risk. Jews, particularly in the West, now enjoy an unparalleled degree of security and cultural freedom in part because of the connection the Jews feel toward Israel, and the recognition that the country is committed to their protection and well being.[95]

In less than 60 years, Israel has become the strongest Jewish community in the world. The country has the right and obligation to "promote and strengthen" the Jewish character of the state as this is based on the concept of national self-determination. This idea does not mean that every citizen in the country must belong to a particular national or ethnic group. The state has the right to protect itself physically and culturally against assimilation or attempts to attack and destroy it. The claim of self-determination "is not a matter of abstract rights talk. Rather, such claims must be addressed according to demographic, societal and political realities that prevail both in the Middle East and in other parts of the world."[96]

The state also has a responsibility to safeguard the rights of non-Jewish minorities. They should be treated fairly, with respect, and their safety and well-being should be ensured. These obligations do not require, however, the termination of the Jewish character of the state.

Espousing a national identity—ethnonationalism—is not unusual. Most states formally identify with a specific religious or cultural tradition of their predominant groups. Many European countries, for example, explicitly identify as Protestant or Catholic; many Muslim countries are classified as an "Islamic Republic," while in the United States only Christian holidays are officially observed. Israel alone is castigated for reflecting the identity of the Jewish people.[97]

As part of an effort to maintain ethnic dominance, many countries have a differential immigration policy. Armenia, Bulgaria, Croatia, Finland, Germany, Hungary, Ireland, Israel, Serbia and Turkey offer automatic or fast-track citizenship to members of their own dominant group living outside the country. Chinese immigration laws give ethnic Chinese residing overseas preference and benefits. Citizens in the former colonies of Spain and Portugal are granted favorable treatment in their immigration applications to those countries. Individuals who are not citizens of Japan or Slovakia, but who are members of the leading ethnic group, are given official identification documents enabling them to reside and work in the country.

Americans who view such policies as an infringement of universalist standards and thus repugnant, would be considered "provincial" in the rest of the world.[98]

The responsibility of a democratic state is to embody the preferences of the majority, providing they do not impinge on the rights of the minority. Each country protects its own cultural and religious characteristics that are seen by some of its citizens as either "neutral" or at times "alienating." The banning of headscarves for Muslim women and skullcaps for Jews in French schools is a prominent example.[99]

French Catholics were willing to accept a secular society, but not one that would allow extensive multiculturalism. In Israel, Arabs and Jews tend to live in separate communities. Arabs and Israelis share the view that no one should be compelled to live in a bicultural community or one where they would be the minority culture.[100]

A very significant number of countries in the world are built around the self-determination of a particular religious or national group; some examples are Russians, Armenians, Sunni Muslims, Irish, Japanese, Han Chinese, and Poles. Minorities exist in practically all of these countries with their own culture and language. In the U.S., the relations between minority groups are generally peaceful. Ethnic clashes in the Balkans or in Iraq are examples of where the dominant group is in conflict with the rights of a sizable and periodically antagonistic domestic minority. In Czechoslovakia, the citizens decided to divide the country—one state for Czechs, the other for Slovaks. This same solution occurred in a more brutal form in the former Yugoslavia, in Armenia and in other states of the former Soviet Union.[101]

To understand the justification for Jewish settlement, we must distinguish between "rights" and "liberties," concepts advanced by

Wesley Newcomb Hohfeld, an American jurist. Hohfeld postulates that we may talk "of *liberty* when there is no obligation to act or refrain from acting in a certain manner. A *right*, on the other hand, means that others have an obligation not to interfere with, or to grant the possibility of, my acting in a certain manner." As long as the actions of the Jews who settled in the Land of Israel "were legal and nonviolent," Jewish settlers "were at liberty to enlarge their numbers among the local population, even with the declared and specific intent of establishing the infrastructure for a future Jewish state."[102]

The liberty to establish an infrastructure in the Land of Israel was far more justified than that of the Spanish and English who settled the American continent. Palestine was a far more justifiable destination for Jews than Argentina or Uganda. Unlike colonists, Jews had a preexisting connection to the land, returning to an area where they were once the sovereign power.[103]

POSITION 5: THE P.L.O. COVENANT

To prove their claim that Israel has no right to exist, the Arab narrative distorts the historical record in a number of ways. The P.L.O., for example, asserts that Jews do not have any historical connection to the Land of Israel and do not possess the fundamental qualifications to be considered a nation.

The P.L.O. was established by the Arab states as another means to destroy all of Israel. On November 13, 1979, Rafiq Natshe, a P.L.O. operative in Saudi Arabia and later speaker of the Palestinian Legislative Council, confirmed this in the Saudi daily newspaper *al-Riad*: "The Palestinian revolution was born in 1965 from a strategic concept of liberating all Palestine, and the revolution will not change this, whatever the pressures put on it. The best solution is for the Palestinians to return to their homeland and the Jewish foreigner to the country of his birth…Any Palestinian entity to be established on any part of the Palestinian territories will be a starting point for the liberation of the Palestinian territories in all of Palestine."[104]

The Palestinian National Charter (1968), which outlines their guiding principles, makes this clear:

> Article 20:...Claims of historical or religious ties of Jews with Palestine are incompatible with the facts of history and the true conception of what constitutes statehood. Judaism, being a religion, is not an independent nationality. Nor do Jews constitute a single nation with an identity of its own; they are citizens of the states to which they belong.

Article 22 states:

> Zionism is a political movement organically associated with international imperialism and antagonistic to all action for liberation and to progressive movements in the world. It is racist and fanatic in its nature, aggressive, expansionist, and colonial in its aims, and fascist in its methods. Israel is the instrument of the Zionist movement, and geographical base for world imperialism placed strategically in the midst of the Arab homeland to combat the hopes of the Arab nation for liberation, unity, and progress. Israel is a constant source of threat vis-à-vis peace in the Middle East and the whole world...[105]

Approved in June 1964 and amended in 1968, the Charter was used to justify actions against Israel for being the embodiment of evil. The conditions of the 1993 Oslo Accords stipulated the removal of the anti-Israel clauses.[106] Throughout the 1990s, the Arabs resisted making these changes in the Charter.[107] Ziad Abu Ziad, a senior P.L.O. spokesman, explained why it was impossible to change the Charter: "Israel must not demand that the P.L.O. alter its covenant, just as the P.L.O. does not demand that the Jewish nation cancel the Bible."[108]

Yehoshafat Harkabi, a leading Israeli scholar, added that the articles in the Charter are so absolute and "deeply ingrained" that agreeing to live in peace with Israel is an "anathema" and totally incompatible with their core beliefs.[109]

After more than five years of extreme pressure from Israel and the U.S., the P.L.O. agreed to an alternative solution that still allowed a significant number of the odious passages to remain practically as they were. This permitted the P.L.O. to adhere sufficiently to its obligations so that the Israelis would fulfill their part of the agreement, while at the same time assuring their followers that their fundamental goals to liberate Palestine were unchanged.[110]

Rejecting Israel's right to exist is also found in the Palestinian Authority (PA) media and in the 12th grade school books introduced by the PA Ministry of Education at the end of 2006. Students are taught, "Palestine's war ended with a catastrophe that is unprecedented in history, when the Zionist gangs stole Palestine and expelled its people from their cities, their villages, their lands and their houses, and established the State of Israel."[111]

Israel is referred to as "the Zionist Entity" and the "Zionist Enemy." Islamists see Israel as an occupying power, not only on the West Bank and Gaza since 1967, but also in all of Israel proper since 1948. Israel thus resides on land belonging to Islam, transforming the conflict from a national dispute to a "Jihad for Allah…[a] struggle between Muslims and their enemies."[112]

For Hamas cleric Muhsen Abu 'Ita, jihad means the destruction of the Jews in Israel. "The annihilation of the Jews of Palestine is one of the most splendid blessings for Palestine. This will be followed by a greater blessing, Allah be praised, with the establishment of a Caliphate that will rule the land and be pleasing to men and God."[113]

Since the Arabs maintain that Israel has no legitimacy, the country does not appear on any Arab maps. In its place, covering Israel-proper, Gaza and the West Bank, there is a country called Palestine, defined as a state with access to the Mediterranean and Red seas. They have literally wiped Israel off the map.[114]

Mahmoud al-Zahar, a co-founder of Hamas, said Hamas would use the PA educational system to indoctrinate Arab students with their ideology when he noted "they would turn every facet of life into resistance [i.e., chiefly indoctrinating violence and terrorism]. Education will deal with the culture of resistance. We will not tell them that Palestine is a state whose coastline runs from Rafah to Khan Yunis. We will tell them that it runs from Rafah in the south to Ras al-Nakura [Rosh Hanikra, Israel's northern seacoast border with Lebanon] in the north, and that Palestine's western border is the [Mediterranean] sea and its eastern border the [Jordan] river..."[115]

Unfortunately, Hamas' efforts have been successful. A poll of young people, ages 18-25, who studied under the PA, found that 84-93% of Palestinian youth rejected Israel's right to exist.[116] Denying the Jews their historical connection to the Land of Israel, calling them "monkeys and pigs," and disseminating the *Protocols of the Elders of Zion*—which accuses Jews of controlling the world—creates a dehumanizing, toxic and hate-filled environment.[117] From an Islamic perspective there is no urgency or need to reach an agreement with Israel, which would by definition contravene the foundations of Muslim religious ideology.[118]

Those who thought Hamas would eschew terrorism after assuming the reins of the government misread the fervor of their religious commitment and determination to destroy the Jewish state. Being responsible for the welfare of their people by having to provide housing, health care, education, security and employment, and working with their neighbors and enemies has not tempered their

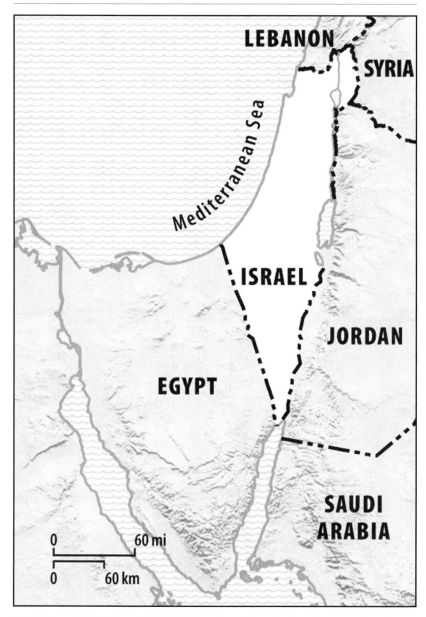

1979-Present—On March 26, 1979, Israel and Egypt signed a peace treaty on the White House lawn. Israel returned the Sinai Peninsula territory to Egypt. Courtesy of Eli Hertz

violent conduct. Instead, Hamas leaders have used their political power to force their will on those under Hamas rule.[119]

The Eternal Bond Between Jews and the Land of Israel

The eternal bond between the Jews and the Land of Israel was eloquently described in the Peel Commission report of 1937:

> While the Jews had thus been dispersed over the world, they had never forgotten Palestine. If Christians have become familiar through the Bible with the physiognomy of the country and its place-names and events that happened more than two thousand years ago, the link which binds the Jews to Palestine and its past history is to them far closer and more intimate. Judaism and its ritual are rooted in those memories. Among countless illustrations it is enough to cite the fact that Jews, wherever they may be, still pray for rain at the season it is needed in Palestine. And the same devotion to the Land of Israel, *Eretz Israel*, the same sense of exile from it, permeates Jewish secular thought. Some of the finest Hebrew poetry written in the Diaspora has been inspired, like the Psalms of the Captivity, by the longing to return to Zion.[1]

The report acknowledged that this connection was not only "spiritual or intellectual," because Jews were living in Palestine "always or almost always" since the demise of the Jewish State. During the Arab reign, there were a considerable number of Jewish communities in the major cities. Even though small in number, the Jews in Eastern Europe considered that they were being represented by this "remnant of their race who were keeping a foothold in the land against the day of the coming of the Messiah."[2]

The groups of messianic *aliyot* that settled in Palestine from the period of the Crusades to the nineteenth century were a minor segment of world Jewry, yet were quite important, in part because of the renowned individuals involved, the broad range of Diaspora communities that participated, and the frequency with which these waves of migrations occurred. They were drawn by a "messianic impulse" and "a belief in the centrality of the land," which became "an axis of Jewish spiritual life."[3]

The Jews, who never established a homeland in any other area, and never relinquished the right to Palestine, did not believe that the establishment of a Jewish homeland was subject to an Arab veto. Palestine had never been a separate and independent Arab political entity. For a number of centuries, the area was under the caliphates that ruled from afar, and had experienced thirteen conquests. Following the exile of the Jews, historical accounts by archeologists, writers and travelers have never mentioned a Palestinian people or any tribe that had a political, national, spiritual or geographical connection to the land.[4]

In 1857, Herman Melville described Judea as "one accumulation of stones-Stony mountains & stony plains; stony torrents & stony roads; stony walls & stony fields, stony houses & stony tombs, stony eyes & stony hearts." A *National Geographic* reporter referred to Palestine in 1916 as a collection of "old cities, old ruins, old roads, old men, and old women."[5]

When Félix Bovet, a professor of Hebrew at the university in Neuchâtel, Switzerland, visited Palestine in 1861, he found "in the midst of the general decadence of the Ottoman Empire, Palestine has fallen even lower than the rest; it is decadence in decadence."[6]

Although the Jews did not request an agreement with the Arabs, they recognized that consent was only possible if the Arabs understood that it was not a requisite condition. Return meant unrestricted growth through immigration, and the right to develop a majority if economic conditions justified it.[7]

Chaim Weizmann told the Anglo-American Committee of Inquiry on Palestine in 1947 that all the Jews wanted a place where they can say, "'Well, here we are, we stand and fall by what we do here;' a place where we build up everything from the bottom upwards. That it is why it is ours, in Goethe's words…'What you have inherited from your parents, acquire it in order to possess it.'"[8]

In response to the extensive Arab opposition to the increase of Jewish immigration Weizmann, replied that they were trying to practice "rough human justice." Under the circumstances, injustice was inevitable, he claimed, but given how the Arabs emerged after the war with eight countries and millions of square miles, how could they begrudge the Jews their own state with just 8,000 square miles?[9]

Some of this antagonism might have been mitigated somewhat, Weizmann said, if a more resolute approach had been taken toward the Arabs from the beginning. The U.N. could have reminded the Arab world that they owed their freedom from Ottoman rule to the Associated Powers after World War I, and to the Allies after World War II. If the Allied Powers decided to give the Jews, what Lord Balfour called this "little notch," to live in as a nation, the Arab states should have accepted it. Instead of adopting a firm policy toward the Arabs, one of "apology and vacillation" became the norm, Weizmann lamented.[10]

The issue of the Jewish contribution to the war effort also had to be taken into account. Weizmann described the *Yishuv*'s involvement modestly, but their support was invaluable to the armies fighting in the western desert. The Middle East was cut off from the West, with even military and civilian supplies having to come through the Cape of Good Hope and Port Said.[11] In contrast, many Arabs, including the Palestinian Mufti, allied themselves with the Ottomans in World War I and with the Nazis in World War II.

"TWO NATIONS WARRING IN THE BOSOM OF A SINGLE STATE"

From the very beginning of the return of Jews to Palestine, a confrontation between the Jews and the Arabs was inevitable because of the insurmountable differences between the two competing national movements. As Colonel Frederick H. Kisch, a British officer in World War I and chairman of the Palestine Zionist Executive in Jerusalem, recorded in his diary on May 20, 1923, "The pan-Arab movement is at present a danger and will remain so until we succeed in coming to terms with the Arabs and bringing our respective national aspirations into harmony with each other."[12]

Relations with the Arabs, he thought, would improve and "develop naturally from the bankruptcy of the policy of [Arab] extremists."[13] When an Arab informant told him that "anti-Zionism had become a sort of religion in the country," Kisch suggested a counter-propaganda effort including the creation of a first-rate and friendly Arabic paper, increased interaction between the Magrebi Sephardic community and the Arabs, and economic interdependence between Arabs and Jews.[14]

Convinced of the existence of a silent and moderate Arab minority that desired a political accord with the Jews, the Zionist Executive continually tried to find common ground between the two communities.[15] Some Jews assumed that the Jewish return would be realized peacefully, since the Arabs would benefit significantly from the economic development as a result of Jewish investment in Palestine. Many believed in the idea that, "to the Arab race Palestine is a mere corner. To the Jews, it is the only place."[16]

The search for the elusive moderate Arab leaders is not new. In June 1938, Sir John Shuckburgh of the Colonial Office was asked about Arab moderates. Shuckburgh recalled the saying of the late Lord John Morley, that, in times of unrest, "moderates are always at a discount." The condition in Palestine, Shuckburgh noted, "was unhappily one in which extremists held the limelight and moderates had little influence."[17]

Alec S. Kirkbride, District Commissioner of the Galilee and Acre, added that there were a number of moderates who were prepared to cooperate with the British, even though they disagreed with the British mandatory policy. It was "impossible" to estimate their exact number, however, because "they were naturally disinclined to come into the open."[18]

The Arabs had a different view. On October 18, 1919, Musa Kazim Pasha al-Husaini, the mayor of Jerusalem, explained: "We are opposed to any rights for Jews...I speak not only for myself but also for all my brothers, the Arabs..."[19] Years later, Jamal al-Husaini reiterated this point. It would be, he said, a "gross error to believe that Arab and Jew may come to an understanding if only each of them exchanges his coat of extremism for another of moderation. When the principles underlying two movements clash, it is futile to expect their meeting halfway."[20]

George Antonius, a major proponent of Arab nationalism, concluded that: "But the logic of facts is inexorable. It shows that no room can be made in Palestine for a second nation except by dislodging or exterminating the nation in possession."[21]

McMAHON-HUSSEIN CORRESPONDENCE

While Arabs often base their claims to Palestine on the McMahon-Hussein correspondence that occurred prior to the Balfour Declaration, the evidence demonstrates that McMahon never explicitly promised

Palestine to the Arabs and the Arabs never upheld their end of the agreement. McMahon, Churchill and two other Colonial secretaries, confirmed that there was never any intention to refer to Palestine in the correspondences.[22] Moreover, Mr. Ormsby-Gore, Secretary of State for the Colonies, acknowledged that, "the McMahon correspondence was fully in the mind of His Majesty's and the Allied Governments when the Balfour Declaration was made."[23]

Four years after this correspondence, Emir Feisal, King Hussein's son, concurred with the British position. On January 3, 1919 Feisal and Chaim Weizmann signed an agreement at the Versailles Peace Conference that said:

> [M]indful of the racial kinship and ancient bonds existing between the Arabs and the Jewish people, and realizing that the surest means of working out the consummation of their natural aspirations is through the closest possible collaboration in the development of the Arab State and Palestine, and being desirous further of confirming the good understanding which exists between them, have agreed to the following articles:[24]

Article I of the agreement stipulates an exchange of "Arab and Jewish duly accredited agents" between the "the Arab State," and "Palestine," implying Jewish sovereignty over Palestine."[25]

Article IV states: "All necessary measures shall be taken to encourage and stimulate immigration of Jews into Palestine on a large scale, and as quickly as possible to settle Jewish immigrants upon the land through closer settlement and intensive cultivation of the soil."[26]

In a letter to Felix Frankfurter, then a Zionist delegate to the Paris Peace Conference, on March 3, 1919, Feisal wanted to "wish the Jews a most hearty welcome home." He acknowledged the simultaneous development of Jewish and Arab liberation movements and that "having suffered similar oppressions at the hands of powers stronger than themselves," he would take the first step towards the attainment of their national ideals together."[27]

He thanked Weizmann for having been "a great helper of our [Arab] cause," and hoped "the Arabs may soon be in a position to make the Jews some return for their kindness." Glaringly omitting any talk of Palestinian nationhood, Feisal declared,

> We are working together for a reformed and revived Near East, and our two movements complete one another. The Jewish movement is national and not imperialist. Our movement is national and not imperialist, and there is room in Syria for us both. Indeed, I think that neither can be a real success without the other.[28]

When Emir Abdullah of Trans-Jordan travelled from Jenin to Lydda, he "was astonished at what [he] saw at the Jewish colonies...They have colonized the sand dunes, extracted their water, quickened them to life and transformed them into a paradise."[29]

Ironically, Arabs at the time bristled at the name "Palestine," since they considered it an integral part of Greater Syria. People in the region viewed the divisions made by the French in Syria-Lebanon and by the British in Palestine as completely artificial.[30]

This period was short-lived. As pan-Arabism spread throughout the Arab world, the Palestinians asserted themselves as Arabs, and not as Syrians from the south. During the British Mandate and for many years later, they and their organizations expressed their national identity as Arabs and not as Syrians or Palestinians.[31]

Even some P.L.O. leaders rejected a separate Palestinian identity. On March 3, 1977, Zuhair Muhsin, the head of the P.L.O.

Military Operations Department, proclaimed:

> [T]here are no differences between Jordanians, Palestinians, Syrians, and Lebanese...We are one people. Only for political reasons do we carefully underline our Palestinian identity. For it is of national interest for the Arabs to encourage the existence of the Palestinians against Zionism. Yes, the existence of a separate Palestinian identity is there only for tactical reasons. The establishment of a Palestinian state is a new expedient to continue the fight against Zionism and for Arab unity.[32]

In view of these facts, the application of the Wilsonian principle of self-determination "is a figment of historical imagination," according to Julius Stone, one of the world's foremost legal theorists. "Palestinian national self-recognition" was a new phenomenon, occurring approximately in 1966 with the adoption of the Palestinian National Charter.[33]

The Charter attempted to play a double-game by asserting that Palestinians were "an integral part of the Arab nation" to whom the land had been allocated, and that the Palestinians were separate people who "possess their legal right to their homeland."(Articles I-V). Accordingly, the Charter declared that Jews who "had normally resided in Palestine until the beginning of the Zionist invasion will be considered Palestinians." Those who were not would obviously be forced to leave.[34]

Not surprisingly, the Charter excluded any mention of the Arab conquest of Palestine by force in 666 CE or of King David's reign over Israel in the 10th century BCE. Doing so would have provided the Jewish people with an indisputable claim to Palestine, and cast "any Arab pretensions of title with the taint of an unlawful breach by past armed invasion of Jewish rights of self-determination. There is…no reason why a half-century…is any more expendable than a millennium or so."

One could even argue "*qui prior est tempore prior est iure* [He who is prior in time is stronger in right]. The facts to which principles are applied may change as completely in a half-century as in a millennium." In other words, if any part of the past is to be resurrected, why is one part more important than the other?[35]

The Muslim world has purposefully elevated the sanctity of the al-Aqsa Mosque in Jerusalem and the sacredness of the city (al-Quds) by reviving ancient traditions "from oblivion." As a result, hundreds of thousands of more Muslims have been visiting al-Aqsa during the month of Ramadan than ever before. Motivation for this increase is a feeling of "political duty" as much as from a conviction in the power of the mosque.[36]

While exaggerating the importance of Jerusalem in Islamic tradition, Arabs have also systematically questioned Jewish ties to Jerusalem, the Temple Mount, and other holy sites. Others will acknowledge the Jewish link, but argue that the Jews betrayed their faith and therefore have forfeited their sovereign rights to the land. Moreover, they argue, Muslim rule for 14 centuries outweighs a brief presence 2,000 years ago.[37]

In the past, scholars have ignored extremist challenges to and rejection of Israeli nationalism assuming their views were limited to a radical fringe.[38] Yet the failure to respond forcefully and adequately to the spurious Arab narrative has allowed Arabs and their allies to shape the debate about Israel's legitimacy. There is rarely a political price to pay or a public reproach for espousing Israel's annihilation. With little or no restraints, Arabs are free to promote their fabrications as facts at the U.N., on college campuses, and in the media. Challenging these distortions will not stop Arab vilification of Israel, but unless a vigorous attempt is made to repudiate these lies, the public will assume they are true. Ignoring the enemies of Israel will not make them disappear.[39]

The Arab/Israeli conflict is about Israel's right to exist, not the size of the Jewish state. When the armies of Egypt, Lebanon, Transjordan, Iraq Syria, and elements of the Saudi and Yemen military attacked the nascent state of Israel in May 1948, their objective was to destroy Israel.[40]

David Ben-Gurion, Israel's first prime minister, recognized that "the Arab people will not be reconciled to the fact that six hundred thousand Jews defeated them; and this will remain a critical issue for us for a long time." He also recognized the Arabs would not be deterred from liquidating the Jewish State—that they would take every opportunity to achieve a strategic advantage, and that they believed time was on their side:

> It should not be assumed that the defeat has restrained them from [wishing to] extirpate us from our land...They are certain, with some justification that time is on their side...ten, fifty, a hundred or two hundred years. They have a classic example right here in the country—the eleventh-century Crusader conquest. A Christian state rose...[and] thrived for decades, [but] eventually the Muslim world overpowered and totally annihilated it.[41]

Subsequent wars in 1967 (Six Day War), and 1973 (Yom Kippur War), suicide attacks by terrorists who blow up innocent Israelis on buses, in cafes, restaurants, pizza shops, parks, shopping malls, and rocket attacks from the Gaza Strip have all had the same objective: the destruction of the Jewish state. The myth of Jews being colonialists encouraged the belief that, like their European forbearers, the Israelis would retreat to their former countries after being attacked. This is the foundation upon which the campaign of terror was begun.[42]

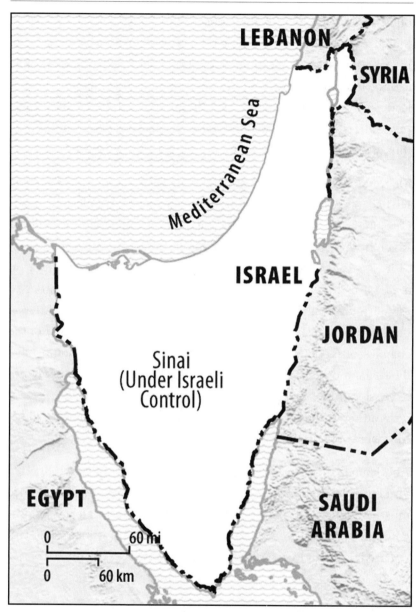

1973—Israel's boundaries following the Yom Kippur War. In a clear act of aggression, Egypt and Syria attacked the State of Israel, but were driven away. Courtesy of Eli Hertz

Unlike the Nazis, who sought to keep the scope of the Final Solution from the world, the Arabs publicly declare their intent to wipe Israel off the map in their media, mosques, schools and charters.[43] In March 2006, Hamas' Yusuf Rizka, Palestinian Authority Minister of Information, said: "We cannot recognize Israel. The land of Palestine is ours and not for Jews."[44] Jews are viewed as intruders. As Hamas leader Isma'il Abu Shanab noted: "In our view, there is not a single person in Israel whom we don't view as a usurper of our land," and, thus, a compelling target for Hamas' campaign of violence.[45]

Mahmud Al-Zahar, a Hamas leader in Gaza, assured viewers on Hizballah's Al-Manar television in January 2006 that "Palestine means Palestine in its entirety from the [Mediterranean] Sea to the [Jordan] River, from Ra's Al-Naqura to Rafah. We cannot give up a single inch of it. Therefore, we will not recognize the Israeli enemy's [right] to a single inch."[46] For Hamas, liberating all of Palestine in order to establish an Islamic state means a holy war against Israel. Anyone daring to sign away even "a grain of sand in Palestine in favor of the enemies of God...who have seized the blessed land" should have their "hand be cut off." Thus, "every negotiation with the enemy is a regression from the [Palestinian] cause, concession of a principle, and recognition of the usurping murders' false claim to a land in which they were not born."[47]

Abu Hamza, the *nom de guerre* of a senior leader of Islamic Jihad, a virulent organization backed by Iran and Syria, declared, "Resistance must continue until we uproot the occupation from all the land of Palestine...from the sea to the river." The future Palestinian state will replace Israel, not live in peace next to it.[48]

THE IMPASSE WILL CONTINUE

The existence of a political will to achieve and sustain peace is the key question. Concessions required are a deterrent for those Israelis who do not want to part with territories won in defensive wars and view Judea and Samaria as part of their patrimony. Others dismiss the idea of negotiated peace with leaders who speak of conditional acceptance of Israel. Still others believe that negotiations are futile because even conciliatory statements by Arabs mask their hidden agenda of annihilation of the Jewish state, and thus genuine peace is a utopian dream. A two-state settlement is viewed by some as fundamentally unstable and would fail regardless of intentions.[49]

More and more Israelis see sustained peace as a fantasy given the vehement anti-Israel rhetoric espoused by Arab political and religious leaders, the Arab media and educators in Palestinian schools.[50] Every Jewish civilian killed or injured as a result of a terrorist attack undermines Israel's feeling of security. It also raises the question as to whether the Palestinian Arabs are addicted to indiscriminate violence and if this enmity is unrelenting and irreconcilable.[51]

When asked at the start of the Arab Revolt how long will it take before peace would prevail, Moshe Beilinson, a journalist for Histadrut's newspaper *Davar*, replied in a June 1936 article:

> Until the most fervent warrior in the enemy camp realizes that there is no means by which to break Israel's power in its land, because it has necessity and living truth on its side. Until they know that there is no other way but to make peace with Israel. This is the purpose of our struggle.[52]

Most problems are not generally resolved. They are endured, outlasted, avoided, discarded out of fatigue, and finally replaced by more urgent issues. R.H. Tawney writes:

> It is the tragedy of a world where man must walk by sight that the discovery of the reconciling formula is always left to the future generations, in which passion has cooled into curiosity, and the agonies of peoples have become the exercise of schools. The devil who builds bridges does not span such chasms till much that is precious has vanished down for ever.[53]

Acknowledgments

There are a number of people and institutions I wish to thank for their significant assistance while writing this book. Generous support was provided by David Messer, Steven Alevy, the Reuben and Rose Mattus and Doris and Kevin Hurley Foundation, the Hodie and Saul Kahn Foundation, Jance Weberman, Rachel Eliyahu, Rabbi David Herman, and Shaare Tfiloh Congregation in Baltimore, Maryland.

Special thanks to Josh Strobel who assisted me at the British National Archives in London. At Harvard University Gabe Scheinmann and John Collins, Reference/Documents Librarian at Lamont Library, were enormously helpful. The staff of the Central Zionist Archives in Jerusalem also provided important assistance.

Jordana Palgon, Gabe Scheinmann, and Dr. Phillip Sieradski assisted with the preliminary editing. Dr. Andrew G. Bostom and Ed Dauber offered invaluable insights. Eli Hertz graciously provided the maps. Thanks to Atara Chouake for her work on the manuscript.

Special thanks to Scott Korman, Danny Rubin, Heshy Seif, Milton Sonnenberg and Dr. Arnold Yagoda for their encouragement throughout this project. Special thanks also to Dr. Ben Chouake for his invaluable insights.

The concern and tenacity of Lynne Rabinoff, my literary agent, is especially appreciated.

I owe a special debt of gratitude to Jim Fletcher, my friend, editor and the publisher of Balfour Books and to Thomas Sharp of Blue Channel Media. Their commitment to telling the truth about Israel, the Middle East, and the Arab-Israeli conflict and to publishing this book is very much appreciated and shows the depth of their commitment to historical truth.

Endnotes

INTRODUCTION ENDNOTES

1. Alex Grobman, *Nations United: How the UN Undermines Israel and the West* (Green Forest, Arkansas: Balfour Books, 2006); Dore Gold, *Towers of Babble: How The United Nations Has Fueled Global Chaos*, (New York: Crown Forum, 2004); Yehuda Z. Blum, *For Zion's Sake*, (New York: Herzl Press, 1987); Anne Bayefsky, "Forsaking Israel," *National Review*, (December 11, 2007); Anne Bayefsky, "U.N. vs. Israel," *National Review*, (April 20, 2004); Yohanan Manor, *To Right a Wrong: The Revocation of the UN General Assembly Resolution 3379 Defaming Zionism*, (New York: Shengold Publishers, Inc., 1996.)

2. Yaacov Herzog, *A People That Dwells Alone*, (New York: Sanhedrin Press, 1975), 127.

3. Rael Jean Isaac, "Why It Would Be a Catastrophe to Solve the Arab-Israel Conflict," *American Thinker*, (February 16, 2007).

4. Hillel Halkin, "The Peace Planners Strike Again," *Commentary* (January 2008):13.

5. Martin Indyk, *Innocent Abroad: An Intimate History of American Peace Diplomacy in the Middle East*, (New York: Simon and Shuster, 2009); David Pollock, ed., "Prevent Breakdown, Prepare for Breakthrough: How President Obama Can Promote Israeli-Palestinian Peace," The Washington Institute for Near East Policy, (December 2008); Barry Rubin, "What They Say Isn't What You Hear," *JewishWorldReview.com*. (December 15, 2008.); Jane Lampman, "Can religion improve peace

prospects in the Middle East?" *Christian Science Monitor*, (December 20, 2007); "Secretary Condoleeza Rice: Interview Roundtable with Radio, Television and Wires," (November 21, 2007), U.S. State Department; Bret Stephens, "The Annapolis Fiasco," *The Wall Street Journal*, (November 20, 2007); Harvey Sicherman, "Endgame for Palestine," *ISN Security Watch*, (July 31, 2007); Rubenstein, op. cit.; Zalman Shoval, "The Jordanian Option," *The Washington Times*, (July 27, 2007); Carlos Fraenkel, "Teaching Plato in Palestine: Can Philosophy Save the Middle East? *Dissent*, (Spring 2007); Neal Kozodoy, ed., *The Mideast Peace Process: An Autopsy*, (New York: Encounter, Books, 2006); Rabah Halabi, ed., *Israeli and Palestinian Identities in Dialogue: The School for Peace Approach*, (New Brunswick, New Jersey: Rutgers University Press, 2004.); David Makovsky, "Taba mythchief," *National Interest*, (Spring 2003); Barry Rubin, "The Terror And The Pity: Yasir Arafat And The Second Loss of Palestine," *Middle East Review of International Affairs*, vol. 6, no. 1, (March 2002); Yossi Klein Halevi, *At the Entrance to the Garden of Eden: A Jew's Search For God With Christians and Muslims In The Holy Land*, (New York: William Morrow, 2001); Avraham Sela, *The Decline of the Arab-Israeli Conflict: Middle East Politics and the Quest for Regional Order*, (Albany, New York: State University Press of New York, 1998); Geoffrey R. Watson, *The Oslo Agreements: International Law and the Israeli-Palestinian Peace Agreements*, (New York: Oxford University Press, 2000); Edward W. Said, *Peace and its Discontents: Essays on Palestine in the Middle East Peace Process*, (New York: Vintage Books, 1995); Richard N. Haass, *Conflicts Unending: The United States and Regional Disputes*, (New Haven: Yale University Press, 1990), 30-56; Mohamed Sid-Ahmed, *After The Guns Fall Silent: Peace or Armageddon in the Middle East*, (London: Croom Helm, 1976), 67-77, 112-115; Kenneth W. Stein and Samuel W. Lewis, "Mediation in the Middle East," in *Managing Global Chaos: Sources of and Responses to International Conflict*, Chester A. Crocker, and Fen Osler Hampson with Pamela Aall, (Washington, D.C.: United States Institute of Peace, 1999), 463-473; Neil Lochery, "Learning the Lessons: Peacemaking in Israel and Northern

Ireland," *Israel Affairs*, vol. 12, issue 2, (April 2006): 234-252; Ruth
Lapidoth, *Autonomy: Flexible Solutions To Ethnic Conflict*, (Washington,
D.C. United Sates Institute of Peace, 1996); Kenneth W Stein, *Heroic
Diplomacy: Sadat, Kissinger, Begin, and the Quest for Arab-Israeli Peace*,
(New York: Routledge, 1999); Karen A. Feste, *Plans for Peace: Negotiation
and the Arab-Israeli Conflict*, (New York: Praeger, 1991); Laura Zittrain
Eisenberg and Neil Caplan, *Negotiating Arab-Israeli Peace: Patterns,
Problems, Possibilities*, (Bloomington, Indiana: Indiana University Press,
1998); Steven L. Spiegel, *The Other Arab-Israeli Conflict: Making America's
Middle East Policy, from Truman to Reagan*, (Chicago, Illinois: The
University of Chicago Press, 1985); Ira Sharkansky, "The Potential of
Ambiguity: The Case of Jerusalem," *Israel Affairs*, vol. 3, issues 3 and 4,
(Spring 1994):187-199; Yaacov Bar-Simon-Tov, *Israel and the Peace Process
1977-1982: In Search of Legitimacy for Peace*, (Albany, New York: State
University of New York, 1994).

6.   Haim Shaked, "Continuity and Change: An Overview in *The Arab-
Israeli Conflict Perspectives*, Alvin Z. Rubinstein, ed., 2nd edition
(New York: HarperCollins, 1991), 191-193, 197; Shlomo Avineri, "The
Palestinians and Israel," *Commentary*, vol. 49, no. 6, (June 1970):34-35;
Elie Kedourie, "Where Arabism and Zionism Differ," *Commentary*,
(June 1960): 32-36; Walid Khalidi, "The Palestine Problem: An
Overview," *Journal of Palestine Studies*, vol. 21, issue 1, (Autumn
1991):5-6; Walid Khalidi, "The Arab Perspective" in *The End of the
Palestine Mandate*, William Roger Louis and Robert W. Stookey,
eds., (Austin Texas: University of Texas Press, 1986), 104-136; I.F.
Stone, "Holy War," The New York Review of Books, vol. 9, no. 2,
(August 3, 1967); Shlomo Ben-Ami, *Scars of War, Wounds of Peace: The
Israeli-Arab Tragedy*. (New York: Oxford University Press, 2006), 7;
H.R. Trevor-Roper, "Jewish and Other Nationalisms," *Commentary*,
(January 1963):15-21; Aharon Cohen, *Israel and the Arab World*, (Boston,
Massachusetts: Beacon Press, 1976); Hedva Ben-Israel, "Zionism and
European Nationalisms: Comparative Aspects," *Israel Studies*, vol. 8,
no. 1, (April 2003):91-104; Anthony D. Smith, "Sacred Territories and

National Conflict," *Israel Affairs*, issue 4, (Summer 1999):13- 31; Barry Rubin, *The Arab States and the Palestine Conflict*, (New York: Syracuse University Press, 1981); in the late 1960s or early 1970s a prominent Knesset committee heard a lecture from a professor of biology from the Weizmann Institute on the "compulsion in animate beings to possess and defend" territory. The lecture was based on a best seller by Robert Audrey, *The Territorial Imperative*, (New York: Dell Publishing Company, Inc., 1966). The reference to the Knesset meeting is found in Simha Flapan, ed., *When Enemies Dare To Talk: An Israeli-Palestinian Debate*, (London: Croom Helm, Ltd., 1979), 91-92; the issue of the territorial instinct is also discussed by Itzhak Galnoor in his book, *The Partition of Palestine: Decision Crossroads in the Zionist Movement*, (Albany, New York: State University of New York Press, Albany, 1995), 7-8; Claude Klein, "Zionism Revisited," *Israel Affairs*, vol. 11, no. 1, (January 2005): 238-253.

7.   David Mamet, *The Wicked Son: Anti-Semitism, Self-Hatred, And The Jews*, (New York: Schocken Books, 2006), 4-7, 10-11, 16.

CHAPTER 1 ENDNOTES

1.   Moshe Gil, *A History of Palestine*, 634-1099, (New York: Cambridge University Press, 1997), 1-2, 12.

2.   Arie Morgenstern, "Dispersion and The Longing For Zion, 1240-1840," in *New Essays On Zionism*, David Hazony, Yoram Hazony, and Michael Oren, eds., (New York: Shalem Press, 2006), 308; Arie Morgenstern, *Hastening Redemption: Messianism And The Resettlement Of The Land Of Israel*, (New York: Oxford University, 2006).

3.   Morgenstern, Dispersion and The Longing For Zion, 1240-1840," op. cit., 308.

4.   Ibid.

5.   Ibid.

6.   Gil, *A History of Palestine*, 634-1099, op. cit., 1-2, 12.

7. Ibid., 2, 68-72.

8. Ibid., 73-74.

9. Ibid., 4.

10. Ibid., 3-4, 105-106.

11. Bernard Lewis, *From Babel To Dragomans: Interpreting The Middle East*, (New York: Oxford University Press, 2004), 60; Gil, A History of Palestine, 634-1099 op. cit., 11.

12. Gil, *A History of Palestine*, 634-1099, op. cit., 11.

13. Ibid., 21.

14. Ibid., 26-31, 221.

15. Ibid., 43.

16. Ibid., 1, 113- 114; Bernard Lewis, "The Palestinians and the PLO: A Historical Approach," *Commentary*, vol. 59, no 1, (January 1975):32; Bernard Lewis, "Palestine: On the History and Geography of a Name," *The International History Review*, (January 1980): 1-12.

17. Gil, *A History of Palestine*, 634-1099, op. cit., 114.

18. Ibid., 92-96.

19. Ibid., 98-100; for an in-depth analysis of how the Arabs have elevated the importance of Jerusalem by "reconstructing history and beliefs by using early Islamic traditions," see Yitzhak Reiter, *Jerusalem and Its Role in Islamic Solidarity*, (New York: Palgrave Macmillan, 2008).

20. Gil, *A History of Palestine*, 634-1099, op. cit., 92-96.

21. Ibid., 171-189, 212-220, 500-501.

22. Ibid., 203.

23. Ibid., 205-207

24. Ibid., 335-347, 370-378, 387-421.

25. Ibid., 826-837; Martin Gilbert, *Exile and Return: The Struggle for a Jewish Homeland*, (Philadelphia and New York: J.B. Lippincott Company), 11.

26. Gilbert, *Exile and Return: The Struggle for a Jewish Homeland*, op. cit., 11.

27. Ibid., 12.

28. Ibid.

29. Morgenstern, "Dispersion And The Longing For Zion, 1240-1840." op. cit., 312.

30. Ibid., 312-313; Gilbert, *Exile and Return: The Struggle for a Jewish Homeland*, op. cit., 12.

31. Morgenstern, "Dispersion And The Longing For Zion, 1240-1840," op. cit., 314-315.

32. Gilbert, *Exile and Return: The Struggle for a Jewish Homeland*, op. cit., 17.

33. Ibid., 19-20.

34. Ibid.

35. Ibid., 17.

36. Ibid., 18-19.

37. Morgenstern, "Dispersion And The Longing For Zion, 1240-1840," op. cit., 319.

38. Ibid.

39. Gilbert, *Exile and Return: The Struggle for a Jewish Homeland*, op. cit., 19.

40. H.H. Ben Sasson, ed., *A History of the Jewish People*, (Cambridge, Massachusetts: Harvard University Press, 1976), 635.

41. Gilbert, *Exile and Return: The Struggle for a Jewish Homeland*, op. cit., 19.

42. Morgenstern, "Dispersion and the Longing For Zion, 1240-1840," op. cit., 320.

43. Ibid., 323-324.

44. Ibid., 325.

45. Ibid.

46. Ben Sasson, *A History of the Jewish People*, op. cit., 634.

47. Morgenstern, "Dispersion and the Longing For Zion, 1240-1840," op. cit., 325.

48. Ibid.

49. Ibid., 329.

50. Ibid., 329-330.

51. Ibid.

52. Ibid.

53. Ibid., 332.

54. Ibid.

55. Ibid., 334-335.

56. Ibid., 336.

57. Ibid.

58. Morgenstern, *Hastening Redemption*, op. cit., 207.

59. Morgenstern, "Dispersion And The Longing For Zion, 1240-1840," op. cit., 344.

60. Heschel, *Israel: An Echo of Eternity*, op. cit., 56-57; Ben Gurion, David, "Ben-Gurion and De Gaulle: An Exchange of Letters," *Midstream*, (February 1968): 12.

61. Tudor Parfitt, *The Jews In Palestine 1800-1882*, (Suffolk, England: Royal Historical Society, 1987), 218-219.

62. Rabbi Joseph Schwarz, *A Descriptive Geography and Brief Historical Sketch of Palestine*, (For Sixteen Years A Resident in the Holy Land) (Philadelphia, Pennsylvania: A Hart, 1850), 373-374; Parfitt, *The Jews in Palestine 1800-1882*, op. cit., 220; Michael Avi-Yonah, *A History of Israel and the Holy Land*, (New York: Continuum International Group, 2001).

63. Parfitt, *The Jews in Palestine 1800-1882*, op. cit., 221.

64. Ibid. For an understanding of the role of the dhimmis, see Bat Ye'or, *Eurabia: The Euro-Arab Axis*, (Teaneck, New Jersey: Fairleigh Dickinson University Press, 2005), 9; Bat Ye'or, *Islam and Dhimmitude: Where Civilizations Collide*, (Teaneck, New Jersey: Fairleigh Dickinson University Press, 2002); Wilfred Cantwell Smith, *Islam In Modern History*, (New York: Mentor Books, 1957); Daniel Pipes, "Islam and Islamism-Faith and Ideology," *National Interest*, (Spring 2000).

65. David Kushner, "Zealous Towns in Nineteenth-Century Palestine," *Middle Eastern Studies*, vol. 33, no. 3, (July 1997):597.

66. Finn, *Stirring Times or Records from Jerusalem Consular Chronicles of 1853 to 1856*, vol. I, (London: C. Kegan Paul and Company, 1878), 237, 390; James Finn to the Earl of Clarendon, F.O. 78/962 (29, April 1853).

67. Finn, *Stirring Times or Records from Jerusalem Consular Chronicles of 1853 to 1856*, vol. II, Elibron Classic Series, 2005, (Originally Published, London: C. Kegan Paul & Co, 1878), 154; John Mills, *Three Months' Residence at Nablus, and an Account of the Modern Samaritans*, (London: John Murray, 1864).

68. John Lewis Burckhardt, *Travels and the Holy Land*, (London: Association for Promoting The Discovery of The Interior Parts of Africa, 1882), 342; Mary Eliza Rogers, *Domestic Life in Palestine*, (Cincinnati, Ohio: Poe and Hitchcock, 1865):234-236; Beshara Doumani, *Rediscovering Palestine: Merchants and Peasants in Jabal Nablus, 1700-1900*, (Berkeley, California: University of California Press, 1995).

69. Walter Keating Kelly, *Syria and the Holy Land: Their Scenery and Their People*, (Chapman and Hall, 1847), 389-390; Rabbi Joseph Schwarz, *A Descriptive Geography and Brief Historical Sketch of Palestine*, op. cit., 396-401; James Finn to Viscount Palmerston, F.O. 78/839 (27 September 1850); James Finn to Viscount Palmerston, F.O.78/874 (1 July 1851); James Finn to the Earl of Malmesbury, F.O. 78/1382 (July 8, 1858).

70. Finn, *Stirring Times*, vol. I, op. cit., 107-110; Jonathan Frankel, *The Damascus Affair: Ritual Murder, Politics, and the Jews in 1840*, (New York: Cambridge University Press, 1997).

71. Finn, *Stirring Times*, vol. I, op. cit., 107-110.

72. James Finn to Lord Palmerston, F.O. 78/705 (13 March 1847).

73. Finn, *Stirring Times*, vol. I, op. cit., 108-109.

74. William T. Young to Viscount Palmerston, Jerusalem, (25 May, 1839): F.O. 78/368; James Finn to the Earl of Clarendon, F.O.78/962 (19, July, 1853); James Finn to Lord Stratford De Redcliffe, F.O.195/369 (13 October 1853).

75. William T. Young to Viscount Palmerston, Jerusalem, (25 May, 1839): F.O. 78/368, op. cit.

76. Finn, Stirring Times, vol. I, op. cit.,118 -119.

77. William T. Young to Viscount Palmerston, Jerusalem, (25 May, 1839), F.O. 78/368). In other words, "the prejudice of the Christian against the Jew in Jerusalem amounts to fanaticism....."; William T. Young to Colonel Patrick Campbell, F.O.78/368 (19 April, 1839); On Easter Day 1848, a Jew was recognized in the Church of the Holy Sepulchre and was almost beaten to death by members of the Christian community who had come to pray. James Finn to Viscount Palmerston, F.O. 78/755 (27 April 1848); James Finn to Viscount Palmerston, F.O. 78/755 (2 May 1848).

78. Young to Viscount Palmerston, Jerusalem, (25 May, 1839), op. cit.; Claude Reignier Condor, Tent Work in Palestine: A Record of Discovery and Adventure, vol. 1, (London: Richard Bentley and Son, 1878): 338-339; James Finn to Earl of Malmesbury, F.O. 195/604 (8 November, 1858).

79. James Finn, Stirring Times, vol. I, op. cit., 105-106. Throughout Finn's 17 years in Palestine, his "singular" and "unsurpassed" efforts to protect the Jews were prompted not only by his feelings towards them, but by his appreciation that this community had "a germ of development for future time," Isaiah Friedman, "Lord Palmerston and the Protection of Jews in Palestine 1839-1851," Jewish Social Studies, vol. 30, no. 1, (January 1968): 38.

80. Parfitt, The Jews in Palestine, op. cit.,195-196,198.

81. Neville J. Mandel, The Arabs and Zionism Before World War I, (Berkeley, California: University of California Press), 54; Derek Hopwood, The Russian Presence In Syria and Palestine 1843-1914, (New York: Clarendon Press, Oxford University Press, 1969): 117-118.

82. Ibid.

83. Ibid., 53.

84. Karsh and Karsh, *Empires of the Sand: The Struggle for Mastery in the Middle East*, 1789-1923, op. cit., 162-163.

85. Ibid., 164-165; Feroz Ahmad, *The Young Turks: The Committee of Union and Progress in Turkish Politics, 1908-1914*, (New York: Columbia University Press, 2008).

86. Friedman, *Germany, Turkey, Zionism: 1897-1918*, (New Brunswick, New Jersey: Transaction Publishers, 1998), 32-37; Alexander Scholch, "Britain In Palestine, 1838-1882: The Roots of the Balfour Declaration," *Journal of Palestine Studies XXX*, no. 1, (Autumn 1992):40; Ruth Kark, *American Consul in the Holy Land 1832-1914*, (Jerusalem: The Magnes Press / The Hebrew University and Detroit, Michigan: Wayne State University Press, 1994); James Finn, Stirring Times, vol. II, op. cit., 281; Yehoshua Ben-Arieh, *The Rediscovery of the Holy Land in the Nineteenth Century*, (Jerusalem: The Magnes Press / The Hebrew University and Detroit, Michigan: Wayne State University Press, 1979),11-13; Abraham David, *To Come to the Land: Immigration and settlement in 16th-Century Eretz-Israel*, (Tuscaloosa, Alabama: The University of Alabama Press, 1999); Gorny, *Zionism and the Arabs, 1882 — 1948: A Study of Ideology*, (New York: Oxford, 198),14

87. Ruth Kark, *American Consul in the Holy Land 1832-1914*, (Jerusalem and Detroit, Michigan: The Magnes Press / The Hebrew University, Jerusalem Wayne State University Press, 1994), 61-63.

88. Gorny, *Zionism and the Arabs, 1882 — 1948: A Study of Ideology*, op. cit., 14; Alexander Scholch, "Britain In Palestine, 1838-1882: The Roots of the Balfour Declaration," op. cit., 40; Kark, *American Consul in the Holy Land 1832-1914*, op. cit., 55-67; Friedman, *Germany, Turkey, Zionism: 1897-1918*, op. cit., 32-37; James Finn, *Stirring Times*, vol. II, op. cit., 281; Alexander Scholch, *Palestine in Transformation: 1856-1882: Studies in Social, Economic and Political Development*, 47-70.

89. Friedman, *Germany, Turkey, Zionism: 1897-1918*, op. cit., 32-33.

90. Colonel Patrick Campbell to William T. Young, (28 May, 1839) F.O. 78/368 (no. 6).

91. Isaiah Friedman, "Lord Palmerston and the Protection of Jews in Palestine 1839-1851," op. cit., 24, 28-29, 33.

92. A.M. Hyamson, *Palestine Under The Mandate*, (London: Methuen and Company, Ltd., 1950), 6.

93. Ibid., 7-8; Friedman, "Lord Palmerston and the Protection of Jews in Palestine 1839-1851," op. cit., 24-25.

94. Scholch, *Palestine in Transformation: 1856-1882*, op. cit., 42-43, 45-48; It is important to note that there were a number of Christian colonization ideas and plans that were articulated, 48-53; Yaron Perry, *British Mission to the Jews in Nineteenth Century Palestine*, (New York: Routledge, 2003), 2-3.

95. David Ben-Gurion, "Ben-Gurion and De Gaulle: An Exchange of Letters," op. cit., 13; Michael Graetz, *The Jews in the Nineteenth Century France: From the French Revolution to the Alliance Israelite Universelle*, (Palo Alto, California: Stanford University Press, 1996).

96. Gorny, *Zionism And The Arabs: 1882-1948*, op. cit., 2-3; Arieh Bruce Saposnik, *Becoming Hebrew: The Creation of a Jewish National Culture in Ottoman Palestine*, (New York: Oxford University Press, 2008); Ben Halpern and Jehuda Reinharz, *Zionism and the Creation of a New Society*, (New York: Oxford University Press, 1998); S. Ilan Troen, *Imagining Zion: Dreams, Designs, and Realities in a Century of Jewish Settlement*, (New Haven, Connecticut: Yale University Press, 2003), 3-14.

97. Morgenstern, "Dispersion and the Longing For Zion, 1240-1840," op. cit., 337.

98. Ibid., 340.

99. Ibid.

100. Ibid., 340-341

101. Ibid.

102. Ibid., 341.

103. Ibid.

104. Ibid.

105. Gorny, *Zionism And The Arabs: 1882-1948*, op. cit., 2, 5.; See also Israel
     Kolatt, "The Organization of the Jewish Population of Palestine and
     the Development of its Political Consciousness Before World War I,"
     in *Studies on Palestine during the Ottoman period*, Moshe Ma'oz, ed.,
     (Jerusalem: The Magnes Press and The Hebrew University, 1975), 211-
     245.

106. Troen, *Imagining Zion: Dreams, Designs, and Realities in a Century of
     Jewish Settlement*, op. cit., 51.

107. Gorny, *Zionism And The Arabs: 1882-1948*, op. cit., 11; Emile
     Marmorstein "European Jews in Muslim Palestine," in *Palestine and
     Israel in the 19th and 20th Centuries,* Elie Kedourie and Sylvia G. Haim,
     eds., (London: Frank Cass, 1982), 1-14.

108. David Vital, *The Origins of Zionism*, (Oxford, England: Clarendon Press,
     1975), 89, 90-91,97.

109. Shlomo Avineri, *The Making of Modern Zionism: The Intellectual Origins of
     the Jewish State*, (New York: Basic Books, 1981), 5,13.

110. Ibid., 88.

111. Gorny, *Zionism And The Arabs: 1882-1948*, op. cit., 12.

112. Ibid., 12.

113. Ibid., 13; Gur Alroey, "Journey to Early-Twentieth-Century Palestine
     as a Jewish Immigrant Experience," *Jewish Social Studies*, vol. 9, no. 2,
     (January 2003), 28-64.

114. Kenneth W. Stein, *The Land Question in Palestine, 1917-1939*, (Chapel
     Hill: North Carolina: The University of North Carolina Press, 1984), 3.

115. R. Harari, "Report on the Economic and Commercial Situation of
     Palestine," (March 31, 1921), (Jerusalem: Greek Convent Press, 1922),
     17; George Adam Smith, *Historical Geography of the Holy Land*, (London:
     The Fontana Library), 269-283.

116. R. Harari, "Report on the Economic and Commercial Situation of
     Palestine," op. cit.,17; George Adam Smith, *Historical Geography of the
     Holy Land*, op. cit., 269-283.

CHAPTER 2 ENDNOTES

1. Friedman, *The Question of Palestine*, op. cit., 330; Richard H.S. Crossman, "Gentile Zionism And The Balfour Declaration," *Commentary*, vol. 33, no. 6 (June 1962): 487-494; Richard H.S. Crossman, "The Balfour Declaration 1917-1967," *Midstream*, (December 1967):21-28; Letter from Lord Curzon to Lloyd George, October 9, 1920, (Rohan Butler, and J.P.T. Bury, eds., *Documents on British Foreign Policy 1919-1939 , First Series*, (January 1920-March 1921), Vol. XIII, (London: Her Majesty's Stationery Office,1963): 376.

2. Efraim Karsh and Inari Karsh, *Empires of the Sand: The Struggle for the Mastery in the Middle East*, 1789-1923, (Cambridge, Massachusetts: Harvard University Press, 1999), 173.

3. Marie Syrkin, "Who Are the Palestinians?" *Midstream*, (January 1970), 6; Daniel Pipes, "Palestine for the Syrians?" *Commentary*, (December 1986).

4. Eli E. Hertz, *Reply*, (New York: Myths and Facts, 2005), 24; See Yehoshua Porath, *The Palestinian Arab National Movement: From Riots to Rebellion*, vol. 2, (London: Frank Cass and Company, (1977), 81-82; *Hopwood*, op. cit., 200-201.

5. Syrkin, "Who Are the Palestinians?" op. cit.

6. www.yahoodi.com/peace/palestinians.html; Al Liwa, a Jerusalem daily newspaper, reported that "...Palestine is an inseparable and integral part of Syria and we are fighting for its complete independence"; Mustafa Kabha, *The Palestinian Press as Shaper of Public Opinion 1929-1939: Writing up a Storm*, (Portland Oregon: Vallentine Mitchell, 2007), 178.

7. Syrkin, "Who Are the Palestinians?" op. cit., 6.

8. Ibid., 6-7.

9. Harris O. Schoenberg, *A Mandate For Terror: The United Nations and the PLO*, (New York: Shapolsky Publishers, Inc., 1989), 15.

10. Hertz, *Reply*, op. cit., 24.

11.   Friedman, *The Question of Palestine*, op. cit., 330-331.

12.   Ibid., 33.

13.   Ibid., 331-332.

14.   C. Ernest Dawn, "The Amir of Mecca Al-Husayn Ibn-'Ali and the
      Origin of the Arab Revolt," *Proceedings of the American Philosophical
      Society*, vol. 104, no. 1, (February 1960): 12; Karsh and Karsh, *Empires
      of the Sand: The Struggle for the Mastery in the Middle East, 1789-1923*,
      op. cit. 2, 176, 185-186; Eli Kedourie, *In the Anglo-Arab Labyrinth: The
      McMahon-Husayn Correspondence and its Interpretations 1914-139*,
      (London and Portland, Oregon: Frank Cass Publishers, 2000), 4-7, 11.

15.   McMahon, quoted in Kedourie, *In the Anglo-Arab Labyrinth*, op. cit.,1;
      Karsh and Karsh, *Empires of the Sand: The Struggle for the Mastery in
      the Middle East, 1789-1923*, op. cit., 3, 208; to appreciate the problems
      Hamilton encountered see, Michael and Eleanor Brock, eds., *H.H.
      Asquith: Letters to Venetia Stanley*, (New York: Oxford University Press,
      1985), 373-375, 438-440, 598; Philip Magnus, *Kitchener: Portrait of an
      Imperialist*, (New York E.P. Dutton and Company, 1968), 324-330.

16.   Karsh and Karsh, *Empires of the Sand: The Struggle for the Mastery in the
      Middle East, 1789-1923*, op. cit., 3, 208.

17.   Kedourie, *In the Anglo-Arab Labyrinth*, op. cit., 14-16, 35-38.

18.   Ibid., 16.

19.   Ibid., 16-17.

20.   Ibid., 19.

21.   Ibid., 19-20.

22.   Karsh and Karsh, *Empires of the Sand: The Struggle for the Mastery in the
      Middle East, 1789-1923*, op. cit., 188-189.

23.   Alexander Aaronsohn, *With The Turks in Palestine*, (infomotions.com,
      1916), chapter 6; for more information about Dr. Otis, see Ruth Kark,
      American Consuls in the Holy Land, op. cit, 33-334.

24.   Meinertzhagen, *Middle East Diary 1917-1956*, op. cit., 7.

25.   Ibid., 192, 194, 229.

26. Friedman, *The Question of Palestine*, op. cit., 330.

27. Ibid.

28. Meinertzhagen, *Middle East Diary 1917-1956*, op. cit., 168-169.

29. Philip Graves, *Palestine, the Land of Three Faiths*, (London: Jonathan Cape, 1923), 112-113.

30. Isaiah Friedman, "Arnold Toynbee: Pro-Arab or Pro-Zionist?" *Israel Studies*, vol. 4, no. 1, (Spring 1999): 75.

31. Ibid., 211.

32. Ibid., 212.

33. Ibid.

34. Ibid., 213.

35. Ibid.

36. Ibid., 213, 214, 222.

37. Ibid., 215-221.

38. Ibid., 215-216.

39. Ibid., 221; See Charles D. Smith, "The Invention of A Tradition: The Question of Arab Acceptance of the Zionist Right to Palestine during World War I," vol. XXII, no. 2, *Journal of Palestine Studies*, (Winter 1993): 48-61.

40. Karsh and Karsh, *Empires of the Sand: The Struggle for the Mastery in the Middle East, 1789-1923*, op. cit., 237.

41. Ibid., 237.

42. Ibid., 238.

43. Kedourie, *In the Anglo-Arab Labyrinth*, op. cit., 86-87.

44. Ibid., 87

45. Ibid.

46. Karsh and Karsh, *Empires of the Sand: The Struggle for the Mastery in the Middle East, 1789-1923*, op. cit., 242.

47. Friedman, *The Question of Palestine*, op. cit., 21.

48. A. Henry McMahon, "Independence of The Arabs: The 'McMahon Pledge,'" *The London Times*, (July 23, 1947), 17.

49. "Report of the Palestine Royal Commission: Report of the presented by the Secretary of State for the Colonies to the United Kingdom Parliament by Command of His Britannic Majesty," (July 1937), op. cit., Chapter II: 20.

50. "Report of a Committee Set Up to Consider Certain Correspondence Between Sir Henry McMahon and The Sharif of Mecca In 1915 and 1916 Presented by the Secretary of State for the Colonies to Parliament by Command of His Majesty," (March 1939), London: His Majesties Stationery Office.

51. Ibid.

52. Karsh and Karsh, *Empires of the Sand: The Struggle for the Mastery in the Middle East*, 1789-1923, op. cit., 239.

53. "Report of a Committee Set Up to Consider Certain Correspondence Between Sir Henry McMahon and The Sharif of Mecca In 1915 and 1916," op. cit.

54. Ibid.

55. Ibid.

56. Ibid.

57. "Report of the Palestine Royal Commission: presented by the Secretary of State for the Colonies to the United Kingdom Parliament by Command of His Britannic Majesty," (July 1937), op. cit., Chapter II, 41; Friedman, op. cit., 331.

58. "Report of a Committee Set Up to Consider Certain Correspondence Between Sir Henry McMahon and The Sharif of Mecca In 1915 and 1916," op. cit.

59. Ibid.

60. Ibid.

61. "Report of a Committee Set Up to Consider Certain Correspondence Between Sir Henry McMahon and The Sharif of Mecca In 1915 and 1916," op. cit.

62. Kedourie, op. cit., 4-25; See also telegram to Sir Edward Grey on May 14, McMahon, Ibid., 24.

63. Ibid., 25.

64. Friedman, op. cit., 7, 290-291.

65. Ibid; James Renton, *The Zionist Masquerade: The Birth of the Anglo-Zionist Alliance*, 1914-1918, (New York: Palgrave Macmillan, 2007), 2-5, 69-71; Christopher Sykes, *Two Studies of Virtue*, (New York: Alfred A. Knopf, 1953), 183-186; Efraim and Inari Karsh, *Empires of the Sand: The Struggle for the Mastery in the Middle East, 1789-1923*, op. cit., 252; Gilbert, *Exile and Return*, op. cit., 105; Conor Cruise O'Brien, *The Siege: The Saga of Israel and Zionism*, (New York: Touchstone Book, 1986), 123-126; Leonard Stein, op. cit., 549-550; Mayir Vereté, "The Balfour Declaration and its Makers," in *From Palmerston to Balfour: Collected Essays of Mayir Vereté ed.*, Norman Rose, (Portland, Oregon: Frank Cass and Company, 1992), 1-38, 204-226; George Lichtheim, "Winston Churchill and Zionism," *Midstream*, (Spring 1959), 19-29; Jehuda Reinharz, "The Balfour Declaration and its Maker," *The Journal of Modern History*, vol. 64, no. 3, (September 1992): 455-499; Ronald Sanders, *The High Walls of Jerusalem: A History of the Balfour Declaration And The Birth of The British Mandate For Palestine*, New York: Holt and Winston, 1983), 615. One of the books used to enlist support of Jews in England to Zionism was edited by historian Harry Sacher and partially financed by Edmond de Rothschild, Zionism and the Jewish Future, (London: John Murray, 1916); British Prime Minister Lloyd George wrote that "The Zionist leaders gave us a definite promise that, if the Allies committed themselves to giving facilities for the establishment of a national home for the Jews in Palestine, they would do their best to rally to the Allied cause Jewish sentiment and support throughout the world. They kept their word in the letter and the spirit, and the

only question that remains is now whether we mean to honour ours..
. .There is no better proof of the value of the Balfour Declaration as a
military move than the fact that Germany entered into negotiations
with Turkey in an endeavor to provide an alternative scheme which
would appeal to the Zionist." Lloyd George, *The Truth About the
Peace Treaties*, Vol. II, (London: Victor Gollancz, 1938), 1139-1142. In a
broadcast on May 23, 1939 about the White Paper, Lloyd George added
additional information about what prompted the British to adopt this
policy: "Twenty-five years ago, the British empire became engaged in
a life and death struggle against the most formidable military empire
in the world, for the vindication of international right. In 1917, that
conflict reached a critical stage, when the issue appeared more than
doubtful. The scales of victory seemed then to weigh down in favour
of the German militarists. The leaders on both sides of this conflict
were straining in every effort to rally all available forces and resources,
internal and neutral, on their side to achieve a decision. The Allies and
their foes alike realised the undoubted influence and opportunities
which the Jews, their descendants of the great dispersal, could exert
at vital points in the vast battle area.. .. The Jews have honourably
kept their part of the bargain." Silas S. Perry, *Britain Opens a Gateway*,
(London: Museum Press Limited, 1944), 94-95.

66.   Stuart A. Cohen, *English Zionists and British Jews: The Communal Politics
of Anglo-Jewry, 1895-1920*, (Princeton, New Jersey: Princeton University
Press, 1982), 229.

67.   "Memorandum by Felix Frankfurter of an Interview in Mr. Balfour's
Apartment, 23 rue Nitot, Paris, on Tuesday, June 24th, 1919 at 4:45
p.m.," E.L. Woodward and Rohan Butler, *Documents on British Foreign
Policy 1919-1939*, First Series, 1919, Vol. IV, (London: Her Majesty's
Stationary Office, 1952), 1276-1278.; Renton, *Zionist Masquerade: The
Birth of the Anglo-Zionist Alliance, 1914-1918*, op. cit., 3.

68.   Ibid., 69.

69. Martin Gilbert, *Winston S. Churchill, 1874-1965*, (London: William Heinemann Ltd, 1975), 652-653; Renton, op. cit., 69; Sir Herbert Samuel took issue with this reasoning in his memoirs, and suggested there were other justifications for issuing the Balfour Declaration. Viscount Samuels, *Memoirs*, (London: The Cresset Press, 1945), 146-148; In her diary entry of March 18, 1936, Baffy (Blanche) Dugdale, Balfour's niece, wrote "It was "Eretz Israel (the land of Israel) which converted A.J.B. [Arthur James Balfour]," *Baffy: The Diaries of Blanche Dugdale 1936-1947*, N.A. Rose ed., (London: Vallentine, Mitchell,1973), 9; Michael Makovsky notes that in addition to humanitarian relief, Churchill recognized that Jews needed some kind of territorial entity, a Jewish political entity, as a safe haven. *Churchill's Promised Land: Zionism and Statecraft* (New Haven, Connecticut: Yale University Press, 2007), 58-59, 61-63, 68, 86-87.

70. "Introduction by The Rt. Hon. A.J. Balfour, M.P." in *History of Zionism: 1600-1918*, by Nahum Sokolow, (New York: KTAV Publishing House, 1969), LIV.

71. Meinertzhagen, *Middle East Diary 1917-1956*, (New York: Thomas Yoseloff), 1958,9; In his diary entry of December 30, 1917, Sir Francis Bertie, the British Ambassador to Paris, wrote that French diplomat Paul Cambon said "...that Balfour explained his support of Zionism as partly financial and partly political and also sentimental-viz., the necessity to conciliate the American Jews who have gone in for Palestine and who can supply money for loans, and his own feeling that it would be an interesting experiment to reconstitute a Jewish kingdom. Cambon reminded him of the prophecy that a King of the Jews would be the end of the world. Balfour thinks that such a dénouement would be still more interesting!" Bertie's own view entered on June 1, 1919, was that "a Jew State in Palestine would be the gathering together there of all the scum of the Jewish populations of Russia, Poland, Germany, Hungary, and what has been the Austrian Empire -- which scum has been active in Bolshevist propaganda

and might have to emigrate after Peace." Lady Algernon Gordon Lennox, Ed., *The Diary of Lord Bertie of Thame*, Vol. II, (London: Hodder Stoughton, 1924.): 233, 329-330.

72. John Barnes and David Nicholson, eds., *Leo Amery Diaries Volume I: 1896-1929*, 169, 171-172; John Grigg, *Lloyd George: War Leader, 1916-1918*, (New York: Penguin Books, 2003), 352-357.

73. Ibid., 169-170; Grigg, op. cit., 352; William Roger Louis, *In the Name of God: Leo Amery and the British Empire in the Age of Churchill*, (New York: W.W. Norton, 1992), 72-74.

74. Barnes and Nicholson, *Leo Amery Diaries Volume I: 1896-1929*, op. cit., 559.

75. Leopold Amery, "The White Paper Debate, House of Commons, WWI, the British entered into four "main undertakings concerning the subsequent attribution of Territory in Asia Minor," E.L. Woodward and Rohan Butler, *Documents on British Foreign Policy 1919-1939*, First Series, 1919, Vol. IV, (London: Her Majesty's Stationery Office, 1952), 635.

76. Friedman, *The Question of Palestine*, op. cit., 325.

77. Meinertzhagen, op. cit., 25-26.

78. Stein, *The Balfour Declaration*, op. cit., 649-650.

79. Friedman, *The Question of Palestine*, op. cit., 326.

80. Quoted in Makovsky, *Churchill's Promised Land: Zionism and Statecraft*, op. cit., 154-155.

81. Gilbert, *Winston S. Churchill: 1874-1965*, op. cit., 536, 655-659.

82. Graves, *Palestine, the Land of Three Faiths*, op. cit., 158-160, 241.

83. Ibid., 565.

84. Meinertzhagen, op. cit., 197.

85. George Kirk, *A Survey of International Affairs: The Middle East 1945-1950*, (New York: Oxford University Press, 1954), 331.

86. Meinertzhagen, op. cit., 171.

CHAPTER 3 ENDNOTES

1. Extracts From Speech Delivered By H.E. *The High Commissioner For Palestine on 3 June, 1921,"* T.N.A. CO 733/7: 255-256

2. Extract From Speech On The Middle East By Mr. W. Churchill On the 14th June, 1921 T.N.A. CO 73 3/7: 256- 258.

3. Meinertzhagen, op. cit., 101.

4. An Interim Report on the Civil Administration of Palestine During the Period 1st July, 1920-30th June, 1921, op. cit.; Anita Shapira, *Land and Power*, op. cit., 110.

5. Basheer M. Nafi, Arabism, *Islamism and the Palestine Question.1908-1941: A Political History*, (Reading, England: Ithaca Press, 1998), 71.

6. Wasserstein, *Herbert Samuel: A Political Life*, (Oxford, England: Clarendon Press, 1992), 230-245.

7. Shapira, *Land and Power*, op. cit., 110-111; An Interim Report on the Civil Administration of Palestine During the Period 1st July, 1920-30th June, 1921, op. cit.; Caplan, *Futile Diplomacy: Early Arab-Zionist Negotiation Attempts, 1913-1931*, vol. one, op. cit., 48-49.

8. Ibid., 50-51.

9. Wasserstein, *Herbert Samuel: A Political Life* op. cit., 256-260.

10. Wasserstein argues that it was Samuel's ability to convince the Conservative British Government to remain in Palestine, adhere to the basic policies of the Balfour Declaration and support Samuel's plan to foster Zionist growth conditioned by "conciliation of Arab opposition," that enabled the Jews to establish a "a viable semi-autonomous economy, an underground army, and the embryonic institutions of a national state." Had Samuel not pursued this policy, the British might have been willing to abandon the Zionist experiment.

11. Ibid., 260-262.

12. Shapira, *Land and Power*, op. cit., 112.

13. Ibid., 113.

14. Ibid., 114.

15. Gilbert, *Winston S. Churchill, 1874-1965*, op. cit., 564-566; Moussa Kazim
     El Husseini to the Secretary of State for the Colonies (February 21,
     1922); "Palestine: Correspondence with the Palestine Arab Delegation
     and the Zionist Organization: Presented to Parliament by Command of
     His Majesty." (London: His Majesty's Stationery Office, 1922): 446-448.

16. Ibid.; Moussa Kazim El Husseini to the Secretary of State for the
     Colonies, (February 21, 1922), op. cit., 448; J.E. Shuckburgh, "The
     Colonial Office to the Palestine Arab Delegation," (March 1, 1922)
     (London: His Majesty's Stationery Office): 450-451. At a cabinet
     meeting on August 17, where the future of the Palestine Mandate
     was discussed, it was agreed at one point, "...that the Arabs had no
     prescriptive right to a country which they failed to develop to the best
     advantage."

17. Gilbert, *Winston S. Churchill, 1874-1964*, op. cit., 629.

18. Ibid.

19. Ibid., 629-630.

20. Ibid., 630.

21. J.E. Shuckburgh to the Zionist Organization Enclosure in No.5.
     Palestine Correspondence with the Palestine Arab Delegation and the
     Zionist Organization Presented to Parliament by Command of His
     Majesty June 1922, (London: His Majesty's Stationery Office, (June 3,
     1922): 463.

22. J.E. Shuckburgh, The Colonial Office to the Palestine Arab Delegation,
     (April 11, 1922) (London: His Majesty's Stationery Office): 460.

23. "Moussa Kazim El-Husseini to The Palestine Arab Delegation to
     the Secretary of State for the Colonies," (June 17, 1922) (London: His
     Majesty's Stationery Office, 1922), 472.

24. Naomi Cohen, op. cit., 62-63; Kenneth W. Stein, *The Land Question in
     Palestine, 1917-1939*, (Chapel Hill, North Carolina: The University of
     North Carolina Press, 1984), 6-7, 549-552; Norman Rose, ed., *From*

Palmerston to Balfour: Collected Essays of Mayir Vereté, (London: Frank Cass, 1992), 1-26, 204-223; Isaiah Friedman, *The Question of Palestine, 1914-1918: British-Jewish-Arab Relations,* (London: Routledge and Kegan Paul, 1973), 1-7; Michael J. Cohen, "British Strategy and the Palestine Question 1936-39," *Journal of Contemporary History,* vol. 7, issue 3/4 (July-October, 1972): 157-183; Bernard Wasserstein, "The British Mandate in Palestine: Myths and Realities," in *Middle East Lectures,* Martin Kramer, ed., (Tel-Aviv: The Moshe Dayan Center for Middle Eastern and African Studies, 1995):34.

25.   Arthur Ruppin, *Memoirs, Diaries, Letters,* (London: Weidenfeld and Nicolson, 1971), 215-216.

26.   Meinertzhagen to Mr. Shuckburgh, no date. T.N.A. CO 733/7:.147

27.   Meinertzhagen, *Middle East Diary,* op. cit., 101-102.

28.   Ibid., 82.

29.   "Report of the Commission appointed by His Majesty's Government in the United Kingdom of Great Britain and Northern Ireland, with the approval of the Council of the League of Nations, to determine the rights and claims of Moslems and Jews in connection with the Western or Wailing Wall at Jerusalem," (London: His Majesty's Stationery Office, 1930).

30.   "Report On The Political Situation In Palestine During The Month of May 1922," T.N.A. CO 733/22: 391-392.

31.   "Permanent Mandates Commission Minutes of the Seventeenth (Extraordinary) Session," (June 21, 1930).

32.   "Report on the Palestine Disturbances of August, 1929," Presented by the Secretary for the Colonies in Parliament by Command of His Majesty, March, 1930 (London: His Majesty' Stationery Office, 1930): 29, 31; Norman and Helen Bentwich, *Mandate Memories,* 1918-1948, op. cit., 131.

33.   "Report on the Palestine Disturbances of August, 1929," op. cit., 29, 31; Bentwich, op. cit., 131. For 11 months, the bickering festered, Ibid., 32-

46; Naomi W. Cohen, *The Year After The Riots: American Responses to the Palestine Crisis of 1929-1930* (Detroit Michigan: Wayne State University Press, 1988), ii.; Ilan Pappé "Historical Features Haj Amin and the Buraq Revolt," Jerusalem Quarterly File, 18, (2003).

34.   "Report on the Palestine Disturbances of August, 1929," op. cit., 47; Bentwich, *Mandate Memories,* op. cit., 131.

35.   "Report on the Palestine Disturbances of August, 1929," op. cit., pp. 29-30; Permanent Mandates Commission Minutes of the Seventeenth (Extraordinary) Session (June 21, 1930), Online; John Barnes, *The Empire at Bay: The Leo Amery Diaries 1929-1945,* op. cit., 565.

36.   Ronald Storrs, *Orientations.* (Bristol, England: Purnell and Sons, 1939), 344-345.

37.   "Report on the Palestine Disturbances of August, 1929," op. cit., 30.

38.   F. H. Kisch, *Palestine Diary,* (London: Victor Gollancz LTD, 1938), 206.

39.   "Report on the Palestine Disturbances of August, 1929," op. cit., 32.

40.   Ibid., 50-51.

41.   Ibid., 53-54; "Permanent Mandates Commission Minutes of the Seventeenth (Extraordinary) Session," (June 21, 1930), op. cit.

42.   "Report on the Palestine Disturbances of August, 1929, op. cit., 53-55; Permanent Mandates Commission Minutes of the Seventeenth (Extraordinary) Session," (June 21, 1930), op. cit.

43.   "Permanent Mandates Commission Minutes of the Seventeenth (Extraordinary) Session," (June 21, 1930), op. cit.; Report on the Palestine Disturbances of August, 1929, op. cit., 55.

44.   "Report on the Palestine Disturbances of August, 1929," op. cit., 56.

45.   Ibid., 56-58.

46.   Ibid., 56-60, 64, 75.

47.   Ibid., pp. 63-64; Naomi Cohen, *The Year After the Riots,* op. cit., 22.

48.   Ibid., 64-65.

49.   Ibid., 65, 149.

50. Ibid., 65.

51. Naomi Cohen, *The Year After the Riots*, op. cit., ii; "Diary of the first Al-Aqsa Intifada," Al-Ahram Weekly, no. 583 (April 25 - May 1, 2002).

52. Naomi Cohen, *The Year After the Riots*, op. cit., 23.

53. Ibid., 25.

54. Ibid., 42.

55. Shapira, *Land and Power*, op. cit., 177.

56. Norman and Helen Bentwich, *Mandate Memories*, op. cit., 134.

57. Ibid.

58. Ibid., 134-135.

59. Ibid., p.135; for an additional account of what transpired during this period, see Maurice Samuel, *What Happened in Palestine: The Events of August, 1929 Their Background And Their Significance*, (Boston, Massachusetts: The Stratford Company Publishers, 1929).

60. Norman and Helen Bentwich, *Mandate Memories*, op. cit., 133.

61. "Report on the Palestine Disturbances of August, 1929," op. cit., 66, 85-89.

62. Ibid., 65-66.

63. Ibid., 68.

64. Ibid., 68-69; "Report by His Majesty's Government in the United Kingdom of Great Britain and Northern Ireland to the Council of the League of Nations on the Administration of Palestine and Trans-Jordan for the Year 1931," (London: His Majesty's Stationery Office, 1932), 758-762.

65. Shapira, *Land and Power*, op. cit., 173-174.

66. Ibid., 186.

67. Ibid., 174.

68. Ibid., 182, 187.

69. Ibid., 173, 180, 182, 188.

70. Meinertzhagen to Mr. Shuckburgh, no date, T.N.A. CO 733/7, 147-148.

71.   Isaiah Friedman, "Arnold Toynbee: Pro-Arab or Pro-Zionist?" op. cit., 74.

72.   Lord Samuel, "Report on the Administration of Palestine 1920-1925," quoted in Rony E. Gabbay, A Political Study of the Arab-Jewish Conflict: The Arab Refugee Problem, (Geneva: Librairie E. Droz, 1959), 31; Ronald Storrs, The Memoirs of Sir Ronald Storrs, (New York: G.P. Putnam's Sons, 1937), 366-367.

73.   Gilbert, Exile and Return, op. cit., 164; In the summer of 1930, Pinhas Rutenberg, president of the Va'ad Leumi (National Council) suggested the British impose a solution by establishing a Jewish and an Arab council to deal with their internal issues. High Commissioner Sir John Chancellor, who was no friend of the Zionists, intervened to convince the Colonial Office to prevent this from happening. Caplan, Futile Diplomacy, vol. one, op. cit., 101-103; Daniel P. Kotzin, "An Attempt to Americanize the Yishuv: Judah L. Magnes in Mandatory Palestine," Israel Studies, vol. 5, no. 1, (April 2000): 9-11.

74.   Shapira, Land and Power, op. cit., 219.

75.   Gilbert, Exile and Return, op. cit., 164; "League of Nations Permanent Mandates Commission: Minutes Of The Thirty-Second (Extraordinary) Session Devoted To Palestine," (July 30-August 18, 1937). Historian Martin Bunton found that "A review of the published law reports during the mandate reveals the significance of land disputes that took place not as formative political struggles between Arab and Jew, but between government and land owners, or among Arab landowners themselves. It is estimated that 70 percent of land transactions registered during the mandate consisted of intra communal transfers. Only 30 percent consisting by Arabs to Jews." Martin Bunton, Colonial Policies In Palestine, 1917-1936, (New York: Oxford University Press, 2007), 3-7, 203-204; Jacob Metzer, The Divided Economy of Mandatory Palestine, (News York: Cambridge University Press, 1998), 85-94; The Land Policy of the Zionist Organization is found in: A. Granovsky, Land Settlement in Palestine, (London: Victor Gollancz, LTD., 1930).

76. Shapira, *Land and Power*, op. cit., 219.

77. Gilbert, *Exile and Return*, op. cit., 164.

78. Shapira, *Land and Power*, op. cit., 220.

79. Ibid.

80. Ibid., 220-221, 229; "League of Nations Permanent Mandates Commission: Minutes Of The Thirty-Second (Extraordinary) Session Devoted To Palestine," (July 30-August 18, 1937), op. cit.

81. Ibid.

82. Ibid., 224, 227-228; "League of Nations Permanent Mandates Commission: Minutes Of The Thirty-Second (Extraordinary) Session Devoted To Palestine," (July 30-August 18, 1937), op. cit.

83. Shapira, *Land and Power*, op. cit., 222.

84. Ibid., 230.

85. Ibid., 236, 237, 244, 247.

86. Ibid.

87. Ibid., 231-233.

88. Ibid., 250-257.

89. "Palestine: A Study of Jewish, Arab, and British Policies," vol. two, op. cit., 859-860.

90. Gabbay, "A Political Study of the Arab-Jewish Conflict: The Arab Refugee Problem," op. cit., 36; Kenneth W. Stein, "The Intifada and the 1936-39 Uprising: A Comparison," *Journal of Palestine Studies*, vol. 19, no. 4, (Summer 1990): 79; Nafi, "Arabism, Islamism and the Palestine Question, 1908-1941: A Political History," op. cit., 280-281.

91. Stein, "The Intifada and the 1936-39 Uprising: A Comparison," op. cit., 79-80.

92. Nafi, "Arabism, Islamism and the Palestine Question, 1908-1941: A Political History," op. cit., 283.

93. Sir Alec Seath Kirkbride, *A Crackle Of Thorns: Experiences in the Middle East*, (London: John Murray, 1956), 98; *Palestine: A Study of Jewish, Arab, and British Policies*, op. cit., vol. two, 876.

94. Gilbert, *Exile and Return*, 187, 197, 205. For a description of the "real war" that was being waged, see Albert Viton, "It's War in Palestine," *The Nation* (October 1, 1938), 320-323.

95. Gilbert, *Exile and Return*, op. cit., 187, 197, 204.

96. Ibid., 204-205, 207.

97. Ibid., 185-186.

98. Gabbay, "A Political Study of the Arab-Jewish Conflict: The Arab Refugee Problem," op. cit., 37; Shai Lachman, "Arab Rebellion and Terrorism in Palestine 1929-39: The Case of Sheikh Izz al-Din al-Qassam and his Movement," in *Zionism And Arabism in Palestine and Israel*, eds. Elie Kedourie and Sylvia G. Haim, eds., (London, England: Frank Cass, 1982), 52-99.

99. Gabbay, "A Political Study of the Arab-Jewish Conflict: The Arab Refugee Problem," op. cit., 37.

100. Ibid.

101. Bauer, *From Diplomacy to Resistance: A History of Jewish Palestine, 1930-1945*, op. cit., 46-47; Arieh J. Kochavi, "Britain's Image Campaign against the Zionists," *Journal of Contemporary History*, vol. 36, no. 2001, 294.

102. Gilbert, *Exile and Return*, op. cit., 229.

103. Ibid., 230.

104. Martin Gilbert, *Churchill and the Jews: A Lifelong Friendship*, (New York: Henry Holt and Company, 2007), 277-278.

105. Ibid., 255

CHAPTER 4 ENDNOTES

1. David Yisraeli, "The Third Reich and Palestine," in *Palestine and Israel In the 19th and 20th Centuries*, Elie Kedourie and Sylvia G. Haim, eds., (Totowa, New Jersey: Frank Cass, 1982), 3, 111.

2. "Palestine Royal Commission Report Presented by the Secretary of State for the Colonies to Parliament by Command of His Majesty," (London: His Majesty's Stationery Office, July 1937), 175, 178-181; Elie Kedourie, *The Chatham House Version and other Middle-Eastern Studies*, new edition, (Hanover, New Hampshire: University Press of New England, 1984), 69, 72-73; Viscount Samuel, *Memoirs*, (London: The Cresset Press, 1945), 167-168; Uri M. Kupferschmidt, *The Supreme Muslim Council: Islam Under the British Mandate for Palestine*, (Boston and Leiden: Brill, 1985), 1-16.

3. Palestine Royal Commission Report, 1937, op. cit., 178, 181.

4. Bernard Lewis, *Semites and Anti-Semites An Inquiry into Conflict and Prejudice*, (New York: W.W. Norton and Company, 1986), 147.

5. Ibid.

6. Ibid., 147-148; *Kabha*, op. cit., 142-145, 191-195.

7. Matthias Küntzel, *Jihad and Jew-Hatred: Islam, Nazism and The Roots of 9/11*, (New York: Telos Press Publishing, 2007), 28-29.

8. "The Jewish Case Before The Anglo-American Committee Of Inquiry On Palestine As Presented By The Jewish Agency For Palestine: Statements and Memoranda," op. cit., 360, 363.

9. Ibid., 361.

10. Ibid.

11. Matthias Küntzel, "National Socialism and Anti-Semitism in the Arab World," *Jewish Political Studies Review, Jewish Center For Public Affairs*, vol. 17, issues 1-2 (Spring 2005); Küntzel, *Jihad and Jew-Hatred: Islamism, Nazism and the Roots of 9/11*, op. cit, 20-21.

12. Lewis, *Semites and Anti-Semites*, op. cit., 145.

13. Ibid., 145-146; Küntzel, *Jihad and Jew-Hatred: Islamism, Nazism and the Roots of 9/11*, op. cit., 260.

14. Lewis, *Semites and Anti-Semites*, op. cit., 140.

15. Andrew Roth, "The Mufti's New Army," *The Nation*, (November 16, 1946), 552; Robert Wistrich, *Muslim Anti-Semitism: A Clear and Present Danger*, (New York: American Jewish Committee, 2002), 47.

16. Lewis, *Semites and Anti-Semites*, op. cit., 146.

17. Küntzel, *Jihad and Jew-Hatred: Islamism, Nazism and the Roots of 9/11*, op. cit., 28-29.

18. Ibid., 29.

19. Ibid., 28-29.

20. Bernard Lewis, *The Crisis of Islam: Holy War and Unholy Terror*, (New York: The Modern Library, 2003), 59-60.

21. Gilbert, *Winston S. Churchill*, op. cit., vol. IV, 564.

22. Yisraeli, "The Third Reich and Palestine," in *Palestine and Israel In the 19th and 20th Centuries*, op. cit., 3, 111.

23. Ibid., 179-180; see also Wolfgang G. Schwanitz, "The Jinnee and the Magic Bottle": Fritz Grobba and the German Middle East Policy, 1900-1922," in *Germany and the Middle East, 1871-1945*, Wolfgang G. Schwanitz, ed. (Princeton, New Jersey: Markus Wiener Publishers, 2004), 101-104.

24. Küntzel, *Jihad and Jew-Hatred: Islamism, Nazism and the Roots of 9/11*, op. cit., 31; Kenneth W. Stein, "The Intifada and the 1936-39 Uprising: A Comparison." *Journal of Palestine Studies*, vol. 19, no. 4, (Summer 1990): 64-85.

25. Küntzel, *Jihad and Jew-Hatred: Islamism, Nazism and the Roots of 9/11*, op. cit., 4.

26. Ibid.

27. Ibid., 104, 106-109.

28. Ibid.

29. Ibid.

30. Ibid.

31. Ibid., 30.

32. Joseph B. Schechtman, *The Mufti and the Fuehrer: The Rise and Fall of Haj Amin el-Husseini*, (New York: Thomas Yoseloff, 1965), 110-114.

33. Jorge Garcia-Granados, *The Birth of Israel: The Drama As I Saw It*, (New York: Alfred A. Knopf, 1948), 204-205; Daniel Carpi, "The Mufti of Jerusalem, Amin el-Husseini, and His Diplomatic Activity during World War II (October 1941-July 1943)," *Studies in Zionism*, Number 7, (Spring 1983): 104; Zvi Elpeleg, *The Grand Mufti: Haj Amin Al-Hussaini*, (Portland, Oregon: Frank Cass and Company, Ltd. 1993), 66; Wolfgang G. Schwanitz, "Germany's Middle East Policy," *The Middle East Review of International Affairs*, vol. 11, no. 3, article 4/9, (September 2007).

34. Daniel Carpi, "The Mufti of Jerusalem, Amin el-Husseini, and His Diplomatic Activity during World War II (October 1941-July 1943); *Studies in Zionism*, Number 7, (Spring 1983), 104; Zvi Elpeleg, *The Grand Mufti: Haj Amin Al-Hussaini*, (Portland, Oregon: Frank Cass and Company, Ltd. 1993), 66; Wolfgang G. Schwanitz, "Germany's Middle East Policy," *The Middle East Review of International Affairs*, vol. 11, no.3, article 4/9 (September 2007).

35. Carpi, "The Mufti of Jerusalem, Amin el-Husseini, and His Diplomatic Activity during World War II (October 1941-July 1943)," op. cit., 104-107.

36. Ibid., 108-109; Zvi Elpeleg, *The Grand Mufti: Haj Amin Al-Hussaini*, (Portland, Oregon: Frank Cass and Company, Ltd. 1993), 66; Wolfgang G. Schwanitz, "Germany's Middle East Policy," op. cit.

37. Dan Michman, *Holocaust Historiography: A Jewish Perspective*, Portland, Oregon: Vallentine Mitchell, 2003), 112; Christopher R. Browning, *The Origins of The Final Solution: The Evolution of Nazi Jewish Policy*, September 1939 - March 1942,(Lincoln, Nebraska: University of Nebraska Press 2004), 406.

38. "German Chancellor Adolf Hitler and Grand Mufti Haj Amin al-Husseini: Zionism and the Arab Cause," (November 28, 1941) in *The Israeli-Arab Reader*, Walter Laqueur and Barry Rubin, eds. (New York: Penguin Books, 2008), 51-55.

39. Robert Wistrich, *Hitler's Apocalypse: Jews and The Nazi Legacy* (New York: St. Martin's Press, 1985), 164-165.

40. Jeffrey Herf, *The Jewish Enemy: Nazi Propaganda During World War II And The Holocaust*, (Cambridge, Massachusetts: The Belknap Press of Harvard University, 2006), 158-159; Küntzel, *Jihad and Jew-Hatred: Islamism, Nazism and the Roots of 9/11*, op. cit., 35.

41. Küntzel, *Jihad and Jew-Hatred: Islamism, Nazism and the Roots of 9/11*, op. cit., 35

42. Herf, *The Jewish Enemy: Nazi Propaganda During World War II And The Holocaust*, op. cit., 159.

43. Ibid., 172-173.

44. Schechtman, *The Mufti and the Fuehrer: The Rise and Fall of Haj el-Husseini*, op. cit., 127.

45. Ibid., 173, 180

46. Ibid., 173.

47. Antonio J. Munoz, ed., *The East Came West: Muslim, Hindu, and Buddhist Volunteers in the German Armed Forces 1941-1945*, (Bayside, New York: Axis Europe Books, 2001), 14-17.

48. Ibid.

49. "The Jewish Case before the Anglo-American Committee of Inquiry on Palestine as Presented By the Jewish Agency for Palestine: Statements and Memoranda," op. cit.,109-110.

50. Schechtman, *The Mufti and the Fuehrer: The Rise and Fall of Haj Amin el-Husseini*, op. cit., 127-147.

51. Ibid.

52. "The Jewish Case before the Anglo-American Committee of Inquiry on Palestine as Presented By the Jewish Agency for Palestine: Statements

and Memoranda," op. cit., 110; Eliahu Epstein, "Middle East Munich," *The Nation*, (March 9, 1946), 288.

53. Robert Satloff, *Among The Righteous: Lost Stories From The Holocaust's Long Reach Into Arab Lands*, (New York: PublicAffairs, 2006), 86-87.

54. Ibid.

55. "The Jewish Case before the Anglo-American Committee of Inquiry on Palestine as Presented By the Jewish Agency for Palestine: Statements and Memoranda," op. cit., 134.

56. Raul Hilberg, *The Destruction of European Jewry*, third edition, vol. II, (New Haven, Connecticut: Yale University Press, 2003.), 846-84; Bartley C. Crum, *Behind the Silken Curtain: A Personal Account of Anglo-American Diplomacy in Palestine and the Middle East*, (Port Washington, New York: Kennikat Press, Inc., 1947), 110-111; Yehuda Bauer, *Jews For Sale? Nazi-Jewish Negotiations, 1933-1945*, (New Haven, Connecticut: Yale University Press, 1994), 88, 100.

57. Bauer, Jews For Sale, op. cit., 88, 100; Küntzel,. *Jihad and Jew-Hatred: Islamism, Nazism and the Roots of 9/11*, op. cit., 36.

58. "The Jewish Enemy: Nazi Propaganda During World War II And The Holocaust," op. cit., 243.

59. Lewis, *Semites and Anti-Semites: An Inquiry into Conflict and Prejudice*, op. cit., 156-157; Schechtman, *The Mufti and the Fuehrer: The Rise and Fall of Haj Amin el-Husseini*, op. cit., 160; The Jewish Case before the Anglo-American Committee of Inquiry on Palestine as Presented By the Jewish Agency for Palestine: Statements and Memoranda op. cit., 110; Bartley C. Crum, a San Francisco attorney and a member of the Anglo-American Committee on Palestine who visited the Nuremberg Trials, reports that "Nazi records show that, accompanied by [Adolf Eichmann], the Grand Mufti, incognito visited the gas chambers of Auschwitz, where hundreds of thousands of Jews were exterminated." Bartley C. Crum, Behind the Silken Curtain: A Personal Account of Anglo-American Diplomacy in Palestine and the Middle East, op. cit.,

110: Rafael Medoff, "The Mufti's Nazi years Examined," *The Journal of Israel's History*, vol. 17, no. 3, (1996):329-333.

60.   Gerhard Höpp, "Arab Inmates in Nazi Concentration Camps," in *Germany and the Middle East, 1871-1945*, Wolfgang G. Schwanitz, ed., (Princeton, New Jersey: Markus Wiener Publishers, 2004), 221.

61.   Peter Z. Malkin and Harry Stein, *Eichmann in My Hands*, (New York: Warner Books, 1990), 38; David G. Dalin and John F. Rothmann, *Icon of Evil*, (New York: Random House, 2008), 181, footnote 46 and 47.

62.   Höpp, "Arab Inmates in Nazi Concentration Camps," op. cit., 217-221; Wolfgang G. Schwanitz, "Amin al-Husaini and the Holocaust, What Did the Grand Mufti Know?" *World Politics Review*, (May 8, 2008).

63.   Herf, Jeffrey, *The Jewish Enemy: Nazi Propaganda During World War II And The Holocaust*, op. cit., 243.

64.   Dalin and Rothmann, *Icon of Evil*, op. cit., 170-171.

65.   Schechtman, *The Mufti and the Fuehrer: The Rise and Fall of Haj Amin el-Husseini*, op. cit., 17-18.

66.   Benny Morris, *The Road To Jerusalem: Glubb Pasha, Palestine and the Jews*, (London and New York: I.B. Tauris Publishers, 2002), 33-34.

67.   Daphne Trevor, *Under The White Paper: Some Aspects of British Administration In Palestine From 1939 to 1947*, (Jerusalem: The Jerusalem Press, LTD, 1948), 139; Küntzel, *Jihad and Jew-Hatred: Islamism, Nazism and the Roots of 9/11*, op. cit., 45-46.

68.   Küntzel, *Jihad and Jew-Hatred: Islamism, Nazism and the Roots of 9/11*, op. cit., 45; I.F. Stone, "The Case of the Mufti," *The Nation*, (May 4, 1946), 527.

69.   Issa Khalaf, *Politics in Palestine: Arab Factionalism and Social Disintegration*, 1939-1948, (Albany, New York: State University of New York Press, 1991), 117; David Pryce-Jones, *Betrayal: France, The Arabs, and The Jews*, (New York: Encounter Books, 2006), 6-67.

70. Khalaf, *Politics in Palestine: Arab Factionalism and Social Disintegration,1939-1948*, op. cit., 117-118; David Pryce-Jones, *Betrayal: France, The Arabs, and The Jews*, op. cit., 62.

71. Khalaf, *Politics in Palestine: Arab Factionalism and Social Disintegration, 1939-1948*, op. cit.; Küntzel, *Jihad and Jew-Hatred: Islamism, Nazism and the Roots of 9/11*, op. cit., 44-45.

72. Küntzel, *Jihad and Jew-Hatred: Islamism, Nazism and the Roots of 9/11*, op. cit.,46-49.

73. The tremendous victory left the Jewish UN delegation aware that the days, months and perhaps even years ahead would be fraught with danger and hardship After the United States and the Russians, who were major protagonists, agreed to the establishment of the Jewish state, several antisemites commented: "Those damn Jews! They even bring America and Russia together when they want something." David Horowitz, *State in the Making*, (New York: Alfred A. Knopf, 1953), 311; *Commentary*, (January 1948): 97- 103; Michael J. Cohen, "Truman, the Holocaust and the Establishment of the State of Israel," *The Jerusalem Quarterly*, no. 23, (Spring 1982):79-94; Arnold Krammer, *The Forgotten Friendship: Israel and the Soviet Bloc 1947-53*, (Urbana: University of Illinois Press, 1974), 16-23.

74. Efraim Karsh, *Arafat's War: The Man and His Battle for Israeli Conquest*, (New York: Grove Press, 2003), 32.

75. Rony E. Gabbay, *A Political Study of the Arab-Jewish Conflict: The Arab Refugee Problem*, (Geneva: Librairie E. Droz, 1959), 55.

76. Ibid., 56; There had also been some discussion in the Arab and world press about using more peaceful diplomatic means of preventing partition, such as withdrawing from the UN, instituting economic sanctions ("oil concessions"), bringing the question to the Security Council and the International Court of Justice, but all suggestions were rejected as not being pragmatic. "Arab World Affairs: Weekly Survey," Number 12(39) CZA S25/9051 (December 12, 1947), 1-4; "World Arab Affairs: Special Issue." op. cit., 3.; Except for Yemen,

all of the other delegations to the conference expressed the need to
resist partition, but differed on the type of response to be taken. No
Arab government could remain in office, they acknowledged, if their
actions were construed as betraying the Arab cause. Whatever form of
resistance that would be adopted, it would inevitably lead to "fighting
and bloodshed." The impression was that most, if not all of the
premiers, would prefer not to use force as long as it did not accept the
establishment of a Jewish State. Given the present situation, they could
not imagine the Jews willing to consider anything less. "Arab World
Affairs: Weekly Survey," Number 12(39) CZA S25/9051 (December 12,
1947), 1-4; "World Arab Affairs: Special Issue," op. cit., 3.

77.   Abraham J. Edelheit, *History of Zionism: A Handbook and Dictionary*,
      (Boulder, Colorado: Westview Press 2000), 250-251.

78.   Joseph Nevo, "The Arabs of Palestine 1947-48: Military and Political
      Activity," *Middle Eastern Studies*, vol. 23, no. 1, (January 1987), 11; Musa
      S. Braizat, *The Jordan –Palestinian Relationship: The Bankruptcy of the
      Confederal Idea*, (London: I. Tauris, 1998), 74.

79.   I. N. Clayton, "Note On Proceedings Of the Meeting Of The Arab
      Premiers In Cairo December 8 to 17th 1947," T.B.N. F.O. 816/115.

80.   Gabby, *A Political Study of the Arab-Jewish Conflict: The Arab Refugee
      Problem*, op. cit., 56; Jon and David Kimche, *Both Sides of the Hill: Britain
      and The Palestine War*, (London: Secker and Warburg, 1960), 80.

81.   Gabby, *A Political Study of the Arab-Jewish Conflict: The Arab Refugee
      Problem*, op. cit. 57.

82.   Ibid., 58.

83.   George Kirk, *The Middle East 1945-1950*, (New York: Oxford University
      Press, 1954), 251.

84.   Ibid; Haim Levenberg, *The Military Preparations Of the Arab Community
      in Palestine 1945-1948*, (Portland, Oregon: Frank Cass, 1993), 179; Yoav
      Gelber, *Palestine 1948: War, Escape and the Emergence of the Palestinian
      Refugee Problem*, (Portland, Oregon: Frank Cass: Sussex Academic Press,
      2001),16.

85. Kirk, *The Middle East 1945-1950*, op. cit., 251.

86. "Memorandum of the 26th December, 1947: The Situation in Palestine," *The Jewish Agency for Palestine*, Jerusalem (CZA S25/9051), 2; "Schedule: Jerusalem," op. cit.,2-3; "Schedule: Palestine General." CZA S25/4148 (May 12, 1947), 1-3.

87. "World Arab Affairs: Special Issue," no. 11, (38) CZA S25/9051 (December 14, 1947), 2, 5, 8.

88. The Arab World: Diary of Events," no. 12, CZA S25/9051 (September 12, 1947 –December 1947), 5-7.

89. Ibid., 24; The Palestinian Arab press preached against land sales to Jews and denounced the practice. At the Muslim Clerics' Convention in January 1935, they declared that anyone involved in land speculation or selling land would be viewed as a heretic and should be removed from the nation of believers. Fatwas were also declared against participating or facilitating the sale of Arab land and all communication with those involved should cease. In October and November 1934, Alef Baa, a Palestinian newspaper published in Damascus with a decidedly anti-Zionist bent, noted that "the economic situation in Palestine is better than that of Syria, mainly due to the sale of Arab lands to Jews." The same reporter also wrote that in areas where Arabs sold land to Jews the economic conditions were better than in locations where they hadn't engaged in such practices. Kabha, op. cit., 114-118, 134.

90. Nevo, "The Arabs of Palestine 1947-48: Military and Political Activity," op. cit., 6.

91. Ibid., 3-6, 12-17.

92. Levenberg, *The Military Preparations Of the Arab Community in Palestine 1945-1948*, op. cit., 113, 154, 180.

93. "Fortnightly Intelligence Newsletter," no. 61, op. cit.

94. "The Arab World: Diary of Events," (September 12, 1947 – December 1947), op. cit., 7; Levenberg, *The Military Preparations Of the Arab Community in Palestine 1945-1948*, op. cit., 113, 154, 180.

95. Ibid.

96. "The Responsibility for the Arab Higher Executive for the Disturbances," CZA S25/4148 (December 16, 1947), 1.

97. "Letter From Egypt," (January 1, 1948), CZA, S25/3569.

98. "The Responsibility for the Arab Higher Executive for the Disturbances," op. cit., 2-3.

99. Ibid.,5; "Fortnightly Intelligence Newsletter," no. 61, (February 13, 1948), T.N.A. W.O. 261/573; Palestinius, "Palestine's Mood After UNSCOP: The Yishuv Ponders Partition," *Commentary*, (October 1947):338-343.

100. Trygve Lie, *In the Cause Of Peace: Seven Years with the United Nations*, (New York: The Macmillan Company, 1954), 165.

101. Shabtai Teveth, "Charging Israel With Original Sin," *Commentary*, (September 1989), 30.

102. "Arab Activities" CZA S25/7733 (March 10, 1948).

103. Ibid.

104. Ibid; "In Syria and Lebanon the Arabs were so delighted by Axis victories that they chanted happily, 'No more mister, no more monsieur, only Allah in heaven, only Hitler on earth.'" Eliahu Ben-Horin, "Have the Arabs a Case?" *The Nation*, (October 20, 1945), 400.

105. John Zimmerman, "Radio Propaganda in the Arab-Israeli War 1948," *The Weiner Library Bulletin*, vol. 27, new series nos. 30/31, (1973/74): 3.

106. "Arab Activities" CZA S25/7733 (March 10, 1948, op. cit.

107. Hilberg, *The Destruction of European Jewry*, op. cit., 1152-1153.

108. Arieh Stav, *Peace: The Arabian Caricature, A Study of Anti-Semitic Imagery*, (New York: Geffen Publishing House, 199), 121.

109. "The Jewish Case Before The Anglo-American Committee Of Inquiry On Palestine As Presented By The Jewish Agency For Palestine: Statements and Memoranda," op. cit., 360.

110. Ibid., 360-361.

111. Ibid., 371.

112. Lewis, *Semites and Anti-Semites An Inquiry into Conflict and Prejudice*, op. cit., 160.

CHAPTER 5 ENDNOTES

1. Anthony Verrier, ed., *Agents of Empire: Anglo-Intelligence Operations 1915-1919 Brigadier Walter Gribbon*, Aaron Aaronsohn and the NILI Ring, (London: Brassey's (UK) Ltd., 1995), 308; *Matthew Hughes, Allenby and British Strategy in the Middle East 1917-1919*, (Portland, Oregon: Frank Cass Publishers, 1999), 91-92.

2. Verrier, *Agents of Empire: Anglo-Intelligence Operations 1915-1919*, op. cit., 7-8; *Hughes, Allenby and British Strategy in the Middle East 1917-1919*, op. cit., 18-22, 43-44.

3. Verrier, *Agents of Empire: Anglo-Intelligence Operations 1915-1919*, op. cit., 308; Alexander Aaronsohn, "Saifna Ahmar, Ya Sultan." *The Atlantic Monthly*, (July 1916), pp. 1-12.; NILI is the Hebrew abbreviation for Netzach Yisrael Lo Yishaker (The Eternal One of Israel Will Not Lie), Samuel I 15:29.

4. Verrier, *Agents of Empire: Anglo-Intelligence Operations 1915 - 1919*, op. cit., .97, 310-311; for an analysis of the work of Sir Wyndham Deeds did on behalf of the Jewish people in Palestine, see Eliahu Elath, Norman Bentwich and Doris May, eds., *Memories of Sir Wyndham Deeds*, (London: Victor Gollancz Ltd, 1958), 24-40.

5. Gilbert, *Exile and Return*, op. cit., 92.

6. Ibid., 290; Chaim Weizmann, *Trial and Error: The Autobiography of Chaim Weizmann*, (New York: Harper and Brothers Publishers), 173-175.

7. Christopher Sykes, *Cross Roads to Israel: Palestine from Balfour to Bevin*, (London: First Nel Mentor Edition, 1967), 220; N.A. Rose "Palestine's Role in Britain's Imperial Defence: An Aspect of Zionist Diplomacy, 1938-39," *The Weiner Library Bulletin*, vol. XXII, no. 4, New Series no. 13, (Autumn 1968): 32-35; Arthur Koestler, *Promise and Fulfillment: Palestine 1917 - 1949*, (London: Macmillan and Company, Ltd 1949), 76-78; Daphne Trevor, *Under the White Paper: Some Aspects of British Administration In Palestine From 1939 to 1947*, (Jerusalem: The Jerusalem Press Ltd, 1948), 52-84).

8. Yehuda Bauer, *From Diplomacy to Resistance: A History of Jewish Palestine 1939-1945*, (Philadelphia: The Jewish Publication Society, 1970), 354; Sykes., op. cit., 220-223; Jewish Brigade Group, Jewish Virtual Library; Howard Blum, *The Brigade: An Epic Story of Vengeance, Salvation, and World War*, (New York: First Perennial Edition, 2002).

9. Bauer, *From Diplomacy to Resistance*, op. cit., 354-355.

10. Pierre Van Paassen, *The Forgotten Ally*, (Top Executive Media, 2005), 138-173: Bauer, *From Diplomacy to Resistance*, op. cit, 114-116, 120-122; Sykes, *Cross Roads to Israel*, op. cit., 228-229; Koestler, *Promise and Fulfillment*, op. cit., 76-77.

11. Bauer, *From Diplomacy to Resistance*, op. cit, 119, 276.

12. Ibid., 121-122.

13. Ibid., 119-120.

14. Ibid., 279.

15. Ibid.

16. Ibid.

17. Ibid., 280.

18. Ibid.

19. Ibid., 281-282.

20. Rivka Ashbel, *As Much As We Could Do: The Contributions Made by the Hebrew University and Jewish Doctors and Scientists from Palestine During*

and After the Second World War, (Jerusalem: The Hebrew University, Mount Scopus Publications, The Magnes Press, 1989),12

21. Charles D. Smith, *Palestine and the Arab-Israeli Conflict,* sixth edition, (Boston: Bedford / St Martin's, 2007),150.

22. Ashbel, *As Much As We Could Do,* op. cit., 13-14.

23. Ibid., 16-17.

24. Ibid., 18-19.

25. Ibid., 19-20.

26. Ibid., 22-26.

27. Ibid., 43-44.

28. Ibid., 44, 63-67.

29. Ibid., 68-69,138-140.

30. Ibid., 68-69,138.

31. Ibid., 92-93, 105, 111-112.

32. Dov Joseph, *The Faithful City: The Siege of Jerusalem,* 1948, (New York: Simon and Shuster, 1960), 8.

33. "The Jewish Case Before The Anglo-American Committee Of Inquiry On Palestine As Presented By The Jewish Agency For Palestine: Statements and Memoranda," (Jerusalem: The Jewish Agency For Palestine, 1947), 471.

34. Ibid., 470.

35. Ibid., 471, 479-481.

36. Ibid., 471.

37. Ibid., 471-472, 477.

38. Ibid., 473-474.

39. Ibid., 478.

40. Ibid., 479.

CHAPTER 6 ENDNOTES

1. Nur Masalha, *The Bible and Zionism: Invented Traditions, Archeology and Post-Colonialism In Israel-Palestine*, (London and New York: Zed Books, 2007); Itamar Marcus and Barbara Crook, "Anti-Semitism Among Palestinian Authority Among Palestinian Authority Academics," (Jerusalem: Institute For Global Jewish Affairs Jewish Affairs-Post-Holocaust and Anti-Semitism), no. 69 (May 2008).

2. Arnon Groiss, "Palestinian Textbooks: From Arafat to Abbas and Hamas." *Center for Monitoring Peace and Cultural tolerance in School Education*, www.edume.org (March 2008); AJC-CMIP Report: Scant Progress in Revising Palestinian Textbooks," American Jewish Committee, (March 20, 2008); Itamar Marcus and Barbara Crook, *From Nationalist Battle To Religious Conflict: New 12th Grade Palestinian Schoolbooks Present a World Without Israel*, Palestinian Media Watch, (February 2007); Itamar Marcus, "Lies, Libels and Historical Revisionism in the Palestinian Authority," *Makor Rishon*, (February 22, 2001)."

3. Alvin Rosenfeld, "Modern Jewish Intellectual Failure: A Brief History," in *The Jewish Divide Over Israel: Accusers and Defenders Alexander, Edward and Paul Bogdanor*, eds., (New Brunswick, New Jersey: Transaction Publishers, 2006), 20-21; Manfred Gerstenfeld, ed., *Academics Against Israel And The Jews*, (Jerusalem: Jerusalem Center for Public Affairs, 2008); Alan Dershowitz, *The Case Against Israel's Enemies*, (Hoboken, New Jersey: John Wiley and Sons, 2008); "'Progressive' Jewish Thought and the New Anti-Semitism," American Jewish Committee, (2007).; see also *Avraham Burg, The Holocaust Is Over; We Must Rise From The Ashes*, (New York: Palgrave Macmillan, 2008).

4. Dore Gold and Jeff Helmreich, "An Answer To The New Anti-Zionists: The Rights Of The Jewish People To A Sovereign State in their Historic Homeland," *Jerusalem Viewpoints*, Jerusalem Center for Public Affairs, no. 507, (November 16, 2003); Three Historical Memoranda Submitted to the United Nations Special Committee On Palestine On Behalf of the

Vaad Leumi General Council of the Jewish Community of Palestine, (Haoman Press, Jerusalem, 1947); The American War Congress and Zionism: Statements by Members of the American War Congress on the Jewish National Movement, (New York: Zionist Organization of America, 1919); For an analysis of Wilson's support, please see Leonard Stein, The Balfour Declaration (London: Vallentine Mitchell, 1961), 504-513; David Vital, Zionism: The Crucial Phase, (Oxford, England; Clarendon Press, 1987), 285-289; Melvin I. Urofsky, *American Zionism From Herzl to the Holocaust*, (Lincoln, Nebraska: University of Nebraska Press, 1975), 215-220; For an analysis of Wilson's support, see Stein 504-513; Reuben Fink, ed. *America and Palestine*, (New York: American Zionist Emergency Council, 1944), 33-35.

5.   Andrew G. Bostom, "Misunderstanding Islamic Antisemitism," *American Thinker*, (May 13, 2008); Andrew G. Bostom, "Jihad and Islamic Antisemitism," *Frontpagemag.com*, (May 22, 2008); Bat Yeor, "Modern Egyptian Jew Hatred: Indigenous Elements and Foreign Influences," in *The Legacy of Islamic Antisemitism*, Andrew G. Bostom, ed., (Amherst, NY: Prometheus Books, 2008), 51-54, 90-97, 150-164, 168-169, 613, 618; Andrew G. Bostom, "From Communism as the 20th Century Islam, to Islam as the 21st Century Communism," *andrewbostom.org/blog* (December 5, 2009); Sivan, Emmanuel, "Islamic Fundamentalism, Antisemitism, and Anti-Zionism," in *Anti-Zionism and Antisemitism in the Contemporary World*, Robert S. Wistrich, ed., (New York: New York University Press, 1990), 74-84; Sylvia G. Haim, ed., *Arab Nationalism: An Anthology*, (Berkeley, CA: University of California Press, 1962), 63-64; email from Andrew Bostom to author, June 17, 2009.

6.   Email from Andrew Bostrom to author June 17, 2009

7.   Ibid; English translation from the State Department Telegram 1763/ Embassy (Cairo) Telegram 1256 D441214

8.   Bostom, *Jihad and Islamic Antisemitism*, op. cit.

9.   Ibid

10. To understand how the city has become a key to the radical Islamists' apocalyptic vision of global jihad, please see Dore Gold, *The Fight For Jerusalem: Radical Islam, the West and the Future of the Holy City*, (Washington, D.C.: Regnery Publishing, Inc., 2007).

11. "Interview with Yasser Arafat," MEMRI Special Dispatch Series-Number 428 (October 11, 2002); Benny Morris, "Camp David and After: An Exchange," (An Interview with Ehud Barak), *The New York Review of Books*, vol. 49, no. 10, (June 13, 2002).

12. Dennis Ross, *The Missing Peace: The Inside Story of the Fight for Middle East Peace*, (New York: Farrar, Straus, and Giroux, 2004), 718; Gidi Greenstein, Dennis Ross, "Camp David: An Exchange," *The New York Review of Books*, vol. 48, no. 14 (September 20, 2001); Edgar Lefkovitz, "NGO: PA Lying about Jews' ties to J'lem," *The Jerusalem Post*, (May 21, 2009); Daniel Pipes, "Constructing a Counterfeit History of Jerusalem," *danielpipes.com*, (March 10, 2008); "A Bone Seal Engraved with the Name Shaul, from the First Temple, was found in the IAA Excavations," *Israel Antiquities Authority*, (May 22, 2009); Hassan Naffa, "It's still about Zionism," *Al-Ahram*, Issue no. 947, Opinion (May 14-20, 2009); Thomas L. Thompson, *The Mythic Past: Biblical Archeology and the Myth of Israel*, (New York: Basic Books, 1999), xv-xvi, 4-7, is a source also quoted to claim Jews have no historical connection to the land of Israel.

13. Ross, *The Missing Peace: The Inside Story of the Fight for Middle East Peace*, op. cit., 718.

14. Yael Yehoshua, "Abu Mazen: A Political Profile," MEMRI Special Report, no. 15, (April 29, 2003).

15. Itamar Marcus and Barbara Cook, "Jews have no historical connection to Western Wall—It's an Islamic site named for Muhammad's horse," *Palestinian Media Watch*, (October 19, 2006).

16. "Arab leader denies temple ever existed," *Jerusalem Post*, (March 10, 2008); "Sheikh Salah: Western Wall belongs to Muslims," YNETnews.

com, (February 18, 2007), Jeremy Sharon, "Writing Jews out of Jerusalem's History," *guardian.co.uk*, (November 1, 2009)

17. Nadia Abu El-Haj, *Facts on The Ground: Archaeological Practice and Territorial Self-Fashioning in Israeli Society*, (Chicago, IL: The University of Chicago Press, 2001), 5.

18. Ibid., 18.

19. Margot Dudkevitch, "Murdered Joseph's Tomb teacher to be buried tomorrow," *Jerusalem Post*, (October 10, 2000); "Palestinians Set Fire to Joseph's Tomb," *Jerusalem Post*, (October 16, 2003); "Trouble in the Holy Land: Arab Vandals Desecrate Joseph's tomb," *WorldNetDaily*, (February 25, 2003).

20. Abu El-Haj, *Facts on The Ground: Archaeological Practice and Territorial Self-Fashioning in Israeli Society*, op. cit., 281; Please also see, Efrat Weiss, "Prayer books at holy site vandalized," *Ynet.com*, (March 9, 2009).

21. El-Haj, *Facts on The Ground: Archaeological Practice and Territorial Self-Fashioning in Israeli Society*, op. cit.,153.

22. Ibid., 148.

23. Harrington, "Bulldozer archeology: Excavation, earthmoving and archeological practice in Israel," op. cit.

24. Mark Ami-El, "The Destruction of the Temple Mount Antiquities," *Jerusalem Letter/Viewpoints Jerusalem Center for Public Affairs*, no. 483, (August 1, 2002; "Q&A on the Temple Mount with Dr. Eilat Mazar," *The Jerusalem Post*, (February 14, 2007); Aaron Klein, "Rachel's Tomb: Back in Business," WorldNetDaily.com, (March 16, 2005); Raphael Israeli, *Green Crescent Over Nazareth: The Displacement of Christians by Muslims in the Holy Land*, (London: Frank Cass Publishers, 2002).

25. Ami-El, *The Destruction of the Temple Mount Antiquities*, op. cit.; Etgar Lefkovits, "Archeologists: Muslim dig damaged Temple wall," *The Jerusalem Post*, (August 31, 2007); Etgar Lefkovits, "Archeologists slam authorities over Muslim dig," *The Jerusalem Post* (August 28, 2007);

Meron Rapoport, "Waqf Temple Mount excavation raises archeologists' protests," Haaretz, (July 11, 2007).

26. Ami-El, *The Destruction of the Temple Mount Antiquities*, op. cit.

27. William G. Dever, *What Did the Biblical Writers Know and When Did They Know It? What Archeology Can Tell Us about the Reality of Ancient Israel*, (Grand Rapids, Michigan: William B. Eerdman Publishing Company, 2001); William G. Dever, "The Identity of Early Israel: A Rejoinder to Keith W. Whitelam," *Journal for the Study of the Old Testament*, vol. 72, (1996): 3-23; Etgar Lefkovits, "Rubble yields silver Temple 'tax' half-shekel," *Jerusalem Post*, (December 18, 2008); "Jerusalem dig uncovers ancient city walls," Thomson Reuters, (September 3, 2008); "A Hoard Comprising Hundreds of Gold Coins was Uncovered in the Excavations the Israel Antiquities Authority is Conducting at the 'Giv'ati Car Park' in the City of David, in the Walls Around Jerusalem National Park," Israel Antiquities Authority in Zikhron Ya'aqov," *Israel Antiquities Authority* (December 2, 2008); "A Rare Hebrew Seal from the First Temple Period was Discovered in Archeological Excavations in the Western Wall," *Israel Antiquities Authority*, (October 30, 2008); "A New Visitor's Path is Inaugurated in Safed," (October 5, 2008); The Southern Wall of Jerusalem that Dates to the Time of the Hasmonean Dynasty was Discovered on Mount Zion," *Israel Antiquities Authority*, (September 3, 2008).

28. El-Haj, *Facts on The Ground: Archaeological Practice and Territorial Self-Fashioning in Israeli Society*, op. cit., 17.

29. Keith W. Whitelam, *The Invention of Ancient Israel: The Silencing of Palestine History*, (New York: Routledge, 1996), 3.

30. Harrington, "Bulldozer archeology: Excavation, earthmoving and archeological practice in Israel," op. cit.

31. Bentwich, *The New-Old Land of Israel*, op. cit.,15.

32. Steven Erlanger, "King David's Palace Is Found, Archaeologist Says," NYT (August 5, 2005)

33. Paul and Dever, *Biblical Archeology*, op. cit., xi.

34. Ibid., x; (Paul and Dever, op. cit.), x.; William G. Dever, *What Did the Biblical Writers Know and When Did They Know It?* *What Archeology Can Tell Us about the Reality of Ancient Israel*, (Grand Rapids, Michigan: William B. Eerdman Publishing Company, 2001).

35. Ibid; Nadav Shragai, "The Latest Damage to Antiquities on the Temple Mount," *Jerusalem Viewpoints*, Jerusalem Center for Public Affairs, vol. 7, no. 32, (February 28, 2008).

36. Nadav Shragai, "The Latest Damage to Antiquities on the Temple Mount," op. cit.; Nadav Shragai, "Group petitions to stop Muslim dig on temple Mount," Haaretz, (September 9, 2007).

37. Rivkah Fishman-Duker, "'Jerusalem: Capital of the Jews:' The Jewish Identity of Jerusalem in Greek and Roman Sources," *Jewish Political Studies Review*, 20:3-4 (Fall 2008):120-.140; for negative attitudes toward Judaism see Martin Goodman, *Rome and Jerusalem: The Clash of Ancient Civilizations*, (New York: Alfred A. Knopf, 2007), 112,372, 471-472.

38. Fishman-Duker, "'Jerusalem: Capital of the Jews:' The Jewish Identity of Jerusalem in Greek and Roman Sources," op. cit., 120-126; Goodman, op. cit., 169, 376, see also 46-52; Dore Gold, *The Fight for Jerusalem: Radical Islam, The West, and the Future of the Holy City*, (Washington, D.C: Regnery Publishing, Inc. 2007); Rivka, Gonen, *Contested Holiness: Jewish, Muslim and Christian Perspectives on the Temple Mount in Jerusalem*, (Jersey City, New Jersey: KTAV Publishing House, Inc., 2003).

39. Ibid., 125-126.

40. Joel Fishman, "The Big Lie and the Media War Against Israel: From Inversion of the Truth to Inversion of Reality," Jewish Center for Public Affairs, *Jewish Political Studies Review*, 19, nos. 1 and 2, (Spring 2007.)

41. Ibid.

42. Nathan Feinberg, *The Arab-Israel Conflict In International Law*, (Jerusalem: The Magnes Press at The Hebrew University, 1970), 21-22.

43. Ibid., 22-23.

44. Ibid., 23-24.

45. Ibid., 25; Eli E. Hertz, "The 86th Anniversary of the Mandate for Palestine," *Mythsandfacts.com*, (July 24, 2008).

46. Gold and Helmreich, "An Answer To The New Anti-Zionists: The Rights Of The Jewish People To A Sovereign State in their Historic Homeland," op. cit.; Treaty of Sevres, *hri.org*.

47. Isaiah Friedman, *The Question of Palestine, 1914-1918: British-Jewish-Arab Relations*, (London: Routledge and Kegan Paul, 1973), 331.

48. Herzog, *A People That Dwells Alone*, op. cit., 128-129; for an analysis of how Zionism differs from other nationalisms, please see Hedva Ben-Israel, "Zionism and European Nationalisms: Comparative Aspects," *Israel Studies*, vol. 8, no. 1, (April 2003): 91-104.

49. Gold and Helmreich, "An Answer To The New Anti-Zionists: The Rights Of The Jewish People To A Sovereign State in their Historic Homeland," op. cit.; Kenneth Levin, The Oslo Syndrome: delusions of a People Under Siege Smith and Kraus, 2005), 307; Kristen Henrard, *Devising an Adequate System of Minority Protection: Individual Human Rights, Minority Rights and the Right to Self-Determination*, (Boston, Massachusetts: Martinus Nijhoff Publishers, 2000), 281-283.

50. Chaim Herzog, "The Lost Element in Arab-Israeli Peace Negotiations," *FrontPageMagazine.com*, (May 2, 2003); Bernard Lewis, "The Other Middle East Problems," in *Middle East Lectures Number One*, Martin Kramer, ed., (Tel-Aviv: The Moshe Dayan Center for Middle East Studies of Tel Aviv University, 1995: 45; "Palestinian Authority TV visualizes a world without Israel: Shows map of Israel covered by Palestinian flag," *Palestinian Media Watch Bulletin*, (October 17, 2007); Itamar Marcus and Barbara Crook, "PA TV Singing to Israel's Destruction," *Palestinian Media Watch Bulletin*, (October 29, 2007).

51. Norman and Helen Bentwich, *Mandate Memories*, 1918-1948, (New York: Schocken Books, 1965), 26.

52. Abba Eban, *Voice of Israel*, (New York: Horizon Press, 1957), 71, 101.

53. Abraham Joshua Heschel, *Israel: An Echo of Eternity*, (New York: Farrar, Straus and Giroux, 1969), 53-55.

54. "The Jewish Case Before The Anglo-American Committee Of Inquiry On Palestine As Presented By The Jewish Agency For Palestine: Statements and Memoranda," (Jerusalem: The Jewish Agency For Palestine, 1947): 266; Earl of Beaconsfield, *Tancred or The Crusade*, (Longmans, Green and Co., 1900), 388.

55. Ibid., 54-55; Kiddushin, 52b; Rabbi J.J. Reines; see Yehuda Leib Hacohen Fishman, ed., *Sefer Ha-Mizrachi* (Jerusalem, 1946), 10.

56. Ibid., 95

57. Heschel, *Israel: An Echo of Eternity*, op. cit., 50-51; See also the prophet Ezekiel's vision of the Dry Bones in chapter 37.

58. Rabbi Joseph B. Soloveitchik, *Kol Dodi Dofek: Listen—My Beloved Knocks*, (New York: Yeshiva University Press, 2006), 31; Aaron Rakeffet-Rothkoff, *The Rav: The World of Rabbi Joseph B. Soloveitchik*, vol. 2, (Jersey City: KTAV, Publishing House, Inc., 1999), 94-96, 116-118, 128-129.

59. Feinberg, *The Arab-Israel Conflict In International Law*, op. cit., 29.

60. David Hazony, "Zion and Moral Vision," in *New Essays On Zionism*, (Jerusalem: Shalem Press, 2006): 170.

61. Theodore Herzl, *The Complete Diaries of Theodor Herzl*, Raphael Patai, ed., vol. I, (New York: Herzl Press and Thomas Yoseloff, 1960), 6-7; Alex Bein, *Theodore Herzl: A Biography of the Founder of Modern Zionism*, (New York: Atheneum, 1962),160-164.

62. Moses Hess, *Rome and Jerusalem*, (New York: Philosophical Library, 1958), 13, 34.

63. Shmuel Almog, *Zionism and History: The Rise of a New Jewish Consciousness*, (New York: St. Martin's Press and The Magnes Press, The Hebrew University, 1987), 23.

64. Ibid., 23, 259; Gideon Shimoni, *The Zionist Ideology*, (Hanover, New Hampshire: Brandeis University Press, 1995), 104-112, 270-285; "Ahad Ha'am "Truth From Eretz Israel," *Israel Studies*, vol. 1, no. 2, (October 2000): 160-181.

65. For an analysis of the Uganda Controversy see, Almog, Zionism and History: The Rise of a New Jewish Consciousness, op. cit., 238-304; David Vital, "The Afflictions of the Jews and the Afflictions of Zionism: The Meaning and Consequences of the 'Uganda' Controversy," In Essential Papers on Zionism, Jehuda Reinharz and Anita Shapira, eds., (New York: New York University Press, 1996), 119-132; Chaim Gans, *A Just Zionism: On the Morality of the Jewish State*, (New York: Oxford University Press, 2008), 37, 41.

66. Arthur Hertzberg, "Anti-Semitism and Jewish Uniqueness," *The B. G. Rudolf Lectures in Judaic Studies*, (April 1973): 19-20; "Contemporary Global Anti-Semitism: A Report Provided to the United States Congress," (Washington, D.C.: Office of the Special Envoy to Monitor Combat Anti-Semitism, U.S. Department of State) March 2008); Dennis MacShane, "The New Anti-Semitism," *The Washington Post* (September 4, 2007): A17; Jeff Jacoby, "The Cancer of Anti-Semitism in Europe," *The Boston Globe*, (March 14, 2004).

67. Jacob Robinson, *Palestine and the United Nations: Prelude to Solution*, (Westport, Connecticut: Greenwood Press, Publishers, 1947), 237; A.B. Yehoshua, Between Right and Right, (Garden City, New York: Doubleday, 1981), 75-106; Gans, *A Just Zionism: On the Morality of the Jewish State*, op. cit., 47.

68. Robinson, *Palestine and the United Nations: Prelude to Solution*, op. cit., 210.

69. Ibid., 211-212.

70. Abba Eban, "Israel, Anti-Semitism and the United Nations," *The Jerusalem Quarterly*, (Fall 1976):114-115; Grobman, *Nations United*, op. cit.; Manor, *To Right a Wrong: The Revocation of the UN General Assembly Resolution 3379 Defaming Zionism*, op. cit.

71. Feinberg, *The Arab-Israel Conflict In International Law*, op. cit., 39; For an analysis of the British War Cabinet discussion of the question of the Mandatory Power, please see Lloyd George, *The Truth About The Peace Treaties*, vol. II, op. cit., 1149-1201; Howard Grief, *The Legal Foundation*

And Borders Of Israel Under International Law, (Jerusalem: Mazo
Publishers, 2008), 136-147. It is important to note that in November
1914, the Ottoman Empire entered the war against Russia, Britain,
and France. The war ended on October 31, 1918 with the defeat of the
Ottoman armies and the subsequent dismemberment of the empire.
Four years later, after additional fighting and upheaval, Turkey
emerged as a state in Anatolia and a small section of Eastern Thrace,
and five new territories including Palestine, under control of Britain
and France called mandates. (D.K. Fieldhouse, *Western Imperialism in
the Middle East 1914-1958,* (New York: Oxford University Press, 2006),
36. As lawyer Howard Grief has noted, "The legal title of the Jewish
people to the mandated territory of Palestine...was acknowledged"
at the San Remo Conference on April 24, 1920 when the Supreme
Council of the Principal Allied Powers (Great Britain, France, Italy and
Japan) agreed to approve the Balfour Declaration of November 2, 1917.
This session completed the work begun at the London Conference in
February 1920, where the boundaries of Palestine were defined as being
from Dan to Beersheba. The Supreme Council met in the Italian resort
city of San Remo from April 18-26. From April 24-25, they decided
the future of all of Turkey's former territories outside of Anatolia
(known as Asia Minor or Asiatic Turkey), which as a result of Turkish
losses of World War I, had ceased to be under control of the Ottoman
Turkish Empire. As a consequence of the San Remo decision, Britain
obligated itself to reconstitute the Jewish National Home in Palestine.
The San Remo resolution was inserted into the Treaty of Sèvres on
August 10, 1920 and then into the Preamble of the Mandate Charter,
which was approved by 52 nations in 1922, and later by other nations
that joined the League of Nations. Although the Treaty of Lausanne,
which replaced the treaty of Sèvres, did not mention the San Remo
resolution, Grief notes that the resolution was still "an independent
act of binding international law." "The Right of self-determination in
regard to Palestine," Grief concluded, "is a right implicit in Article 22
[of the Covenant of the Leagues of Nations] reserved exclusively for

the Jewish people. It was never the intention of the Supreme Council of the Principal Allied Powers that Palestine or any part of it be made the Arab national home, despite the fact that its population then was overwhelmingly Arab, except for Jerusalem which had a Jewish majority. The word 'home' was a mere euphemism for a Jewish State, and it applied to the whole country." Grief, op. cit., 19-21, 27-44, 271, 486, 667- 668; Howard Grief, "Legal Rights and Title of Sovereignty of the Jewish People to the Land of Israel and Palestine Under International Law," Nativ, vol. 2, 2004; The British Secretary's notes of the meetings of the Supreme Council can be found in Rohan Butler, and J.P.T. Bury, eds. Documents on British Foreign Policy 1919-1939, First Series, 1920, Vol. VIII, (London: Her Majesty's Stationery Office, 1958), 156 ff.; for analysis of the principle of self-determination in Article 22 of the League of Nations see Grief, The Legal Foundation And Borders Of Israel Under International Law, op. cit., 69-71; for an analysis of the Smuts Resolution see, David Hunter Miller, The Drafting of the Covenant, (New York: G.P. Putnam's Sons, 1928), 109-117.

72.   Linowitz, "Analysis of a Tinderbox: The Legal Basis for the State of Israel," op. cit., 524.

73.   Feinberg, *The Arab-Israel Conflict In International Law*, op. cit., 39.

74.   Linowitz, "Analysis of a Tinderbox: The Legal Basis for the State of Israel," op. cit., 524-525.

75.   Julius Stone, *Israel and Palestine: Assault on the Law of Nations*, (Baltimore, Maryland: Johns Hopkins University Press, 1981),16.

76.   Quoted in Simon H. Rifkind, et. al., *The Basic Equities of the Palestine Problem*, (New York: Arno Press, 1977), 80.

77.   Official Records of The Second Session Of The General Assembly Supplement No.11: United Nations Special Committee on Palestine. Report Of The General Assembly Volume III Annex A: Oral Evidence Presented At Public Meeting Lake Success, New York. Verbatim Record Of The Sixteenth Meeting (Public), (July 4, 1947).

78.   Ibid.

79. Official Records of the Second Session of the General Assembly Supplement 11 vol. 1 A / 364 United Nations Special Committee on Palestine. Report to The General Assembly, (September 3, 1947). In rejecting partition, Jamal al-Husseini of the Arab Higher Committee said that the decision of the manner and form of independence for Palestine should be made by "the rightful owners of Palestine." It was "illogical" he said, "for the U.N. to be associated with the introduction of an alien body into the established homogeneity, a course which could only produce new Balkans." ("Statement to the AD HOC Committee on the Palestinian Question by the Representative of the Arab Higher Committee, 29, September 1947.") Ruth Lapidoth and Moshe Hirsch, eds. *The Arab-Israel Conflict and its Resolution: Selected Documents,* (Boston: Martinus Nijhoff Publishers, 1992), 57-58.

80. Elihu Lauterpacht, "Jerusalem and the Holy Places," (London: Anglo-Israel Association, 1968):13, 19.

81. The Jewish Case Before The Anglo-American Committee Of Inquiry On Palestine As Presented By The Jewish Agency For Palestine, op. cit., 357.

82. The Jewish Case; *Report Before the Anglo-American Committee Of Inquiry On Palestine,* op. cit., 23.

83. Ibid., 23-24.

84. Ibid., 27.

85. Speeches by Jewish Agency representatives in the General Assembly May 1947 Israel Ministry of Foreign Affairs, *mfa.gov.il* / MFA.

86. "The Speech of Father Nunez Ambassador of Costa Rica in the United Nations on Zionism," CZA S110 / 47:1. Nunez first served as Costa Rican Ambassador to the UN from 1954-1956 and was back in 1975. At one point in his career, he lived in Israel as his country's ambassador.

87. Ibid., 2.

88. Ibid., 3.

89. Ibid., 6-7.

90. Ibid., 7.

91. Robert Alter, "Zionism of the 70's," *Commentary*, (February 1970): 53.

92. Reinhold Niebuhr, "Our Stake in the State of Israel," *The New Republic* (January 4, 1957).

93. Ibid

94. Ibid., 12.

95. Ruth Gavison, "The Jewish State: A Justification" in New Essays On Zionism, David Hazony, Yoram Hazony, and Michael Oren, eds., (New York: Shalem Press, 2006), 9; Ruth Gavison, "Ruth Gavison Offers a Vision of a Democratic, Jewish Israel," UCLA Ronald W. Burkle Center For International Relations, International, *UCLA.edu*/burkle.

96. Gavison, "The Jewish State: A Justification," op. cit:10.

97. Gold and Helmreich, "An Answer To The New Anti-Zionists: The Rights Of The Jewish People To A Sovereign State in their Historic Homeland," op. cit.

98. Jerry Z. Muller, "Us and Them: The Enduring Power of Ethnic Nationalism" *Foreign Affairs*, (March/April 2008.)

99. Gavison, "Ruth Gavison Offers a Vision of a Democratic, Jewish Israel," op. cit.

100. Ibid.

101. Ibid.

102. Gavison, "The Jewish State: A Justification," op. cit: 11-12.

103. Ibid., 12.

104. Quoted in Blum, *For Zion's Sake*, op. cit., 50-51; see also Efraim Karsh, *Arafat's War: The Man and His Battle For Israeli Conquest*, (New York: Grove Press, 2003), 4.

105. Palestinian National Charter.

106. Geoffrey R. Watson, *The Oslo Accords: International Law and the Israeli-Palestinian Peace Agreements*, (New York: Oxford University Press, 2000), 375-376, 366, 380.

107. Ibid., 46-48,105, 203-210; Madeleine Albright, U.S. Secretary of State, noted in 2000 that Arafat "acknowledged Israel's existence but not its moral legitimacy," Madeleine Albright, *Madam Secretary: A Memoir*, (New York: Miramax Books, 2003), 483.

108. Y. Harkabi, *The Palestinian Covenant and it Meaning*, (Totowa, New Jersey: Vallentine, Mitchell, 1979), 12-13, 18; *spiritus-temporis.com* / Palestine-liberation organization.com.

109. Harkabi, *The Palestinian Covenant and it Meaning*, op. cit., 13-14; Menachem Milson, "How to Make Peace with the Palestinians," *Commentary*, (May 1981:27-28; Daniel Pipes, "PLO Acknowledges: Still at War with Israel," *Danielpipes.org*. (October 28, 2008).

110. Efraim Karsh, *Arafat's War: The Man and His Battle for Israeli Conquest*, op. cit., 87-88; "Erekat: We won't accept Jewish Israel" *Jerusalem Post*, (November 12, 2007); "The recognition sham," *Jerusalem Post*, Online Edition (November 14, 2007); Shimon Peres, *Battling For Peace*, (New York: Random House, 1995), 305-306; Jeff Jacoby, "Is Israel a Jewish state?" *The Boston Globe*, (November 14, 2007); John V. Whitbeck, "What 'Israel's right to exist' means to Palestinians," *The Christian Science Monitor*, (February 2, 2007); Joshua Muravchik, "The Holocaust and the Nakba," *Commentarymagazine.com*, (December 2, 2007).

111. Itamar Marcus and Barbra Crook, "PA TV: Putting hatred to music; Rejecting Israel's legitimacy," *Palestinian Media Watch*, (November 6, 2008); Itamar Marcus and Barbra Crook, "Mickey Mouse Again: Disney images adorn studio while mass murder glorified," *Palestinian Media Watch*, (September 9, 2008); Itamar Marcus and Barbra Crook, "PA TV Children's quiz: Teaching About a world without Israel," *Palestinian Media Watch* (September 3, 2008); Itamar Marcus and Barbara Crook, "From nationalist battle to religious conflict: New 12th Grade Palestinian schoolbooks present a world without Israel," *Palestinian Media Watch*, (February 2007); See also Justus Reid and Michael Sussman, "Will the Next Generation of Palestinians Make Peace With Israel?" *Jerusalem Viewpoints*, Jerusalem Center for Public Affairs, no.

537 (December 1, 2005); Itamar Marcus and Barbara Crook, "Seducing Children to Martyrdom," Jerusalem Post, (July 4, 2006); "Palestinian factions denounce Balfour Declaration; demand British apology." Maan *News Agency*, (November 2, 2008).

112. Marcus, "From nationalist battle," op. cit.

113. Hamas Cleric Muhsen Abu 'Ita: "The Annihilation of the Jews in Palestine is One of the Most Splendid Blessings for Palestine," MEMRI Special Dispatch-No. 2087 (October 28, 2008).

114. Ibid; Itamar Marcus and Barbara Crook, "Abbas with PLO flag erasing Israel," Palestinian Media Watch, (January 14, 2008).

115. Al-Rai Al- 'Aam Kuwait, (February 15, 2006) Center for Special Studies, Intelligence and Terrorism Center: News of the Israeli-Palestinian Conflict February 1-15, 2006, Update.

116. Itamar Marcus and Barbara Crook, "Nearly 90% of Palestinian youth deny Israel's right to exist," *Palestinian Media Watch Bulletin*, (February 28, 2007); "Does Israel have the right to exist?" *Near East Consulting*, (February 2007). Perhaps only 20 percent of the entire adult Palestinian population in the Palestinian Authority, Jordan and Lebanon recognizes Israel, but they do not play a significant role in the peace process; Daniel Pipes testimony, "Next Steps in Israeli-Palestinian Peace Process, Testimony presented to: Hearing of the Subcommittee on the Middle East and South Asia of the House Foreign Affairs Committee," (February 14, 2007).

117. Elihu Richter, "The first core issue: incitement," *Jerusalem Post*, (January 19 2008).

118. Raphael Israeli, "Radical Islam and Israel," in *Israel and Ishmael: Studies in Muslim-Jewish Relations*, Tudor Parfitt, ed. (New York: St. Martin's Press, 2000), 226-228; J.B. Barron, Mohammedan Wakfs in Palestine, (Jerusalem: Greek Convent Press (March 1922),.5-9, 15-20; Article 13 Yaakov Lappin, "Expert: No peace with Muslims, ever," *Ynet*, (September 14, 2006); Article 11 of Hamas Charter, 1988; Yosef Tommy Lapid, "Bush's, Peres's rosy scenario," *Jerusalem Post* (July 18, 2007);

Itamar Marcus and Barbara Crook, " PATV lauds Internet site calling for Israel's elimination," Palestinian Media Watch, (March 14, 2008).

119. Gerald Steinberg, "The 'pragmatic' Hamas myth," IMRA (June 20, 2005); Jonathan Ferziger, "Hamas Threatens to End truce Unless Israel Eases Restrictions," *Bloomberg.com*. (December 16, 2008).

CONCLUSION ENDNOTES

1. "Palestine Royal Commission Report," op. cit., 11.

2. Ibid., 11-12.

3. Morgenstern, "Dispersion and the Longing for Zion," op. cit., 308.

4. Yaacov Herzog, *A People that Dwells Alone*, op. cit., 37; Sol Linowitz, "Analysis of a Tinderbox: The Legal Basis for the State of Israel," *American Bar Association Journal*, vol. 43, no. 523, (June 1957): 524; Bernard Lewis, "The Palestinians and the PLO," op. cit., 32-34.; Bernard Lewis, "Palestine: On the History and Geography of a Name.," op. cit., 1-12.

5. Quoted in Sidra DeKoven Ezrahi, *Booking Passage: Exile and Homecoming in the Modern Jewish Imagination*, (Berkeley, California: University of California Press, 2000):37, Walter Lowdermilk, a devout Methodist, who served as assistant chief of the Soil Conservation Service of the U.S., spent more than three months in Palestine in 1939 surveying the land. He found the Jewish pioneers were "colonizing a damaged and wasted land" and building their own economy in a backward and neglected land... denuded of trees and depleted of its natural fertility." In many areas, swamps were drained to remove pestilential malaria. Walter Clay Lowdermilk, "The Land and the People," *The Nation*, (October 4, 1947), 674.

6. Félix Bovet, *Egypt, Palestine, And Phoenicia: A Visit To Sacred Lands*, (New York: E.P. Dutton and Company, 1883), 98, 131-132.

7. "The Jewish Case Before The Anglo-American Committee Of Inquiry On Palestine As Presented By The Jewish Agency For Palestine:

Statements and Memoranda," (Jerusalem: The Jewish Agency For Palestine, 1947), 101, 103.

8. Ibid., 31.

9. Yaacov Herzog, *A People that Dwells Alone*, op. cit., 37.

10. The Jewish Case Before The Anglo-American Committee Of Inquiry On Palestine. op. cit., 27.

11. Ashbel, *As Much As We Could Do*, op. cit., 12-13;

12. Kisch, *Palestine Diary*, op. cit., 58.

13. Ibid., 125, 304.

14. Ibid., 74-75, 395.

15. Ibid., 19-20, 304, 314, 329-330, 394-395, 454-455; for a detailed account of how the Zionist Executive worked with the Arabs, please see Hillel Cohen, *Army of Shadows: Palestinian Collaborators with Zionism*, 1917-1948, (Berkeley, California: University of California Press, 2008), 15-20; Tamir Goren, "Separate or Mixed Municipalities? Attitudes of Jewish Yishuv Leadership to the Mixed Municipality during the British Mandate: The Case of Haifa," *Israel Studies*, vol. 9, no. 1, (April 2004), 101-124; "A Jewish Manifesto to the Arabs," *The Nation* (December 13, 1922), 674.

16. The Jewish Case Before The Anglo-American Committee of Inquiry On Palestine As Presented BY The Jewish Agency For Palestine: Statements and Memoranda Statement by Moshe Shertok, op. cit., 125; Zaki Shalom, David Ben-Gurion, *The State of Israel, and the Arab World, 1949-1956*, (Portland, Oregon: Sussex Academic Press, 2002), 5-6; Aubrey S. Eban, "The Future Of Arab-Jewish Relations," *Commentary*, (September 1948): 205; Shapira, *Land and Power*, op. cit., 139; Kisch, *Palestine Diary*, op. cit., 7, 58, 74-75, 125, 304, 395, 461.

17. League of Nations Permanent Mandates Commission Minutes of the Thirty-Fourth Session including the Report of the Commission to the Council, (June 8-23, 1938).

18. Ibid.; the search for Arab moderates continues. Please see Marwan Muasher, *The Arab Center: The Promise of Moderation*, (New Haven: Yale University Press, 2008); Menachem Milson, "How to Make Peace with the Palestinians," op. cit., 27.

19. Neil Caplan, *Palestine Jewry and the Arab Question: 1917-1925*, (London, England: Frank Cass, 1978), 47-49; Adnan Abu-Ghazaleh, "Arab Cultural Nationalism in Palestine during the British Mandate," *Journal of Palestine Studies*, vol. 1, issue 3, (Spring 1972):51-52.

20. Caplan, *Futile Diplomacy: Early Arab-Zionist Negotiation Attempts, 1913-1931*, vol. one, op. cit., 125-126.

21. George Antonius, *The Arab Awakening, the Story of the Arab National Movement*, (New York: Capricorn Books, 1965), 412.

22. Linowitz, "Analysis of a Tinderbox: The Legal Basis for the State of Israel," op. cit., 525.

23. Rifkind, et. al., *The Basic Equities of the Palestine Problem*, op. cit., 84.

24. Stone, *Israel and Palestine: Assault on the Law of Nations*, op. cit: 13, 147; Felix Frankfurter Reminisces: An Intimate Portrait as Recorded in Talks with Dr. Harlan B. Philips, (New York: A Doubleday Anchor Book, 1962), 185-187.

25. Stone, *Israel and Palestine: Assault on the Law of Nations*, op. cit., 147.

26. Ibid., 147-148.

27. Ibid., 13, Laqueur and Rubin, *The Israel-Arab Reader*, op. cit., 13-16.

28. Ibid., Laqueur and Rubin, *The Israel-Arab Reader*, op. cit., 17-20.

29. Rifkind, et. al., *The Basic Equities of the Palestine Problem*, op. cit., 43-44.

30. Bernard Lewis, "The Palestinians and the PLO: A Historical Approach," *Commentary*, vol. 59, no. 1, (January 1975), 33.

31. Ibid.

32. Stone, *Israel and Palestine: Assault on the Law of Nations*, op. cit., 11.

33. Ibid., 11-12.

34. Ibid.

35. Ibid., 12-13.

36. Reiter, *Jerusalem and Its Role in Islamic Solidarity*, op. cit., 154.

37. Ibid., 154-155.

38. Ruth Gavison, "The Jewish State: A Justification," in *New Essays On Zionism*, David Hazony, Yoram Hazony, and Michael Oren. ed., (Jerusalem: Shalem Press, 2006), 3; for an analysis of Israeli nationalism see Shmuel Almog, "People and Land in Modern Jewish Nationalism," in Essential Papers On Zionism, Jehuda Reinharz and Anita Shapira, eds., (New York: New York University Press, 1996), 46-62; Israel Kolatt, "Theories On Israel Nationalism," In The Dispersion: Surveys And Monographs, (Jerusalem: World Zionist Organization, 1967):13-50; George L. Mosse, "Can Nationalism Be Saved? About Zionism, rightful and Unjust Nationalism," *Israel Studies*, vol. 2, no. 1, (Spring 1997):156-173. Oxford historian H.R. Trevor-Roper saw the return of Jews to Zion as "the last product of Europe nationalism: a product which, since it is a national settlement, not a colonial exploitation, is the most solid and most formidable," "Jewish and Other Nationalisms," *Commentary*, (January 1963): 21.

39. Ruth Wisse, "The Delegitimation of Israel," *Commentary*, (July 1982):30; "Parallel progress needed in Middle East, Ban Ki-moon tells UN meeting," *UN News Service* (March 22, 2007), op. cit., 31,33; Grobman, *Nations United*, op. cit.; Gary A. Tobin, Aryeh K. Weinberg and Jenna Ferer, The Uncivil University, (San Francisco, Institute for Jewish and Community Research, 2005); Ben Shapiro, *Brainwashed: How Universities Indoctrinate America's Youth*, (Nashville, Tennessee: WorldNetDaily Books, 2004); Martin S. Kramer, *Ivory Towers on Sand: The Failure of Middle Eastern Studies in America's Campuses*, (Washington, D.C.: Washington Institute for Near East Policy, 2001.

40. Eli E. Hertz, "Israel's Major Wars: The Legal Aspects of Coming Into Possession of the Territories," (April 24, 2007); Khaled Abu Toameh, "Dhalan to Hamas: Never Recognize Israel," *The Jerusalem Post*, (May 17, 2009); "Hamas will not recognize any agreement signed by

Abbas." The International Middle East Media Center. (May 27, 2009).
The Israelis paid an excessively high price for their independence.
Six thousand Jews were killed, amounting to one percent of the total
Jewish population of the country. This was approximately more than
four times the number of losses sustained by the Americans during
World War II and higher than what the British had suffered. In terms
of the Palestinians, Israel's fatalities were proportionally twice their
percentage. Efraim Karsh, Fabricating Israeli History: The 'New
Historians," Second Revised Edition, (Portland, Oregon: Frank Cass,
1997), 22, 24; Itamar Marcus and Barbara Cook, "Beyond Mere Hatred,"
The Jerusalem Post, (December 15, 2009); Joshua Hersh, "Hezullah's Last
Mission," The 7th General Conference ad Its Ideology of Resistance,
vol. 9, number 15, Jerusalem Center for Public Affairs, (December 15,
2009), 5

41.   Shalom, David Ben-Gurion, *The State of Israel, and the Arab World, 1949-*
      1956, op. cit., 3, 14.

42.   Bernard Avishai, *The Tragedy of Zionism: Revolution and Democracy in the*
      Land of Israel, (New York: Farrar Straus Giroux, 1983), 145-147.

43.   Meir Hatina, "The 'Ulama' and the Cult of Death in Palestine." *Israel*
      Affairs, Volume 12, issue 1, (January 2006): 29-51; "Faysal Al-Husseini
      in his Last Interview: The Oslo Accords Were a Trojan Horse; The
      Strategic Goal is the Liberation of Palestine from [Jordan] River
      to the [Mediterranean] Sea," MEMRI No. 236., (July 6, 2001); Alan
      M. Dershowitz, Why Terrorism Works: Understanding the threat,
      responding to the challenge, (New Haven, Connecticut: Yale University
      Press, 2002), 81-82; Barbara Victor, *Army of Roses: Inside The World Of*
      Palestinian Women Suicide Bombers, (New York: Rodale, 2003); Luca
      Ricolfi, "Palestinians, 1981-2003" in *Making Sense of Suicide Missions*,
      (New York: Oxford University Press, 2006), Diego Gambetta, ed.,77-
      129.; Oliver and Steinberg, *The Road to Martyrs' Square: A Journey Into*
      The World of The Suicide Bomber, op. cit.; Amnon Rubenstein, "Suicide,
      the path to national salvation," *The Jerusalem Post*, (May 21, 2008);

Bostom, Andrew G., "Jihad and Islamic Antisemitism," *Frontpagemag. com*, op. cit.

44. Yehudit Barsky, *Hamas: The Islamic Resistance Movement of Palestine*, (New York: American Jewish Committee, 2006), 1.

45. Ibid., 9.

46. Ibid; See also "Hamas Representative in Lebanon, Osama Hamdan: We Will Not Accept a Solution in which Haifa, Jaffa and Acre Will Remain Israeli Cities," *Al-Manar TV*, Lebanon, MEMRI Clip Number 1441, (April 2, 2007); "Hamas: We won't waive an inch of Palestinian land," Ezzedeen Alqassam Brigades Information office, (September 12, 2007); Matthew Levitt, *Hamas: Politics, Charity, and Terrorism in the Service of Jihad*, (New Haven, Connecticut: Yale University Press, 2007), 8-9, 19-20; Shaul Mishal and Avraham Sela, *The Palestinian Hamas: Vision, Violence, and Coexistence*, (New York: Columbia University Press, 2000), 50-53; Meir Hatina, *Islam and Salvation In Palestine: The Islamic Jihad Movement*, (Tel-Aviv: The Moshe Dayan Center for Middle Eastern and African Studies, Tel-Aviv University, 2001), 18-19; Rachel Ehrenfeld and Alyssa A. Lappen, "The Truth about the Muslim Brotherhood," *FrontPageMagazine.com*, (June 16, 2006); Boaz Ganor, "Hamas—The Islamic Resistance Movement in the Territories," Jerusalem Center for Public Affairs, *Survey of Arab Affairs*, Number 27, (February 2, 1992); Zvi Mazel, "How Egypt Molded Modern Radical Islam," *Jerusalem Issue Brief*, Jerusalem Center for Public Affairs, vol. 4, no. 18, (February 16, 2005); "Hamas Demonstrations against Annapolis in Gaza Strip," Ma'an News Agency (November 23, 2007); Nidal al-Mughrabi, "Hamas slams Annapolis, vows to keep fighting Israel," Reuters (November 26, 2007); "Hamas celebrates 22nd anniversary since founding," *BBC News*, (December 14, 2009); "Hamas TV teaches kids to kill Jews," *Palestinian Media Watch Bulletin*, (September 23, 2009)

47. Mishal and Sela, *The Palestinian Hamas: Vision, Violence, and Coexistence*, op. cit.,51.

48. Steve Gutin, "Islamic Jihad: No Peace With Israel," *WashingtonPost.com*, (October 11, 2007).

49. Mark A. Heller and Sari Nusseibeh, *No Trumpets, No Drums: A Two-State Settlement of the Israeli-Palestinian Conflict*, (New York: Hill and Wang, 1991), 150-151; for analysis why a two-state solution is seen as unrealistic, see Caroline Glick, "Our Vision in Act Three," *Jerusalem Post*, (July 10, 2007); Benny Elon, "It's the Palestinian state, Stupid," *The Jerusalem Post*, (July 10, 2007); Leslie Susser, "Is two-state solution still viable," JTA (July 9, 2007); Julie Stahl, "Two-State Solution to Israeli-Palestinian Conflict Not Viable, Experts Say," (July 5, 2007), *CNS News Com*; "Ya'alon: Two State Solution Irrelevant," *Jerusalem Post*, (January 22, 2007); Giora Eiland, "Rethinking the Two-State Solution," *The Washington Institute for Near East Policy*, (September 2008))

50. Heller and Sari Nusseibeh, *No Trumpets, No Drums: A Two-State Settlement of the Israeli-Palestinian Conflict*, op. cit.,150-151.

51. Ibid., 18, 34.

52. Quoted in Moshe Ya'alon, "Israel and the Palestinians: A New Strategy," Azure. no. 34, (Autumn 2008); Ethan Bronner, "Poll Shows Most Palestinians Favor Violence Over Talks," NYT (March 19, 2008); Moshe Ya'alon, "Ya'alon: For Arabs we're all settlers," *Ynetnews.com*, (November 22, 2008); "The Palestinian and the Jewishness of the state," *Jerusalem Media Center*, (January 20, 2008); Demands by Israeli Arabs to dismantle the Jewish state can be found in their declarations: "The Future Vision of The Palestinian Arabs in Israel," (December 2006); An Egalitarian Constitution for All," (2006); "A Democratic Constitution "(March 2007); and "The Haifa Declaration," (May 15, 2007; Hillel Halkin," The Jewish State and Its Arabs," *Commentary*, (January 2009):30-37.

53. Talmon, *Israel Among The Nations*, op. cit., 190.

Bibliography

BOOKS

Aall, Pamela, Chester A. Crocker, and Fen Osler Hampson, eds., *Managing Global Chaos: Sources of and Responses to International Conflict*, Washington, D.C.: United States Institute of Peace Press, 1999.

Aaronsohn, Alexander, *With The Turks in Palestine*, Infomotions.com, 1916, Abdullah of Jordan. *My Memoirs Completed*, Translated by Harold W. Glidden, London: Longman, 1978.

Abu El-Haj, Nadia, *Facts on the Ground: Archaeological Practice and Territorial Self-Fashioning in Israeli Society*. Chicago, IL: University of Chicago Press, 2001.

Abu-Lughod I., *The Transformation of Palestine*. Chicago, Illinois: Northwestern University Press, 1971.

Aburish, Said K., *A Brutal Friendship: The West and the Arab Elite*. London: Indigo, 1997.

Adler, Joseph, *Restore the Jews to Their Homeland: Nineteen Centuries in the Quest for Zion, Northvale*, VT: Jason Aronson, 1997.

Ahmad, Feroz, *The Young Turks: The Committee of Union and Progress in Turkish Politics, 1908-1914*. New York: Columbia University Press, 2008.

Ajami, Fouad, *The Arab Predicament: Arab Political Thought and Practice Since 1967*, Cambridge: Cambridge University Press, 1992.

Albright, Madeleine, *Madam Secretary: A Memoir*. New York: Miramax Books, 2003.

Albright, William Foxwell, *From The Stone Age to Christianity: Monotheism and the Historical Process*, New York: Doubleday Anchor Books, Second Edition, 1957.

Aldington, Richard, *Lawrence of Arabia: A Biographical Enquiry*, Chicago, IL: Henry Regnery Company, 1955.

Alexander, Edward, and Paul Bogdanor, eds., *The Jewish Divide Over Israel: Accusers and Defenders*, New Brunswick, NJ: Transaction Publishers, 2006.

Almog, Samuel, ed., *Zionism and the Arabs*. Jerusalem: Zalman Shazar Institute Press, 1983.

Almog, Samuel, *Zionism and History: The Rise of a New Jewish Consciousness*, New York: St. Martin's Press, 1987.

Alon, Mati, *Holocaust and Redemption*, Victoria, BC: Trafford, 2003.

Alroy, Gil Carl, ed., *Attitudes Toward Jewish Statehood in the Arab World*, New York: American Academic Association For Peace In The Middle East, 1971.

Antonius, Georges, *The Arab Awakening, the Story of the Arab National Movement*, New York: Capricorn Books, 1965.

Ardrey, Robert, *The Territorial Imperative*, New York: Dell Publishing Company, 1966.

Arens, Moshe, *Broken Conflict: American Foreign Policy and the Crisis Between the U.S. and Israel*, New York: Simon and Schuster, 1995.

Armstrong, Karen, *The Battle for God*, New York: Alfred A. Knopf, 2000.

Armstrong, Karen, *Jerusalem: One City, Three Faiths*, New York: Ballantine, 1997.

Aronson, Shlomo, *Conference and Bargaining In the Middle East: An Israeli Perspective*, Baltimore and London: John Hopkins University Press, 1974.

Arzt, Donna E., *Refugees into Citizens: Palestinians and the End of the Arab-Israeli Conflict*, New York: Council on Foreign Relations, 1997.

Asali, KJ, ed., *Jerusalem in History*, Brooklyn, NY: Olive Branch Press, 1990.

Ashbel, Rivka, *As Much As We Could Do*, Jerusalem: Magnes Press of the Hebrew University, 1989.

Ashrawi, Hanan, *This Side of Peace*, New York: Simon and Schuster, 1995.

Ashton, Nigel, *King Hussein of Jordan: A Political Life*, New Haven, CT: Yale University Press, 2008.

Ateek, Naim Stifan, and Rosemary Radford Ruether, *Justice and Only Justice: A Palestinian Theology of Liberation, Maryknoll*, New York: Orbis Books, Ltd., 1999.

Atiyah, Edward, *The Arabs: The Origins, Present Conditions, and Prospects of the Arab World*, Baltimore, MD: Penguin Books, Inc., Revised edition, 1958.

Auron, Yair, *The Banality of Indifference: Zionism and the Armenian Genocide*, Piscataway, NJ: Transaction Publishers, 2000.

Avineri, Shlomo, *The Making of Modern Zionism: The Intellectual Origins of the Jewish State*, New York: Basic Books, 1981.

Avishai, Bernard, *The Tragedy of Zionism: Revolution and Democracy in the Land of Israel*, New York: Farrar Straus Giroux, 1985.

Avneri, Arieh L., *The Claim of Dispossession: Jewish Land-Settlement and the Arabs 1878-1948*, New Brunswick, NJ: Transaction Books, 2006.

Avnery, Uri, *Israel Without Zionists: A Plea for Peace in the Middle East*, New York: The Macmillan Company, 1968.

Ayalon, Ami, *The Press in the Arab Middle East: A History*, New York: Oxford University Press, 1995.

Baker, A.J., *Arab Israeli Wars*, New York: Hippocrene Books, 1981.

Baker, James A. III, *The Politics of Diplomacy: Revolution, War and Peace, 1989-1992*, New York: G.P. Putnam's Sons, 1995.

Baldwin, Neil, *Henry Ford and the Jews: The Mass Production of Hate*, New York: Public Affairs, 2001.

Ball, George W., and Douglas B. Ball, *The Passionate Attachment: America's Involvement with Israel, 1947 to the Present*, New York: W. W. Norton, 1992.

Baram, Philip J., *The Department of State in the Middle East 1919-1945*, Philadelphia, PA: University of Pennsylvania, 1978.

Bard, Mitchell G., *The Complete Idiot's Guide to Middle East Conflict*, New York: Alpha Books, 1999.

Barnes, John and David Nicholson, *The Empire at Bay: The Leo Amery Diaries 1929-1945*, London: Hutchinson and Company, Ltd., 1988.

Barnett, Michael N., *Dialogues in Arab Politics: Negotiations in Regional Order*, New York: Columbia University Press, 1998.

Barron, J.B., *Mohammedan Wakfs*, Jerusalem: Greek Covenant Press, March 1922.

Bauer, Yehuda, *From Diplomacy to Resistance: A history of Jewish Palestine 1939-1945*, Philadelphia: Jewish Publication Society, 1970.

Bauer, Yehuda, *The Jewish Emergence from Powerlessness*, Toronto and Buffalo: University of Toronto Press, 1979.

Bauer, Yehuda, *Jews for Sale: Nazi-Jewish Negotiations, 1933-1945*, New Haven, CT: Yale University Press, 1994.

Beaconsfield, Earl of, *Tancred Or The Crusade*, London: Longmans, Green and Co. 1900

Begin, Menachem, *The Revolt: Story of the Irgun*, Jerusalem: Steimatzky's Agency Limited, 1951.

Bein, Alex, ed., *Arthur Ruppin: Memoirs, Diaries, Letters*, London: Weidenfeld and Nicolson, 1971.

Bein, Alex, *The Jewish Question: Biography of a World Problem*, Madison, New Jersey: Fairleigh Dickinson University Press, 1990.

Ben-Ami, Shlomo, *Scars of War, Wounds of Peace: The Israeli-Arab Tragedy*, New York: Oxford University Press, 2006.

Ben-Ami, Yitshaq, *Years of Wrath, Days of Glory: Memoirs from the Irgun*, New York: Robert Speller and Sons, 1982.

Ben-Arieh, Yehoshua, *The Rediscovery of the Holy Land in the Nineteenth Century*, Jerusalem, Israel: Magnes Press of the Hebrew University, Israel Exploration Society; Detroit, MI: Wayne State University Press, 1979.

Ben-Dor, Gabriel and David B. Dewitt, eds., *Conflict Management in the Middle East*, Lexington, MA: D.C. Heath and Company, 1987.

Ben-Gad, Yitschak, *Roadmap to Nowhere: A Layman's Guide to the Middle East*, Green Forest, AK: Balfour Books, 2004.

Ben-Gurion, David, *Letters to Paula*, Pittsburgh, PA: University of Pittsburgh Press, 1971.

Ben-Gurion, David, *Memoirs*, New York: The World Publishing Company, 1970.

Ben-Gurion, David, *Rebirth and Destiny of Israel*, New York: Philosophical Library, Inc., 1954.

Ben-Meir, Atalia, *Failure or Folly*, Shaarei Tikva: Ariel Center for Policy Research, 2003.

Ben-Tor, Amnon, ed., *The Archaeology of Ancient Israel*, New Haven, CT: Yale University Press, 1992.

Bentwich, Norman, *England in Palestine*, London: Kegan Paul, Trench, Trubner and Company Ltd., 1932.

Bentwich, Norman, *My 77 Years*, Philadelphia, PA: Jewish Publication Society, 1961.

Bentwich, Norman, *The New Old Land of Israel*, London: George Allen and Unwin, Ltd., 1960.

Bentwich, Norman and Helen, *Mandate Memories: 1918-1948*, New York: Schocken Books, 1965.

Benvenisti, Meron, *Jerusalem: The Torn City*, Minneapolis, MN: The University of Minnesota Press, 1976.

Benvenisti, Meron, *City of Stone: The Hidden History of Jerusalem*, Berkeley, CA: University of California Press, 1996.

Benvenisti, Meron, *Conflicts and Contradictions*, New York: Villard Books, 1986.

Benvenisti, Meron, and Thomas L. Friedman, *Intimate Enemies: Jews and Arabs in a Shared Land*, Berkeley, CA: University of California Press, 1995.

Benvenisti, Meron, *Sacred Landscape: The Buried History of the Holy Land Since 1948*, Berkeley, CA: University of California Press, 2000.

Berkowitz, Michael, *Western Jewry and the Zionist Project*, 1914-1933, New York: Cambridge University Press, 1997.

Berkowitz, Michael, *Zionist Cultural and West European Jewry before the First World War*, New York: Cambridge University Press, 1991.

Berman, Aaron, *Nazism, the Jews, and American Zionism*, Detroit, MI: Wayne State University Press, 1990.

Berman, Paul, *Terror and Liberalism*, New York: Norton and Norton and Company, 2003.

Bethell, Nicholas, *The Palestine Trial: The Struggle for the Holy Land*, 1935-48, New York: G.P. Putnam's Sons, 1979.

Bilby, Kenneth W., *New Star in the East*, New York: Doubleday and Company, 1950.

Bishara, Marwan, *Palestine/Israel: Peace or Apartheid: Occupation, Terrorism and the Future*, New York: Zed Books, 2002.

Black, Edwin, *The Transfer Agreement: The Dramatic Story of the Pact Between The Third Reich and Jewish Palestine*, New York: Carroll and Graf Publishers, Inc., 2001.

Blum, Howard, *The Brigade: An Epic Story of Vengeance, Salvation, and WWII*, New York: First Perennial Edition, 2002.

Blum, Yehuda, *For Zion's Sake*, New York: A Herzl Press Publication, 1987.

Blum, Yehuda, *The Juridical Status of Jerusalem*, Jerusalem: The Leonard Davis Institute for International Relations, 1974.

Bolton, John, *Surrender is not an Option: Defending America at the United Nations and Abroad*, New York: Threshold Editions, 2007.

Bonsal, Stephen, *Suitors and Suppliants: The Little Nations at Versailles*, New York: Prentice-Hall, Inc. 1946.

Bostom, Andrew G., ed., *The Legacy of Islamic Antisemitism*, Amherst, NY: Prometheus Books, 2008.

Bourne, K., and D.C. Watt, eds., *Studies in International History*, London: Longmans, Green and Company, Ltd., 1967.

Bovet, Félix, *Egypt, Palestine, And Phoenicia: A Visit To Sacred Lands*, New York: E.P. Dutton and Company, 1883.

Bovis, Eugene H., *The Jerusalem Question*, 1917-1968, Stanford, CA: Hoover Institution Press, Stanford University, 1971.

Beinin, Joel, *Was the Red Flag Flying There? Marxist Politics and the Arab-Israeli Conflict in Egypt and Israel, 1948-1965*, Berkeley, CA: University of California Press, 1990.

Biger, Gideon, *The Boundaries of Modern Palestine*, 1840-1947, New York: Routledge Curzon, 2004.

Bohlen, Charles E., *Witness to History: 1929-1969*, New York: W.W. Norton and Company, Inc., 1973.

Brandeis, Louis D., *Brandeis on Zionism: A Collection of Addresses and Statements by Louis D. Brandeis*, Washington, D.C.: Zionist Organization of America, 1942.

Braizat, Musa S., *The Jordan–Palestinian Relationship: The Bankruptcy of the Confederal Idea*, London: I. Tauris, 1998.

Brock, Michael and Eleanor Brock, eds., *H.H. Asquith: Letters to Venetia Stanley*, New York: Oxford University Press, 1968.

Brog, David, *Standing With Israel*, Lake Mary, FL: Front Line, A Strang Company, 2006.

Bronner, Stephen Eric, *A Rumor About the Jews: Reflections on Antisemitism and the Protocols of the Learned Elders of Zion*, New York: St. Martin's Press, 2000.

Brown, George, *In My Way: The Political Memoirs of Lord George-Brown*, London: Victor Gollancz Ltd., 1971.

Brown, Malcolm, ed., *Secret Dispatches From Arabia and Other Writing By T. E. Lawrence*, London: Bellew Publishing, 1991.

Brown, Michael, *The Israeli-American Connection: Its Roots in the Yishuv*, Detroit, MI: Wayne State University Press, 1996.

Browning, Christopher S., *The Origins of the Final Solution: The Evolution of Nazi Jewish Policy*, September 1939-March 1942, Lincoln, NE: University of Nebraska Press, 2004.

Bunton, Martin, *Colonial Policies in Palestine 1917-1936*, First Series, 1920, Vol. 8, London: Her Majesty's Stationery Office, 1958.

Burckhardt, John Lewis, *Travels and the Holy Land, London: Association for Promoting The Discovery of The Interior Parts of Africa*, 1882.

Caplan, Neil, *Futile Diplomacy*, Vol. 1, Early Arab-Zionist Negotiation Attempts 1913-1931, London: Frank Cass, 1983.

Caplan, Neil, *Futile Diplomacy*, Vol. 2, Arab—Zionist Negotiations and the End of the Mandate, London: Frank Cass, 1986.

Caplan, Neil, *Keeping Faith: Memoirs of a President*, New York: Bantam Books, 1982.

Caplan, Neil, *The Lausanne Conference, 1949: A Case Study in Middle East Peacemaking*, Tel-Aviv: The Moshe Dayan Center for Middle Eastern and African Studies, 1993.

Caplan, Neil, *Palestine and the Arab Question 1917-1925*, London: Frank Cass, 1978.

Carter, Jimmy, *Palestine: Peace Not Apartheid*, New York: Simon and Schuster, 2006.

Cattan, Henry, *Palestine, The Arabs and Israel: The Search for Justice*, London: Longman Group Ltd, 1969.

Cesarani, David, *Major Farran's Hat: The Untold Story of the Struggle to Establish the Jewish State*, (New York: DaCapo Press, 2009)

Chandler, Robert, *Shadow World: Resurgent Russia: The Global New Left, And Radical Islam*, Washington, D.C.: Regnery Publishing, Inc. 2008.

Charters, David, *The British Army and Jewish Insurgency in Palestine*, 1945-1947, Houndsmills and London: Palgrave Macmillan Press, 1989.

Chertoff, Mordecai S., *The New Left and the Jews*, New York: Pitman Publishing Corporation, 1971.

Cheshin, Amir, Bill Hutman and Avi Melamed, *Separate and Unequal: The Inside Story of Israeli Rule in East Jerusalem*, Cambridge, Ma: Harvard University Press, 1999.

Chesterton, G.K., *The New Jerusalem*, Sandy, Ut: Quiet Vision Publishing, 2004.

Chomsky, Noam and Edward W. Said, *Fateful Triangle: The United States, Israel, and the Palestinians*, Cambridge, MA: South End Press, 1999.

Chomsky, Noam, *The Umbrella of U.S. Power: The Universal Declaration of Human Rights and the Contradictions of U.S. Policy*, New York: Seven Stories Press, 1999.

Christison, Kathleen, *Perceptions of Palestine: Their Influence on U.S. Middle East Policy*, Berkeley, CA: University of California Press, 1999.

Christman, Henry M., ed., *The State Papers of Levi Eshkol*, New York: Funk and Wagnalls, 1969.

Churchill, Winston S., *The River War, New York: Award Books*, 1964.

Clarke, Thurston, *By Blood and Fire: The Attack on the King David Hotel*, London: Hutchinson, 1981.

Cleary, Joe, *Literature, Partition, and The Nation State: Culture and Conflict in Ireland, Israel and Palestine*, New York: Cambridge University Press, 2002.

Clifford, Clark M., Eugene V. Rostow, and Barbara W. Tuchman, *The Palestine Question in American History*, New York: Arno Press, 1978.

Clinton, Bill, *My Life*, New York: Alfred A. Knopf, 2004.

Cobban, Helena, *The Palestinian Liberation Organization: People, Power and Politics*, New York: Cambridge University Press, 1984.

Cohen, Aharon, *Israel and the Arab World*, Boston, MA: Beacon Press, 1976.

Cohen, Geula, *Woman of Violence: Memoirs of a Young Terrorist*, 1943-1948, New York: Holt, Rinehart and Winston, 1966.

Cohen, Michael J., *Palestine: Retreat from the Mandate*, New York: Holmes and Meier Publishers, Inc. 1978.

Cohen, Michael J., *Palestine to Israel: From Mandate to Independence*, London: Frank Cass, 1988.

Cohen, Michael J., *Truman and Israel*, Berkeley, CA: University of California Press, 1990.

Cohen, Naomi W., *The Year After the Riots: American Response to the Palestine Crisis of 1929-30*, Detroit, MI: Wayne State University Press, 1988.

Cohen, Stephen P., *Beyond America's Grasp: A Century of Failed Diplomacy in the Middle East*, (New York: Farrar, Straus and Giroux, 2009)

Cohen, Stuart A., *English Zionists and British Jews: The Communal Politics of Anglo-Jewry*, 1895-1920, Princeton, NJ: Princeton University Press, 1982.

Cole, Margaret I, ed., *Beatrice Webb's Diaries 1912-1924*, New York: Longmans, Green and Company, 1952.

Collins, Larry and Dominique Lapierre, *O Jerusalem*, New York: Touchstone Books, 1988.

Conder, Claude Reignier, *Tent Work in Palestine: A Record of Discovery in Palestine*, Vol. 1, Elibron Classics series, 2005, (Originally published: The Committee of Palestine, 1878).

Connor, Walker, *Ethnonationalism: The Quest for Understanding*, Princeton, NJ: Princeton University Press, 1994.

Coogan, Kevin, *Dreamer of the Day: Francis Parker Yockey and the Postwar Fascist International*, Brooklyn, NY: Autonomedia, 1999.

Cook, David, *Understanding Jihad*, Berkeley, CA: University of California Press, 2005.

Crawford, James, *The Creation for States in International Law*, Second Edition, New York: Oxford University Press, 2006.

Crossman, Richard, *A Nation Reborn: The Israel of Weizmann, Bevin, and Ben-Gurion*, London: Hamish Hamilton, Ltd, 1960.

Crossman, Richard, *Palestine Mission: A Personal Record*, New York: Harper and Brothers Publishers, 1947.

Crum, Bartley C., *Behind the Silken Curtain*, New York: Simon and Schuster, 1947.

Dalin, David G., and John F. Rothmann, *Icon of Evil*, New York: Random House, 2008.

David, Abraham, *To Come to the Land: Immigration and settlement in 16th-Century Eretz-Israel*, Tuscaloosa, Alabama: The University of Alabama Press, 1999.

Dayan, Moshe, *Diary of the Sinai Campaign*, New York: Schocken Books, 1965.

Dekel, Efraim, SHAI: *The Exploits of Hagana Intelligence*, New York: Thomas Yoseloff, 1959.

DeNovo, John A., *American Interests and Policies in the Middle East*, 1900—1939, Minneapolis, MN: Minneapolis University Press, 1963.

Dershowitz, Alan, *The Case Against Israel's Enemies*, Hoboken, NJ: John Wiley, 2008.

Dershowitz, Alan, *The Case For Israel*, Hoboken, New Jersey: John Wiley and Sons, 2003.

Dershowitz, Alan, *What Israel Means To Me*, Hoboken, New Jersey: John Wiley, 2006.

Dershowitz, Alan, *Why Terrorism Works: Understanding the Threat and Responding to the Challenge*, New Haven, Connecticut: 2002.

Dever, William G., *Who Were the Early Israelites and Where Did They Come From?* Grand Rapids, MI: William B. Eerdmans Publishing Company, 2003.

Dever, William G., *What Did the Biblical Writers Know and When Did They Know It? What Archaeology Can Tell Us About the Reality of Ancient Egypt*, Grand Rapids, MI: William B. Eerdmans Publishing Company, 2001.

Dodge, Toby, *Inventing Iraq: The Failure of Nation Building and a History Denied*, New York: Columbia University Press, 2003.

Doumani, Beshara, *Rediscovering Palestine: Merchants and Peasants in Jabal Nablus*, 1700-1900, Berkeley, CA: University of California, 1995.

Draper, Theodore, *Israel and World Politics: Roots of the Third Israeli War*, New York: The Viking Press, 1967.

Dumper, Michael, *The Politics of Sacred Space: The Old City of Jerusalem in the Middle East Conflict*, Boulder, CO: Lynne Rienner Publishers, 2002.

Eban, Abba, *Personal Witness: Israel Through My Eyes*, New York: G.P. Putnam, 1992.

Eban, Abba, *The Tide of Nationalism*, New York: Horizon Press, 1959.

Eban, Abba, *Voice of Israel*, New York: Horizon Press, 1957.

Edelheit, Abraham J., *History of Zionism: A Handbook and Dictionary*, Boulder, CO: Westview Press, 2000.

Elath, Eliahu, *Zionism in the UN: A Diary of the First Days*, Philadelphia, PA: Jewish Publication Society, 1976.

Elath, Eliahu, Norman Bentwich and Doris May, eds., *Memories of Sir Wyndham Deeds*, London: Victor Gollancz and the Anglo-Israel Association, 1958.

El-Elini, Roza, *Mandated Landscape: British Imperial Rule in Palestine, 1929-1948*, London: Frank Cass, 2005.

Elishakoff, Isaac and Louis Rene Beres, *The Israel That Can Say No to Self-Annihilation*, Bloomington, IN: 1stBooks Library, 2000.

Elon, Amos, *A Blood-Dimmed Tide: Dispatches from the Middle East*, New York: Columbia University Press, 1997.

Elon, Amos and Sana Hassan, *Between Enemies: A Compassionate Dialogue Between an Israeli and an Arab*, New York: Random House, 1974.

Elpeleg, Zvi, *The Grand Mufti: Haj Amin Al-Hussaini, Founder of the Palestinian National Movement*, London and Portland, OR: Frank Cass, 1993.

El-Sadat, Anwar, *In Search of Identity: An Autobiography*, New York: Harper and Row, 1977.

Emadi, Hafizullah, *Politics of the Dispossessed: Superpowers and Development in the Middle East*, Westport, CT: Praeger, 2001.

Esco Foundation for Palestine, Inc., *Palestine: A Study of Jewish, Arab, and British Policies*, 2 vols. New Haven, CT: Yale University Press, 1947.

Eveland, Wilbur Crane, *Ropes of Sand: America's Failure in the Middle East*, London and New York: W.W. Norton and Company, 1980.

Evensen, Bruce J., *Truman, Palestine, and the Press: Shaping Conventional Wisdom At the Beginning of the Cold War*, Westport, CT: Greenwood, 1992.

Evron, Boas, *Jewish State or Israeli Nation?* Bloomington, IN: Indiana University Press, 1995.

Eytan, Walter, *The First Years: A Diplomatic History of Israel*, New York: Simon and Schuster, 1958.

Ezrahi, Sidra Dekoven, *Booking Passage: Exile and Homecoming in the Modern Jewish Immigration*, Berkeley, CA: University of California Press, 2000.

Ezrahi, Yaron, *Rubber Bullets: Power and Conscience in Modern Israel*, Berkeley, CA: University of California Press, 1998.

Farsoun, Samih K. and Christina Zacharia, *Palestine and the Palestinians*, Boulder, CO: Westview Press, 1998.

Feinberg, Nathan, *On An Arab Jurist's Approach To Zionism And The State Of Israel*, Jerusalem: The Magnes Press, The Hebrew University Press, 1971.

Feinberg, Nathan, *The Arab-Israel Conflict In International Law: A Critical Analysis of the Colloquium of Arab Jurists in Algeria*, Jerusalem: The Magnes Press, The Hebrew University Press, 1970.

Feste, Karen A., *Plans for Peace: Negotiations and the Arab-Israeli Conflict*, New York: Praeger Publishers, 1991.

Feuer, Leon I., *Why A Jewish State*, New York: Richard R. Smith, 1942.

Fieldhouse, D.K., *Western Imperialism in the Middle East 1914-1958*, New York: Oxford University Press, 2006.

Findley, Paul, *Silent No More: Confronting America's False Images of Islam*, Washington, DC: American Educational Trust, 2001.

Findley, Paul, *They Dare to Speak Out: People and Institutions Confront Israel's Lobby*, Atlanta, Georgia: A Cappella Books, 1989.

Finkelstein, Israel and Neil Asher Silberman, *The Bible Unearthed: Archaeology's New Vision of Ancient Israel and the Origin of Its Sacred Texts*, New York: A Touchstone Book, 2001.

Finkelstein, Norman G., *Beyond Chutzpah: On the Misuse of Anti-Semitism and the Abuse of History*, Berkeley California: University of California Press, 2005.

Finkelstein, Norman G., *Image and Reality of the Israel: The Israel-Palestine Conflict*, New York: Verso Books, 1995.

Finn, James, *Stirring Times or Records from Jerusalem Consular Chronicles of 1853 to 1856*, Vol. 1, London: C. Kegan Paul and Company, 1878.

Finn, James, *Stirring Times or Records from Jerusalem Consular Chronicles of 1853 to 1856*, Vol. 2, Elibron Classic Series, 2005, (Originally Published, London: C. Kegan Paul & Co, 1878.).

Flapan, Simha, *The Birth of Israel: Myths and Realities*, New York: Pantheon Books, 1987.

Flapan, Simha, ed., *When Enemies Dare To Talk: An Israeli-Palestinian Debate*, London: Croom Helm, 1979.

Fleischmann, Ellen L., *The Nation and Its "New" Women: The Palestinian Women's Movement 1920-1948*, Berkeley California: University of California Press, 2003.

Fletcher, George P. and Jens David Ohlin, *Defending Humanity: When Force Is Justified and Why*, New York: Oxford University Press, 2008.

Florence, Ronald, *Lawrence and Aaronsohn: T.E. Lawrence, Aaron Aaronsohn, and the Seeds of the Arab-Israeli Conflict*, New York: Viking, 2007.

Fosdick, Harry Emerson, *A Pilgrimage to Palestine*, New York: The Macmillan Company, 1927.

Frankel, Glenn, *Beyond the Promised Land: Jews and Arabs on the Hard Road to a New Israel*, New York: Touchstone Books, 1994.

Frankel, Jonathan, *The Damascus Affair "Ritual Murder," Politics, and the Jews in 1840*, New York: Cambridge University, 1997.

Fraser, T.G., *The Arab-Israeli Conflict*, Second Edition, New York: Palgrave Macmillan, 2004.

Friedland, Roger and Richard Hecht, *To Rule Jerusalem*, Berkeley, CA: University of California Press, 2000.

Friedlander, *Saul, and Mahmoud Hussein, Arabs and Israelis: A Dialogue*, New York: Holmes and Meier, 1975.

Friedman, Isaiah, *Palestine: A Twice-Promised Land?* Vol. 1, The British, the Arabs, and Zionism, 1915-1920, Piscataway, NJ: Transaction Publishers, 2000.

Friedman, Isaiah, *Germany, Turkey, Zionsim: 1897-1918*, Piscataway, NJ: Transaction Publishers, 1998.

Friedman, Isaiah, *The Question of Palestine: British-Jewish-Arab Relations: 1914-1918*, Piscataway, NJ: Transaction Publishers, 1991.

Friedman, Thomas L., *From Beirut to Jerusalem*, New York: Anchor Books, 1990.

Friedman, Thomas L., *Longitudes and Attitudes: Exploring the World after September 11*, New York: Farrar Straus Giroux, 2002.

Friedman, Yohanan, *Tolerance and Coercion in Islam: Interfaith Relations in the Muslim Tradition*, New York: Cambridge University Press, 2003

Fromkin, David, *A Peace to End All Peace: The Fall of the Ottoman Empire and the Creation of the Modern Middle East*, New York: Avon Books, 1989.

Furlonge, Sir Geoffrey, *Palestine Is My Country: The Story of Musa Alami*, New York: Praeger, 1969.

Gabbay, Rony E., *A Political Study of the Arab-Jewish Conflict: The Arab Refugee Problem*, Geneva: Librairie E. Droz, 1959.

Galnoor, Itzhak, *The Partition of Palestine: Decision Crossroads in the Zionist Movement*, Albany, New York: State University of New York Press, 1995.

Gambetta, Diego, ed., *Making Sense of Suicide Missions*, New York: Oxford University Press, 2005.

Ganin, Zvi, Truman, *American Jewry and Israel*, 1945-1948, New York: Holmes and Meir, 1979.

Gans, Chaim, *A Just Zionism: On the Morality of The Jewish State*, New York: Oxford University Press, 2008.

Gans, Chaim, *The Limits of Nationalism*, Cambridge, England: The Press Syndicate of the University of Cambridge, 2003.

Garcia-Granados, Jorge, *The Birth of Israel: The Drama As I Saw It*, New York: Alfred A. Knopf, 1948.

Gelber, Yoav, *Palestine 1948: War, Escape and the Emergence of the Palestinian Refugee Problem*, Portland, OR: Sussex Academic Press, 2001.

Gerson, Allan, *Israel, the West Bank and International Law*, London: Frank Cass. 1978.

Gertz, Nurith, *Myths in Israeli Culture: Captives of a Dream*, London: Vallentine Mitchell, 2000.

Gervasi, Frank, *The Case for Israel*, New York: The Viking Press, 1967.

Gervasi, Frank, *To Whom Palestine?* New York: D. Appleton-Century Company, Inc., 1946.

Gil, Moshe, *A History of Palestine*, 634-1099, Cambridge, England: Cambridge University Press, 1992.

Gilbert, Martin, *Churchill and the Jews: A Lifelong Friendship*, New York: Henry Holt and Company, LLC., 2007.

Gilbert, Martin, *Exile and Return: The Struggle for a Jewish Homeland*, Philadelphia and New York: J.B. Lippincott, 1978.

Gilbert, Martin, *A History of the Twentieth Century: 1952-1999*, Volume 3, New York: William Morrow & Co, 1999

Gilbert, Martin, *Israel: A History*, New York: William Morrow & Company, 1998.

Gilbert, Martin, *Winston S. Churchill*, Vol. 3, The Challenge of War 1914-1916, Boston: Houghton-Mifflin Company, 1971.

Gilbert, Martin, *Winston S. Churchill*, Vol. 4, The Stricken World 1916-1922, London: Heinmann, 1975.

Givet, Jacques, *The Anti-Zionist Complex*, Englewood, New Jersey: SBS Publishing Company, Inc., 1982.

Glubb, John Bagot, *A Soldier with The Arabs*, London: Hodder and Stoughton, 1957.

Gold, Dore, *The Fight for Jerusalem: Radical Islam, the West, and the Future of the Holy City*, Washington, D.C.: Regnery Publishing, Inc., 2007.

Gold, Dore, *Tower of Babble: How The United Nations Has Fueled Global Chaos*, New York: Crown Forum, 2004.

Gold, Dore, *Hatred's Kingdom: How Saudi Arabia Supports the New Global Terrorism*, Washington, D.C.: Regency Publishing, Inc., 2003.

Goldberg, Brett, *A Psalm in Jenin*, Israel: Modan Publishing House, 2003.

Goldmann, Nahum, *The Jewish Paradox: A Personal Memoir of Historic Encounters that Shaped the Drama of Modern Jewry*, New York: Fred Jordan Books/Grosset and Dunlap, 1978.

Goitein, S.D., *Jews and Arab: Their Contacts Through The Ages*, New York: Schocken Books, Inc., 1955.

Gonen, Rivka, *Contested Holiness: Jewish, Muslim and Christian Perspectives on The Temple Mount in Jerusalem*, Jersey City, NJ: KTAV, 2003.

Gordis, Daniel, *Saving Israel: How the Jewish People Can Win a War That May Never End*, Hoboken, New Jersey: John Wiley & Son, Inc., 2009.

Goren, Arthur A, ed., *Dissenter in Zion: From the Writings of Judah L. Magnes*, Cambridge, MA, 1982.

Gorenberg, Gershom, *The End of Days: Fundamentalism and the Struggle for The Temple Mount*, New York: The Free Press, 2000.

Gorny, Yosef, *The British Labour Movement and Zionism 1917-1948*, London: Frank Cass, 1983.

Gorny, Yosef, *Zionism and the Arabs, 1882-1948: A Study of Ideology*, New York: Oxford, 1987.

Gorny, Yosef, *The State of Israel in Jewish Public Thought: The Quest for Collective Identity*, New York: New York University Press, 1994.

Granovsky, A., *Land Settlement in Palestine*, London: Victor Gollancz Ltd., 1930.

Graves, Philip, *Palestine, the Land of Three Faiths*, London: Jonathan Cape, 1923.

Graves, R. M., *Experiment in Anarchy*, London: Victor Gollancz Ltd., 1949.

Gray, Christine., *International Law and the Use of Force*, Third Edition. New York: Oxford University Press, 2008.

Greenberg, Haim, *The Inner Eye*, New York: Jewish Frontier Association, 1953.

Grey, Edward, *Twenty-Five Years*, 1892-1916, New York: Frederick A. Stokes Company, 1925.

Grigg, John, *Lloyd George: War Leader 1916-1918*, New York: Penguin Books, 2002.

Gromyko, Andrei, *Memories: From Stalin to Gorbachov*, London: Arrow Books, 1989.

Grose, Peter, *Israel in the Mind of America*, New York: Random House, 1981.

Guyat, Nicholas, *The Absence of Peace: Understanding the Israeli Palestinian Conflict*, New York: Palgrave, 1998.

Haass, Richard N., *Conflicts Unending: The United States and Regional Disputes*, New Haven, CT: Yale University Press, 1990.

Haass, Richard N., and Martin Indyk, *Restoring The Balance: A Middle East Strategy For The Next President*, Washington, D.C. Brookings Institution Press, 2008.

Haber, Eitan, *Menachem Begin: The Legend and the Man*, New York: Delacorte Press, 1978.

Hadawi, Sami, *Bitter Harvest: Palestine Between 1914-1967*, New York: The New World Press, 1967.

Hadawi, Sami, *Palestinian Rights and Losses in 1948: A Comprehensive Study*, London: Saqi Books, 1988.

Haim, Sylvia G., ed., *Arab Nationalism: An Anthology*, Berkeley, CA: University of California Press, 1962.

Hairn, Yehovada, *Abandonment of Illusions: Zionist Political Attitudes Toward Palestinian Arab Nationalism*, Boulder, CO: Westview Press, 1983.

Halabi, Rabah, ed., *Israeli and Palestinian Identities in Dialogue: The School for Peace Approach*, New Brunswick, NJ: Rutgers University Press, 2004.

Halevi, Yossi Klein, *At The Entrance to the Garden of Eden: A Jew's Search For God With Christians And Muslims In The Holy Land*, New York: HaperCollins, 2001.

Halkin, Abraham S., *Zion in Jewish Literature*, New York: Herzl Press, 1961.

Halkin, Hillel, *Letters to an American Jewish Friend: A Zionist's Polemic*, Philadelphia, PA: Jewish Publication Society, 1977.

Halpern, Ben Reinharz, and Jehuda Reinharz, *A Clash of Heroes: Brandeis, Weizmann, and American Zionism*, New York: Oxford University Press, 1987.

Halpern, Ben Reinharz, *The Idea of a Jewish State, Second Edition*, Cambridge, Massachusetts: Harvard University Press, 1969.

Halpern, Ben and Jehuda Reinharz, *Zionism and the Creation of a New Society*, Hanover and London: Brandeis University Press, 2000.

Halperin, Samuel, *The Political World of American Zionism*, Detroit, MI: Wayne State University Press, 1961.

Hampson, Fen Osler, *Nurturing Peace: Why Peace Settlements Succeed Or Fail*, Washington, D.C.: United States Institute of Peace, 1996.

Harkabi, Yehoshafat, *Arab Attitudes to Israel, Piscataway*, NJ: Transaction Publishers, 1974.

Harkabi, Yehoshafat, *Arab Strategies and Israel's Responses*, New York: The Free Press, 1977.

Harkabi, Yehoshafat, *The Palestinian Covenant and Its Meaning*, Portland, OR: Vallentine Mitchell, 1979.

Harkabi, Yehoshafat, *Palestinians and Israel*, New York: John Wiley and Sons, 1974.

Harris, Lee, *Civilization and Its Enemies: The Next Stage of History*, New York: Free Press, 2004.

Hart, Alan, *Arafat: A Political Biography*, Bloomington and Indianapolis, IN: Indiana University Press, 1989.

Hattis, Susan Lee, *The Bi-National Idea in Palestine during Mandatory Times*, Haifa: Shikmona, 1970.

Hauser, Gideon, *Justice In Jerusalem*, New York: Harper and Row, Publishers, 1966.

Hayward, C.T.R., *Interpretations of the Name Israel in Ancient Judaism and some Early Christian Writings: From Victorious Athlete to Heavenly Champion*, Oxford University Press, 2005.

Hazony, David, Yoram Hazony, and Michael Oren, eds., *New Essays On Zionism*, Jerusalem and New York: Shalem Press, 2006.

Hazony, Yoram, *The Jewish State: The Struggle for Israel's Soul*, New York: Basic Books, 2000.

Heller, Joseph, *The Stern Gang: Ideology, Politics, and Terror, 1940-1949*, London, Frank Cass, 1995.

Heller, Mark A., and Sari Nusseibeh, *No Trumpets, No Drums: A Two-State Solution of the Israeli-Palestinian Conflict*, New York: Hill and Wang, 1991.

Heller, Mark A., *A Palestinian State: Implications for Israel*, Cambridge, MA: Harvard University Press, 1983.

Henrard, Kristen, *Devising an Adequate System of Minority Protection: Individual Human Rights, Minority rights and the Right to Self-Determination*, Boston, MA: Martinus Nijhoff Publishers, 2000.

Herf, Jeffrey, *The Jewish Enemy: Nazi Propaganda During World War II and the Holocaust*, Cambridge, MA: Belknap Press of Harvard University Press, 2006.

Herf, Jeffrey, *Nazi Propaganda For The Arab World*, New Haven, Connecticut: Yale University Press, 2009.

Hertz, Eli E., *Reply*, New York: Myths and Facts Inc., 2005.

Hertzberg, Arthur, *The Fate of Zionism: A Secular Future for Israel and Palestine*, New York: HaperSanFrancisco, 2003.

Hertzberg, Arthur, *Jewish Polemics*, New York: Columbia University Press, 1992.

Hertzberg, Arthur, *The Zionist Idea: A Historical Analysis and Reader*, Philadelphia, PA: Jewish Publication Society, 1997.

Herzog, Chaim, *Who Stands Accused? Israel Answers Its Critics*, New York: Random House, 1978.

Herzog, Yaacov, *A People That Dwells Alone*, New York: Sanhedrin Press, 1975.

Heschel, Abraham Joshua, *Israel: An Echo of Eternity*, New York: Farrar, Straus and Giroux, 1969.

Hilberg, Raul, *The Destruction of European Jews, Third Edition*, New Haven, CT: Yale University Press, 1985.

Hiroyuki, Yanagihashi, ed., *The Concept of Territory in Islamic Law and Thought: A Comparative Study*, London and New York: Kegan Paul International, 2000.

Hirst, David, *The Gun and the Olive Branch*, London: Futura Publications, 1978.

Hoffmeier, James K., *Ancient Israel: The Evidence for the Authenticity for the Wilderness Tradition*, (New York: Oxford Press, 2005)

Hopwood, Derek, *The Russian Presence in Syria and Palestine 1843-1914*, New York: Clarendon Press, Oxford University Press, 1969.

Horowitz, David, *State in the Making*, New York: Alfred A. Knopf, 1953.

Hourani, Albert, *A History of the Arab Peoples*, Cambridge, MA: The Belknap Press of Harvard University Press, 1991.

Hourani, Albert, *The Emergence of the Modern Middle East*, Berkeley, CA: University of California Press, 1981.

Hourani, Albert, Philip S. Khoury, and Mary C. Wilson, *The Modern Middle East*, Berkeley, CA: University of California Press, 1993.

Hughes, Matthew, *Allenby and British Strategy in the Middle East 1917-1919*, Portland, OR: Frank Cass Publishers, 1999.

Humphreys, R. Stephen, *Between Memory and Desire: The Middle East In A Troubled Age*, Berkeley, CA: University of California Press, 1999.

Huneidi, Sarah, *A Broken Trust: Herbert Samuel, Zionism and the Palestinians 1920-1925*, London: I B Tauris & Co Ltd., 2001.

Huntington, Samuel P., *The Clash of Civilizations and the Remaking of World Order*, New York: Touchstone, 1998.

Hurewitz, J.C., *Diplomacy in the Near and Middle East, A Documentary Record*, New York: Van Nostrand, 1956.

Hurewitz, J.C., *Middle East Politics: The Military Dimension*, New York: Praeger, 1969.

Hurewitz, J.C., *The Struggle for Palestine*, New York: Greenwood Press Publishers, 1968.

Husain, Ed, *The Islamist: Why I joined radical Islam in Britain, what I saw inside and why I left*, New York: Penguin Books, 2007.

Hyamson, Albert M., *Palestine Under The Mandate: 1920-1948*, London: Methuen and Company, 1950.

Inbar, Efraim, ed., *Regional Security Regimes: Israel and Its Neighbors*, Albany, NY: State University of New York Press, 1995.

Indyk, Martin, *Innocent Abroad: An Intimate History of American Peace Diplomacy in the Middle East*, New York: Simon and Shuster, 2009.

Israeli, Raphael, *Palestinians Between Nationalism and Islam*, Portland, OR: Vallentine Mitchell, 2008.

Israeli, Raphael, *Green Crescent Over Nazareth: The Displacement of Christians by Muslims in the Holy Land*, London: Frank Cass Publishers, 2002.

Israeli, Raphael, *Jerusalem Divided: The Armistice Regime: 1947-1967*, London: Frank Cass Publishers, 2002.

Israeli, Raphael, *Poison: Modern Manifestations of a Blood Libel*, Lanham, MD: Lexington Books, 2002.

Jochen, Hippler, and Andrea Lueg, *The Next Threat Western Perceptions of Islam*, London: Pluto Press, 1995.

Johnson, Paul, *Modern Times: The World from the Twenties to the Nineties*, New York: Perennial Classics, 2001.

Joseph, Dov, *The Faithful City: The Siege of Jerusalem 1948*, New York: Simon and Schuster, 1960.

Juergensmeyer, Mark, *Terror in the Mind of God*, Berkeley, California: University of California Press, 2000.

Kark, Ruth, *American Consuls in the Holy Land 1832-1914*, Jerusalem, Israel: Magnes Press, The Hebrew University and Detroit, Michigan: Wayne State University Press, 1994.

Kark, Ruth, ed., *The Land That Became Israel: Studies in Historical Geography*, New Haven, Connecticut and Jerusalem: Yale University Press, Magnes Press in The Hebrew University, 1990.

Kark, Ruth, and Michael Oren-Nordheim, *Jerusalem And Its Environs: Quarters, Neighborhoods, Villages*, 1800-1948, Jerusalem and Detroit: Magnes Press in The Hebrew University and Wayne State University Press, 2001.

Karsh, Efraim, *The Arab-Israeli Conflict: The Palestine War 1948*, Botley, Oxford: Osprey Publishing Limited, 2002.

Karsh, Efraim, *Arafat's War: The Man and His Battle for Israeli Conquest*, New York: Grove Press, 2003.

Karsh, Efraim, *Fabricating History: The 'New Historians'" Second Edition*, London: Frank Cass, 2000.

Karsh, Efraim, *Islamic Imperialism: A History*, New Haven, Connecticut: Yale University Press, 2006.

Karsh, Efraim, ed., *Peace In the Middle East: The Challenge for Israel*, Portland, OR: Frank Cass and Company Ltd., 1994.

Karsh, Efraim, and Inari Karsh, *Empires of The Sand: The Struggle For Mastery In The Middle East 1789-1923*, Cambridge, Massachusetts: Harvard University Press, 2001.

Karsh, Efraim, and Gregory Mahler, *Israel At The Crossroads: The Challenge of Peace*, London: British Academic Press, 1994.

Katz, Amnon, *Israel: The Two Halves of the Nation*, Northport, Alabama: Inverted-A, 1999.

Katz, Samuel, *Battleground: Fact and Fantasy in Palestine, Revised Edition*, New York: Taylor Productions, Ltd., 2002.

Katz, Samuel, *Battletruth: The World and Israel*, Israel: Dvir, 1983

Katz, Samuel, *Days of Fire*, New York: Doubleday and Company, 1968.

Katz, Samuel, *The Hollow Peace*, Jerusalem: Dvir and & The Jerusalem Post, 1981.

Katz, Yossi, *Partner to Partition: The Jewish Agency's Partition Plan in the Mandate Era*, London: Frank Cass, 1998.

Kaufman, Menahem, *The Magnes-Philby Negotiations, 1929: The Historical Record*, Jerusalem: Magnes Press in The Hebrew University, 1998.

Kaufman, Menahem, *An Ambiguous Partnership: Non Zionists and Zionists in America*, 1939-1948, Detroit and Jerusalem: Wayne State University Press and The Hebrew University, 1991.

Kedourie, Elie, *In the Anglo-Arab Labyrinth: The McMahon-Husayn Correspondence and its Interpretations 1914-1939*, London and Portland, OR: Frank Cass, 2000.

Kedourie, Elie and Sylvia Haim eds., *Palestine and Israel in the 19th and 20th Centuries*, London: Frank Cass, 1982.

Kedourie, Elie and Sylvia Haim eds., *Zionism and Arabism in Palestine and Israel*, London: Frank Cass, 1982.

Kennedy, Hugh, *The Great Arab Conquests: How The Spread of Islam Changed The World We Live In*, Cambridge, MA: Da Capo Press, 2007.

Khalaf, Issa, *Politics in Palestine: Arab Factionalism and Social Disintegration*, 1939-1948, Albany, NY: State University of New York Press, 1991.

Khalidi, Rashid, *Palestinian Identity: The Construction of Modern National Consciousness*, New York: Columbia University Press, 1997.

Khalidi, Rashid, *Resurrecting Empire: Western Footprints and America's Perilous Path in The Middle East*, Boston, Massachusetts: Beacon Press, 2004.

Khalidi, Walid, ed., *All That Remains: The Palestinian Villages Occupied and Depopulated by Israel in 1948*, Jerusalem: Institute for Palestine Studies 1992.

Khalidi, Walid, *Before Their Diaspora: A Photographic History of the Palestinians*, 1876-1948, Jerusalem: Institute for Palestine Studies, 1991.

Khalidi, Walid, *From Haven to Conquest: Readings in Zionism and the Palestine Problem Until 1948*, Jerusalem: Institute for Palestine Studies, 1987.

Khalidi, Walid, *The Ownership of the U.S. Embassy Site in Jerusalem*, Jerusalem: Institute for Palestine Studies, 2000.

Khoury, Philip S., *Urban notables and Arab nationalism: The politics of Damascus 1860-1920*, New York: Cambridge University Press, 1983.

Kiernan, Thomas, *Arafat: The Man and the Myth*, New York: W.W. Norton and Company, Inc., 1976.

Kimche, Jon, *Palestine or Israel: The Untold Story of Why We Failed*, London: Secker and Warburg, 1973

Kimche, Jon, *The Second Arab Awakening*, London: Thames and Hudson, 1970.

Kimche, Jon, *The Unromantics: The Great Powers and the Balfour Declaration*, London: Weidenfeld and Nicolson, 1968.

Kimche, Jon and David Kimche, *Both Sides of the Hill: Britain and The Palestine War*, London: Secker and Warburg, 1960.

Kimmerling, Baruch, *The Invention and Decline of Israeliness: State, Society and the Military*, Berkeley, CA: The University of California Press, 2001.

Kimmerling, Baruch, ed., *The Israeli State and Society: Boundaries and Frontiers*, Albany, NY: State University of New York Press, 1989.

Kimmerling, Baruch, *Palestinians: The Making of a People*, New York: Free Press, 1993.

Kirk, George, *A Survey of International Affairs: The Middle East 1945-1950*, New York: Oxford University Press, 1954.

Kirk, George, *Survey of International Affairs 1939-1946: The Middle East in the War*, New York: Oxford University Press, 1953.

Kirkbride, Sir Alec Seath, *A Crackle of Thorns: Experiences in the Middle East*, London: John Murray Publishers, Ltd., 1956.

Kisch, F.H., *Palestine Diary*, London: Victor Gollancz Ltd., 1938.

Klein, Aaron, *Schmoozing With Terrorists*, Los Angeles, CA: A WND Book, 2007.

Klein, Menachem, *Jerusalem: The Contested City*, New York: New York University Press, 2001.

Klieman, Aharon, *Compromising Palestine: A Guide to Final Status Negotiations*, New York: Columbia University Press, 2000.

Klieman, Aaron S., *Foundations of British Policy in The Arab World: The Cairo Conference of 1921*, Baltimore, MD: The Johns Hopkins Press, 1970.

Knee, Stuart E., *The Concept of Zionist Dissent in the American Mind*, 1917-1941, New York: Robert Speller & Sons, 1979.

Knohl, Dov, ed., *Siege in the Hills of Hebron: The Battle of the Etzion Bloc*, New York: Thomas Yoseloff, 1958

Koestler, Arthur, *Promise and Fulfillment: Palestine 1917-1949*, London: Macmillan and Company, Ltd., 1949.

Kolinsky, Martin, *Britain's War In The Middle East: Strategy and Diplomacy*, 1936-42, New York: Palgrave, 1999.

Kolinsky, Martin, *Law, Order and Riots in Mandatory Palestine*, 1928-1935, New York: St. Martin's Press, 1993.

Korany, Bahgat and Ali E. Hillal Dessouki, *The Foreign Policies of Arab States: The Challenge of Change, Boulder*, CO: Westview Press, 1991.

Kozodoy, Neil, ed., *The Mideast Peace Process: An Autopsy*, New York: Encounter Books, 2006.

Kramer, Martin, *Middle East Lectures Number One*, Tel-Aviv: The Moshe Dayan Center for Middle East Studies of Tel Aviv University, 1995.

Krammer, Arnold, *The Forgotten Friendship: Israel and the Soviet Bloc 1947-53*, Urbana, IL: University of Illinois Press, 1974.

Kretzmer, David, *The Occupation of Justice: The Supreme Court of Israel and Occupied Territories*, Albany, NY: State University of New York, 2002.

Kupferschmidt, Uri M., *The Supreme Muslim Council: Islam Under the British Mandate for Palestine*, Boston and Leiden: Brill, 1985.

Kurtzer, Daniel C. and Scott B. Lasensky, *Negotiating Arab-Israeli Peace: American Leadership in the Middle East*, Washington, D.C.: United States Institute of Peace Press, 2008.

Kurzman, Dan, *Genesis 1948: The First Arab-Israeli War*, New York: The World Publishing Company, 1970.

Kymlicka, Will, *Politics in the Vernacular: Nationalism, Multiculturalism and Citizenship*, New York: Oxford University Press, 2001.

La Guardia, Anton, *War Without End: Israelis, Palestinians, and the Struggle for a Promised Land*, New York: Thomas Dunne Books, 2001.

Laffin, John, *The P.L.O. Connections*, London: Transworld Publishers, Ltd., 1983.

Lall, Arthur, *The UN and the Middle East Crisis, 1967*, Revised Edition, New York: Columbia University Press, 1970.

Langmuir, Gavin I., *Toward A Definition of Antisemitism*, Los Angles, CA: University of California Press, 1990.

Lapidoth, Ruth, *Autonomy: Flexible Solutions to Ethnic Conflicts*, Washington, D.C.: United States Institute of Peace Press, 1997.

Lapidoth, Ruth, and Moshe Hirsch, eds., *The Arab-Israel Conflict and Its Resolution: Selected Documents*, Boston: Martinus Nijhoff Publishers, 1992.

Lapp, Nancy L., ed., *The Tale of The Tell: Paul W. Lapp*, Pittsburgh, PA: The Pickwick Press, 1975.

Lapp, Paul W., *Biblical Archaeology and History*, New York: The World Publishing Company, 1969.

Laqueur, Walter, *The Changing Face of Anti-Semitism*, New York: Oxford University Press, 2006.

Laqueur, Walter, *Confrontation: The Middle East and World Politics*, New York: Quadrangle, 1974.

Laqueur, Walter, *The Road to Jerusalem: The Arab-Israeli Conflict*, New York: The Macmillan Company, 1968.

Laqueur, Walter, and Barry M. Rubin, eds., *The Israel-Arab Reader: A Documentary History of the Middle East Conflict*, New York: Penguin, 1995.

Latour, Anny, *The Resurrection of Israel: How the Modern State was Born*, New York: The World Publishing Company, 1968.

Lazare, Bernard, *Antisemitism: Its History and Causes*, Lincoln, NE: University of Nebraska Press, 1995.

Lee, Martin A., *The Beast Reawakens*, Boston and New York: Little, Brown and Company, 1997.

Lehrman, Hal, *Israel: The Beginning and Tomorrow*, New York: William Sloane and Associates, 1951.

Leibler, Isi, *The Case For Israel*, Australia: The Executive Council of Australian Jewry, 1972.

Lemche, Niles Peter, *The Israelites in History and Tradition*, Louisville, Kentucky: Westminster John Knox Press, 1998.

Lesch, David W., *The Arab-Israeli Conflict: A History*, New York: Oxford University Press, 2008.

Levenberg, Haim, *The Military Preparations of the Arab Community in Palestine 1945-1948*, London: Frank Cass, 1993.

Levin, Harry, *Jerusalem Embattled: A Diary of the City Under Siege*, London: Cassell, 1997.

Levin, Itamar, *Confiscated Wealth: The Fate of Jewish Property in Arab Land*, Institute of the World Jewish Congress, 2000.

Levin, Kenneth, *The Oslo Syndrome: Delusions of a People Under Siege*, Hanover, NH: Smith and Kraus Global, 2005.

Levine, Lee I., ed., *The Jerusalem Cathedra: Studies In The History, Archaeology, Geography and Ethnography of The Land Of Israel*, Jerusalem: Yad Ben-Zvi Institute and Detroit, MI: Wayne State University Press, 1981.

Levine, Mark, *Overthrowing Geography: Jaffa, Tel Aviv, and The Struggle For Palestine*, 1880-1948, Berkeley, CA: University of California Press, 2005.

Levitt, Matthew, *Hamas: Politics, Charity, and Terrorism in the Service of Jihad*, New Haven, Connecticut: Yale University Press, 2006.

Lewin, Ariel, *The Archaeology of Ancient Judea and Palestine*, Los Angeles, CA: J. Paul Getty Trust, 2005.

Lewis, Bernard, *The Crisis of Islam: Holy War and Unholy Terror*, New York: Modern Library, 2003.

Lewis, Bernard, *Cultures in Conflict: Christians, Muslims and Jews in the Age of Discovery*, New York: Oxford University Press, 1995.

Lewis, Bernard, *From Babel to Dragomans*, New York: Oxford University Press, 2004.

Lewis, Bernard, *Islam and the West*, New York: Oxford University Press, 1994

Lewis, Bernard, *The Jews of Islam*, Princeton, NJ: Princeton University Press, 1987.

Lewis, Bernard, *The Middle East: A Brief History of the Last 2,000 Years*, New York: Touchstone Books, 1997.

Lewis, Bernard, *A Middle East Mosaic: Fragments of Life, Letters and History*, New York: Random House, 2000.

Lewis, Bernard, *The Multiple Identities of the Middle East*, New York: Schocken Books, 2001.

Lewis, Bernard, *Semites and Anti-Semites: An Inquiry into Conflict and Prejudice*, New York: W.W. Norton and Company, 1999.

Lewis, Bernard, *What Went Wrong: Western Impact and Middle Eastern Response*, New York: Oxford University Press, 2001

Lie, Trygve, *In The Cause of Peace: Seven Years with the United Nations*, New York: The Macmillan Company, 1954.

Liebes, Tamar, *Reporting the Arab-Israeli Conflict: How Hegemony Works*, New York: Routledge, 1997.

Likhovski, Assaf, *Law and Identity in Mandate Palestine*, Chapel Hill, NC: University of North Carolina Press, 2008.

Lippmann, Walter, *U.S. War Aims*, Boston, Massachusetts: Little, Brown and Company, 1944.

Litvak, Meir, Ed., *Palestinian Collective Memory and National Identity*, New York: Palgrave Macmillan, 2009.

Locker, Berl, *Covenant Everlasting: Palestine in Jewish History*, New York: Sharon Books, 1947.

Lockman, Zachary, *Comrades and Enemies: Arab and Jewish Workers in Palestine, 1906-1948*, Berkeley, CA: University of California Press, 1996.

Lockman, Zachary, and Joel Benin, eds., *Intifada: The Palestinian Uprising Against Israel Occupation*, Cambridge, Massachusetts: South End Press, 1989.

Lorch, Netanel, *The Edge of the Sword: Israel's War of Independence 1947-1949*, New York: G. P. Putnam's Sons, 1961.

Lorch, Netanel, *One Long War: Arab Versus Jew Since 1920*, Jerusalem: Keter Publishing, 1976.

Louis, William Roger, *The British Empire In The Middle East 1945-1951*, New York: Oxford University Press, 2006

Louis, William Roger, **In The Name Of God, Go!: Leo Amery and the British Empire in the Age of Churchill**, New York: W.W. Norton and Company, 1992.

Louis, William Roger, and Robert W. Stookey, *The End of the Palestine Mandate*, Austin, TX: University of Texas Press, 1986.

Lowdermilk, Walter Clay, *Palestine: Land of Promise*, New York: Harper and Brothers Publishers, 1944.

Lozowick, Yaacov, *Right to Exist: A Moral Defense of Israel's Wars*, New York: Doubleday, 2003.

Lukacs, Yehuda, *The Israeli-Palestinian Conflict: A Documentary Record 1967-1990*, New York: Cambridge University Press, 1992.

Magnus, Philip, *Kitchener: Portrait of an Imperialist*, New York: E.P. Dutton, 1968.

Makiya, Kanan, *Cruelty and Silence*, New York: W.W. Norton and Company, 1993.

Makovsky, David, *Making Peace with the PLO: The Rabin Government's Road to the Oslo Accord*, Boulder, CO: Westview Press, 1996.

Makovsky, David, *Engagement through Disengagement: Gaza and the Potential for Renewed Israeli-Palestinian Peacemaking*, (Washington, D.C.: Washington Institute for Near East Policy, 2005)

Makovsky, Michael, *Churchill's Promised Land: Zionism and Statecraft*, New Haven, CT: Yale University Press, 2007.

Mamet, David, *The Wicked Son: Anti-Semitism, Self-Hatred, and The Jews*, New York: Schocken, 2006.

Mandel, Neville J., *The Arabs And Zionism Before World War I*, Berkeley, CA: University of California Press, 1976.

Mansour, Camille, *Beyond Alliance: Israel in U.S. Foreign Policy*, New York: Columbia University Press, 1994.

Manuel, Frank E., *The Realities of American-Palestine Relations*, Washington, D.C.: Public Affairs Press, 1949.

Ma'oz, Moshe, ed., *Palestinian Arab Politics*, Jerusalem, Israel: The Jerusalem Academic Press for the Harry S Truman Research Institute of The Hebrew University of Jerusalem Mount Scopus, 1975.

Ma'oz, Moshe, ed., *Studies on Palestine During the Ottoman Period*, Jerusalem: Magnes Press, 1975.

Marlowe, John, *Rebellion In Palestine*, London: The Cresset Press, 1946.

Masalha, Nur, *Expulsion of the Palestinians: The Concept of 'Transfer' in Zionist Political Thought*, 1882-1948, Washington, D.C.: Institute for Palestine Studies, 1992.

Masalha, Nur, *Imperial Israel and the Palestinians: The Politics of Expansion Jerusalem*, Institute for Palestine Studies, 2000.

Masalha, Nur, *A Land Without a People: Israel, Transfer and the Palestinians 1946-96*, London: Faber and Faber, 1997.

Masalha, Nur, *The Bible and Zionism: Invented Traditions, Archeology and Post-Colonialism in Israel-Palestine*, New York: Zed Books, Ltd. 2007.

Mazar, Amihai, *Archaeology of the Land of the Bible: 10,000-586 B.C.E.*, New York: Doubleday, 1992.

McCarthy, Andrew C., *Willful Blindness: A Memoir of the Jihad*, New York: Encounter Books, 2008.

McCarthy, Justin, *The Population of Palestine: Population Statistics of The Late Ottoman Period And The Mandate*, New York: Columbia University Press, 1990.

McDonald, James G., *My Mission in Israel: 1948-1951*, New York: Simon and Schuster, 1951.

McGeough, Paul, *Kill Khalid: The Failed Assassination of Khalid Mishal and the Rise of Hamas*, New York: The New Press, 2009.

McGowan, Daniel and Marc H. Ellis, eds., *Remembering Deir Yassin: The Future of Israel and Palestine*, New York: Olive Branch Press, 1998.

Medding, Peter Y., *The Founding of Israeli Democracy*, 1948-1967, New York: Oxford University Press, 1990.

Medoff, Rafael and Chaim I. Waxman, *Baksheesh Diplomacy: Secret Negotiations Between American Jewish Leaders and Arab Officials on the Eve of World War II*, Lanham, MD: Lexington Books, 2001.

Medoff, Rafael and Chaim I. Waxman, *Historical Dictionary of Zionism*, Lanham, Maryland: The Scarecrow Press, 2000.

Medoff, Rafael, *Militant Zionism in America: The Rise and Impact of the Jabotinsky Movement in the United States*, 1926-1948, Tuscaloosa and London: The University of Alabama Press, 2002.

Medoff, Rafael, *Zionism and the Arabs: An American Jewish Dilemma*, 1898-1948, Westport, CT Praeger, 1997

Meinertzhagen, Richard Colonel, *Middle East Diary 1917-1956*, New York: Thomas Yoseloff, 1959.

Meir-Levi, David, *History Upside Down: The Roots of Palestinian Fascism and the Myth of Israeli Aggression*, New York: Encounter Books, 2007.

Mendelsohn, Ezra, *On Modern Politics*, New York: Oxford University Press, 1993.

Metzer, Jacob, *The Divided Economy of Mandatory Palestine*, Cambridge, England: Cambridge University Press, 1998.

Michman, Dan, *Holocaust Historiography: A Jewish Perspective*, Portland, Oregon: Vallentine Mitchell, 2003.

Miller, Aaron David, *The Much Too Promised Land: America's Elusive Search for Arab-Israeli Peace*, New York: Bantam Dell, 2008.

Miller, Rory, *Ireland and the Palestine Question: 1948-2004*, Dublin: Irish Academic Press, 2005.

Mills, Walter, ed., *The Forrestal Diaries*, New York: The Viking Press, 1951.

Minerbi, Sergio I., *The Vatican And Zionism: Conflict in the Holy Land 1895-1925*, New York: Oxford University Press, 1990.

Mishal, Shaul and Avraham Sela, *The Palestinian Hamas: Vision, Violence and Coexistence*, New York: Columbia University Press, 2000.

Mishal, Shaul and Reuben Aharoni, *Speaking Stones: Communiqués from the Intifada Underground*, Syracuse, New York: Syracuse University Press, 1994.

Monroe, Elizabeth, *Britain's Moment in the Middle East*, 1914-1956, London: Chatto and Windus, 1963.

Monroe, Elizabeth, *Philby of Arabia*, London: Pitman, 1973.

Morgenstern, Arie, *Hastening Redemption: Messianism and the Resettlement of the Land of Israel*, New York: Oxford University Press, 2006.

Morris, Benny, *1948 and After: Israel and the Palestinians*, New York: Oxford University Press, 1990.

Morris, Benny, *1948: The First Arab-Israeli War*, New Haven: Yale University Press, 2008.

Morris, Benny, *The Birth of the Palestinian Refugee Problem*, 1947-1949, Cambridge: Cambridge University Press, 1987.

Morris, Benny, *The Birth of the Palestinian Refugee Problem Revisited*, New York: Cambridge University Press, 2004.

Morris, Benny, *Israel's Border Wars: 1949-1956*, Revised and Expanded. New York: Oxford University Press, 2005

Morris, Benny, *Righteous Victims: A History of the Zionist-Arab Conflict*, 1881-1999, New York: Vintage Books, 2001.

Morris, Benny, *The Road to Jerusalem: Glubb Pasha, Palestine and the Jews*, New York and London: I.B. Tauris, 2002.

Mosse, George L., *Confronting the Nation: Jewish and Western Nationalism*, Hanover, NH: Brandeis University Press; University Press of New England, 1993.

Mosse, George L., *Germans and Jews*, New York: Grosset and Dunlap, 1970.

Mossek, Moshe, *Palestine Immigration Policy Under Sir Herbert Samuel: British, Zionist and Arab Attitudes*, London: Frank Cass, 1978.

Muasher, Marwan, *The Arab Center: The Promise of Moderation*, New Haven, CT: Yale University Press, 2008.

Muller, James W., ed., *Churchill as Peacemaker*, Cambridge: Press Syndicate of the University of Cambridge, 1997.

Muravchik, Joshua, *Covering The Intifada: How the Media Reported the Palestinian Uprising*, Washington, D.C.: Washington Institute for Near East Policy, 2003.

Murphy-O'Connor, *The holy land: An Oxford Archaeological Guide*, New York: Oxford University Press. 2008.

Muslih, Muhammad Y., *The Origins of Palestinian Nationalism*, New York: Columbia University Press, 1989.

Muslih, Muhammad Y., *Golan: The Road to Occupation*, Jerusalem: Institute for Palestine Studies, 2000.

Nafi, Basheer M., *Arabism, Islamism, and the Palestine Question 1908-1941: A Political History*, Reading, UK: Garner Publishing Limited, 1998.

Nazzal, Nafez Y. and Laila A. Nazzal, *Historical Dictionary of Palestine*, Lanham, MD: Scarecrow Press, 1997.

Netanyahu, Benjamin, *A Durable Peace: Israel and Its Place Among the Nations*, New York: Warner Books, 2000.

Netanyahu, Benjamin, *A Place Among The Nations: Israel and the World*, New York: Bantam Books, 1993.

Netanyahu, Benjamin, *Fighting Terrorism : How Democracies Can Defeat Domestic and International Terrorists*, New York: Noonday Press, 1997.

Netanyahu, Benjamin, *International Terrorism: Challenge and Response*, Piscataway, NJ: Transaction Publishers, 1981.

Neumann, Emanuel, *In The Arena: An Autobiographical Memoir*, New York: Herzel Press, 1976.

Nicosia, Francis R., *The Third Reich and the Palestine Question*, Piscataway, New Jersey: Transaction Publishers, 2000.

Nir, Yeshayahu, *The Bible and the Image: The History of Photography in the Holy Land*, 1839-1899, Philadelphia, PA: University of Pennsylvania Press, 1985.

Nirenstein, Fiamma, *Terror: The New Anti-Semitism and the War Against the West*, Hanover, New Hampshire: Smith and Kraus Global, 2005.

Norman, Theodore, *An Outstretched Arm: A History of the Jewish Colonization Association*, Boston, MA: Routledge and Kegan Paul, 1985.

Norris, Pippa, Montague Kern, and Marion Just, eds., *Framing Terrorism: The News Media, the Government and the Public*, New York: Routledge, 2003.

Norton, Augustus Richard, *Hezbollah: A Short History*, Princeton, NJ: Princeton University Press, 2007.

Nusseibeh, Sari with Anthony David, *Once Upon a Country: A Palestinian Life*, New York: Farrar, Straus and Giroux, 2007.

O'Brien, Conner Cruise, *The Siege: The Saga of Israel and Zionism*, New York: Simon and Schuster, 1986.

Ofer, Dalia, *Escaping the Holocaust: Illegal Immigration to the Land of Israel*, 1939-1944, New York: Oxford University Press, 1990.

Oliver, Anne Marie and Paul Steinberg, *The Road to Martyr's Square: A Journey into the World of the Suicide Bomber*, New York: Oxford University Press, 2006.

Oren, Michael B., *Power, Faith and Fantasy: America in the Middle East to the Present*, New York: W.W. Norton, 2007.

Oren, Michael B., *Six Days of War: June 1967 and the Making of the Modern Middle East*, New York: Oxford University Press, 2002.

Orni, Efraim, *Geography of Israel*, Philadelphia, PA: The Jewish Publication Society, 1971.

Orr, Akiva, *Israel, Politics, Myths and Identity Crises*, London: Pluto Press, 1994.

Ovendale, Ritchie, *The Origins of the Arab-Israeli Wars*, New York: Longman Group Limited, 1984.

Oz, Amos, *In The Land Of Israel*, New York: Harcourt Brace Jovanovich, 1983.

Oz, Amos, *Israel, Palestine and Peace*, London: Vintage Book, 1994.

Paikert, G.C., *The German Exodus: A Selective Study on the Post World War II Expulsion of German Populations and its Effects*, The Hague: Martinus Nijhoff, 1962.

Palestine, Jewish Agency for and Anglo-American Committee of Inquiry on Jewish Problems in Palestine and Europe, *The Jewish Case before the Anglo-American Committee of Inquiry on Palestine as Presented By the Jewish Agency for Palestine: Statements and Memoranda*, Jerusalem: The Jewish Agency for Palestine, 1947.

Palumbo, Michael, *The Palestinian Catastrophe: The 1948 Expulsion of a People from their Homeland*, London and Boston: Faber and Faber, 1987

Pappé, Ilan, ed., *Israel/Palestine Question: Rewriting Histories*, New York: Routledge, 1999.

Pappé, Ilan, ed., *The Making of the Arab-Israeli Conflict*, 1947-1951, New York and London: I B Tauris, 2001.

Parfitt, Tudor, ed., *Israel and Ishmael: Studies in Muslim Jewish Relation*, New York: St. Martin's Press, 2000.

Parfitt, Tudor, *The Jews In Palestine: 1800-1882*, Suffolk, England: Royal Historical Society, 1987.

Parkes, James, *The Jewish Problem in the Modern World*, New York: Oxford University Press, 1946.

Parkes, James, *Whose Land? A History of the Peoples of Palestine*, New York: Penguin, 1970.

Patai, Raphael, *Journeyman in Jerusalem: Memoirs and Letters*, 1933-1947, Salt Lake City, UT: University of Utah Press, 1992.

Paul, Shalom and William G. Dever, ed., *Biblical Archaeology*, New York: Quadrangle/ The New York Times Press Company, 1974.

Pearlman, Moshe, *Ben Gurion Looks Back*, New York: Simon and Schuster, 1965.

Pearlman, Moshe, *Mufti of Jerusalem: Haj Amin El Husseini, A Father of Jihad*, Philadelphia, PA: Pavilion Press, 2006.

Peleg, Ilan, *The Middle East Peace Process: Interdisciplinary Perspective*, Albany: State University of New York Press, 1998.

Penkower, Monty Noam, *Decision on Palestine Deferred: America, Britain and Wartime Diplomacy 1939-1945*, London: Frank Cass Publishers, 2002.

Penkower, Monty Noam, *The Emergence of Zionist Thought*, Millwood, New York: Associated Faculty Press, 1986.

Penkower, Monty Noam, *The Holocaust and Israel Reborn: From Catastrophe to Sovereignty*, Urbana-Champaign, IL: University of Illinois Press, 1994.

Peres, Shimon, *Battling For Peace: A Memoir*, New York: Random House, 1995.

Peres, Shimon, *David's Sling*, London: Weidenfeld and Nicolson, 1970.

Peres, Shimon, *For The Future of Israel*, Baltimore, MD: Johns Hopkins University Press, 1998.

Phillips, Harlan B., *Felix Frankfurter Reminisces: An Intimate Portrait as Recorded in Talks With Dr. Harlan B. Phillips*, New York: Reynal and Company, 1960.

Poel, Jean Van Der, ed., *Selections from the Smut Papers* (September 1919-November 1934), Vol. 5, New York: Cambridge University Press, 2007.

Polish, David, *'Give Us a King:' Legal-Religious Sources of Jewish Sovereignty*, Hoboken, NJ: KTAV Publishing House, 1989.

Polk, William R., *The United States and the Arab World*, Cambridge, MA: Harvard University Press, 1969.

Porat, Dina and Roni Stauber, *Antisemitism Worldwide*, Tel Aviv: The Stephen Roth Institute for the Study of Contemporary Antisemitism and Racism, 2003.

Porat, Dina, *The Blue and the Yellow Stars of David: The Zionist Leadership in Palestine and the Holocaust 1939-1945*, Cambridge, MA: Harvard University Press, 1990.

Porath, Yehoshua, *The Emergence of the Palestinian Arab National Movement*, 1918-1929, London: Frank Cass, 1974.

Porath, Yehoshua, *The Palestinian Arab National Movement*, 1929-1939, London: Frank Cass, 1977.

Possony, Stefan T., *A Century of Conflict: Communist Techniques of World Revolution*, Chicago, IL: Henry Regnery Company, 1953.

Prior, Michael, *Zionism and the State of Israel: A Moral Inquiry*, New York: Routledge, 1999.

Prittie, Terence, *Whose Jerusalem?* London: Frederick Muller Limited, 1981.

Pryce-Jones, David, *Betrayal: France, The Arabs, And The Jews*, New York: Encounter Books. 2006.

Pryce-Jones, David, *The Closed Circle: An Interpretation of the Arabs*, Chicago: Ivan R. Dee, 2002.

Pryce-Jones, David, *The Face of Defeat: Palestinian Refugees and Guerrillas*, London,Weidenfeld and Nicolson, 1972.

Quandt, William B., *Decade of Decisions: American Policy Toward the Arab-Israeli Conflict, 1967-1976*, Berkeley, CA: University of California Press, 1977.

Quandt, William B., *Fuad Jabber, and Ann Mosely Lesch, The Politics of Palestinian Nationalism*, Berkeley, CA: University of California Press, 1973.

Quigley, John, *Palestine and Israel: A Challenge to Justice*, Durham, NC: Duke University Press, 1990.

Rabin, Yitzhak, *The Rabin Memoirs*, Bnei Brak, Israel: Steimatzky, Ltd., 1979.

Rabinovich, Abraham, *The Yom Kippur War: The Epic Encounter That Transformed The Middle East*, New York: Schocken Books, 2004.

Rabinovich, Itamar, *The Road Not Taken: Early Arab-Israeli Negotiations*, New York: Oxford University Press, 1991.

Rabinovich, Itamar and Jehuda Reinharz, eds., *Israel in The Middle East: Documents and Readings on Society, Politics and Foreign Relations, 1948-Present*, New York: Oxford University, 1984.

Rabinowitz, Dan and Khawla Abu-Baker, *Coffins on Our Shoulders: The Experience of the Palestinian Citizens of Israel*, Berkeley, CA: University of California Press, 2005.

Radosh, Allis and Ronald Radosh, *A Safe Haven: Harry S. Truman and The Founding of Israel*, New York: HarperCollins Publishers, 2009.

Radyshevsky, Dmitry, ed., *The Jerusalem Alternative: Moral Clarity for Ending the Arab-Israeli Conflict*, Green Forest, AR: Balfour Books, 2004.

Ravitzky, Aviezer, *Messianism, Zionism and Jewish Radicalism*, Chicago, Illinois: University of Chicago Press, 1996.

Ray, James Lee, *The Future of America-Israeli Relations: A Parting of the Ways*, Lexington, KY: University of Kentucky Press, 1985.

Reich, Walter, ed., *Origins of Terrorism: Psychologies, Ideologies, Theologies, States of Mind*, Washington, D.C.: Woodrow Wilson Center Press, 1998.

Reinhart, Tanya, *Israel/Palestine: How to End The War of 1948*, New York: Seven Stories Press, 2002.

Reinharz, Jehuda, ed., *Living With Antisemitism: Modern Jewish Responses*, Hanover, New HH: University of New England, 1987.

Reinharz, Jehuda, and Anita Shapira, eds., *Essential Papers on Zionism*, New York: New York University Press, 1996.

Reiter, Yitzhak, *Islamic Endowments in Jerusalem Under British Mandate*, Portland, OR: Frank Cass, 1996.

Reiter, Yitzhak, *Jerusalem and its Role in Islamic Solidarity*, New York: Palgrave Macmillan, 2008.

Reiter, Yitzhak, *Regional Majority: Palestinian Arabs Versus Jews in Israel*, Syracuse, NY: Syracuse University Press, 2009

Renton, James, *The Zionist Masquerade: The Birth of the Anglo-Zionist Alliance*, 1914-1918, New York: Palgrave Macmillan, 2007

Rice, Michael, *False Inheritance: Israel in Palestine and the Search For a Solution*, London and New York: Kegan Paul International, 1994.

Rifkind, Simon H., et. al., *The Basic Equities of the Palestine Problem*, New York: Arno Press, 1977.

Robinson, E. and E. Smith, *Biblical Researches in Palestine and In the Adjacent Regions: Journal of Travels In The Year 1838*, Volume II, Boston, MA: Crocker and Brewster, 1856.

Robinson, Jacob, *Palestine and The United Nations: Prelude to Solution*, Westport, CT: Public Affairs Press, 1947.

Rodinson, Maxime, *Cult, Ghetto, and State: The Persistence of the Jewish Question*, London: Al Saqi Books, 1983.

Rogan, Eugene L. and Avi Shlaim, eds., *The War for Palestine: Rewriting the History of 1948*, Cambridge: Cambridge University Press, 2001.

Rogers, Mary Eliza, *Domestic Life in Palestine*, Cincinnati, OH: Poe and Hitchcock, 1865.

Romann, Michael, *Living Together Separately: Arabs and Jews In Contemporary Jerusalem*, Princeton, NJ: Princeton University Press, 1991.

Roosevelt, Kermit, *Arabs, Oil and History: The Story of the Middle East*, New York: Harper and Brother Publishers, 1949.

Rose, N.A., ed., *Baffy: The Diaries of Blanche Dugdale 1936-1947*, London: Vallentine, Mitchell, 1973.

Rose, N.A., *The Gentile Zionists: A Study in Anglo-Zionist Diplomacy 1929-1939*, London: Frank Cass, 1973.

Rose, Norman, *Chaim Weizmann: A Biography*, New York: Viking Penguin Books, 1986.

Rose, Norman, ed., *From Palmerston to Balfour: Collected Essays of Mayir Verete*, Portland, OR, 1992.

Ross, Dennis, *The Missing Peace: The Inside Story of the Fight for Middle East Peace*, New York: Farrar, Straus and Giroux, 2004.

Ross, Dennis and David Makovsky, *Myths, Illusions, and Peace: Finding a New Direction for America in the Middle East*, (New York: Viking/Penguin, 2009)

Rotenstreich, Nathan, *Essays on Zionism and the Contemporary Jewish Condition*, New York: Herzl Press, 1980.

Rubin, Barry, *The Arab States and the Palestine Conflict*, Syracuse: Syracuse University Press, 1981.

Rubin, Barry, and Judith Colp Rubin. *Yasir Arafat: A Political Biography*. New York: Oxford University Press, 2003.

Rubinstein, Alvin Z., ed., *The Arab-Israeli Conflict: Perspectives, Second Edition*, New York: HarperCollins, 1991.

Rubinstein, Amnon, *From Herzl to Rabin: The Changing Image of Zionism*, New York: Holmes & Meier Publishers, Inc., 2000.

Rubenstein, Danny, *The People of Nowhere: The Palestinian Vision of Home*, New York: Random House, 1991.

Ruppin, Arthur, *Three Decades of Palestine: Speeches and Papers on the Upbuilding of the Jewish National Home*, Westport, CT: Greenwood Press Publishers, 1975.

Rusk, Dean, *As I Saw It*, New York: Penguin Books, 1990.

Safran, Nadav, *From War to War: The Arab-Israeli Confrontation*, 1948-1967, Indianapolis, IN: Pegasus, 1969.

Safran, Nadav, *Israel : The Embattled Ally*, Cambridge, MA: Belknap Press, 1978.

Said, Edward W., *Covering Islam: How the Media and the Experts Determine How We See the Rest of the World*, New York: Vintage Books, 1997.

Said, Edward W., *End of the Peace Process: Oslo and After*, New York: Pantheon Books, 2000.

Said, Edward W., *Out of Place: A Memoir*, New York: Vintage Books, 2000.

Said, Edward W., *Peace and Its Discontents: Essays on Palestine in the Middle East Peace Process*, New York: Vintage Books, 1995.

Said, Edward W., *The Politics of Dispossession*, New York: Vintage Books Edition, 1995.

Said, Edward W., *The Question of Palestine*, New York: Vintage Books, 1992.

Said, Edward and Christopher Hitchens, eds., *Blaming the Victims: Spurious Scholarship and the Palestinian Question*, New York: Verso, 1989.

Salinas, Moises F., *Planting Hatred, Sowing Pain: The Psychology of the Israeli-Palestinian Conflict*, Westport, CT: Praeger, 2007.

Salzman, Philip Carl, *Culture and Conflict in the Middle East*, Amherst, New York: Humanity Books, 2008.

Sanders, Ronald, *The High Walls of Jerusalem: A History of the Balfour Declaration and the Birth of the British Mandate for Palestine*, New York: Holt, Rinehart and Winston, 1983.

Saposnik, Arieh Bruce, *Becoming Hebrew: The Creation of a Jewish National Culture in Ottoman Palestine*, New York: Oxford University Press, 2008.

Satloff, Robert, *Among The Righteous: Lost Stories From The Holocaust's Long Reach Into Arab Lands*, New York: PublicAffairs, 2006.

Sayigh, Rosemary, *Palestinians: From Peasants to Revolutionaries*, London: Zed Press, 1979.

Schafer, Peter, *Attitudes Toward the Jews in the Ancient World*, Cambridge, MA: Harvard University Press, 1997.

Scham, Paul, Walid Salem, and Benjamin Pogrund, eds., *Shared Histories: A Palestinian Dialogue*, Jerusalem: Palestinian Center for the Dissemination and Community Development (Panorama) and the Yakar Center for Social Concern, 2005.

Schechtman, Joseph B., *The Mufti and the Fuehrer*, New York: Thomas Yoseloff, 1965.

Schmidt, Sarah, Horace M. Kallen: *Prophet of American Zionism*, Brooklyn, New York: Carlson Publishing Inc., 1993.

Schoenbaum, David, *The United States and the State of Israel*, New York: Oxford University Press, 1993.

Schoenfeld, Gabriel, *The Return of Anti-Semitism*, San Francisco, CA: Encounter Books, 2003.

Scholch, Alexander, *Palestine In Transformation 1856-1882: Studies In Social, Economic and Political Development*, Washington, D. C.: The Institute for Palestine Studies, 1993.

Schwanitz, G. Wolfgang, ed., *Germany and the Middle East: 1871-1945*, Princeton, NJ: Markus Wiener Publishers, 2004.

Schwarz, Rabbi Joseph, *A Descriptive Geography and Brief Historical Sketch of Palestine, (For Sixteen Years A Resident in the Holy Land)*. (Philadelphia, PA: A Hart, Late Cary and Hart, 1850.

Seabury, Paul, *The Wilhelmstrass: A study of German Diplomats Under Nazi Rule*, Berkeley, California: University of California Press, 1954.

Segel, Binjamin W. and Richard S. Levy, eds., *A Lie and a Libel: The History of the Protocols of the Elders of Zion*, Lincoln, NE: University of Nebraska Press, 1996.

Segev, Tom, 1949, *The First Israelis*, New York: Henry Holt, 1998.

Segev, Tom, *One Palestine, Complete: Jews and Arabs Under the British Mandate*, New York: Metropolitan Books, 2000.

Segev, Tom, *The Seventh Million: The Israelis and the Holocaust*, New York: Hill and Wang, 1993.

Segev, Tom, *The United States and the Jewish State Movement: The Crucial Decade*, 1939-1949, New York: Herzl Press, 1966.

Sela, Avraham, *The Decline of the Arab- Israeli Conflict: Middle East Politics and the Quest for Regional Order*, Albany, NY: State University of New York, 1998.

Seliktar, Ofira, *Doomed to Failure? The Politics and Intelligence of the Oslo Process*, (Santa Barbara, CA: ABC CLIO, 2009)

Shahak, Israel, *Jewish History, Jewish Religion: The Weight of Three Thousand Years*, London: Pluto Press, 1994.

Shalom, Zaki, *David Ben-Gurion: The State of Israel, and the Arab World*, 1949-1956, Brighton and Portland: Sussex University Press, 2002.

Shamir, Yitzhak, *Summing Up: An Autobiography*, London: Weidenfeld and Nicolson, 1994.

Shanks, Hershel, *The City of David: A Guide to Biblical Judaism*, Washington, D.C.: The Biblical Archeology Society, 1975.

Shanks, Hershel, *Recent Archaeology in the Land of Israel*, Washington, D.C. Biblical Archaeology Society, 1985.

Shapira, Anita, *Land and Power: The Zionist Resort to Force 1881-1948*, New York: Oxford University Press, 1992.

Shapiro, Yonathan, *Leadership of the American Zionist Organization. 1897-1930*, Urbana, IL: University of Illinois Press, 1971.

Sharabi, Hisham, *Palestine and the Israelis: The Lethal Dilemma*, New York: Pegasus, 1969.

Sharansky, Natan, *The Case for Democracy: The Power of Freedom to Overcome Tyranny and Terror*, New York: PublicAffairs, 2004.

Sharef, Zeev, *Three Days*, London: W.H. Allen, 1962.

Sharon, Ariel and David Chanoff, *Warrior: The Autobiography of Ariel Sharon*, New York: A Touchtone Book, 2001.

Shaw, Walter S., *Report of the Commission on the Palestine Disturbances of August 1929*, London: His Majesty's Stationery Office, 1930.

Shepherd, Naomi, *Ploughing Sand: British Rule in Palestine 1917-1948*, New Brunswick, NJ: Rutgers University Press, 2000.

Shepherd, Robin, *A State Beyond the Pale, Europes Problem with Israel*, London: Weidenfeld and Nicolson, 2009.

Shermer, Michael and Alex Grobman, *Denying History: Who Says the Holocaust Never Happened and Why Do They Say It?* Berkeley, CA: University of California Press, 2000.

Shimoni, Gideon, *The Zionist Ideology, Hanover: Brandeis University Press*, University Press of New England, 1995.

Shindler, Colin, *The Triumph of Military Zionism: Nationalism and the Origins of the Israeli Right*, New York: Palgrave Macmillan, 2006.

Shipler, David K., *Arab and Jew: Wounded Spirits in a Promised Land*, New York: Penguin, 1987.

Shpiro, David H., *From Philanthropy to Activism: The Political Transformation of American Zionism in the Holocaust Years 1933-1945*, New York: Pergamon Press, 1994.

Shulewitz, Malka Hillel, *The Forgotten Millions: The Modern Jewish Exodus from Arab Lands*, London and New York: Continuum International, 2000.

Sicker, Martin, *Between Hashemites and Zionists: The Struggle for Palestine*, 1908-1988, New York: Holmes and Meier, 1989.

Sid-Ahmed, *Mohamed, After The Guns Fall Silent: Peace or Armageddon in the Middle East*, London: Croom Held, Ltd., 1976.

Silberstein, Laurence J., *The Postzionism Debates: Knowledge and Power in Israeli Culture*, New York: Routledge, 1999.

Silver, Abba Hillel, *Vision and Victory: A Collection of Addresses by Dr. Abba Hillel Silver*, 1942-1948, New York: The Zionist Organization of America, 1949.

Simpson, John Hope, *Report on Immigration, Land Settlement and Development*, London: His Majesty's Stationery Office, 1930.

Singer, Max and Aaron Wildavsky, *The Real World Order: Zones of Peace, Zones of Turmoil*, Chatham, NJ: Chatham House Publishers, Inc., 1993

Sivan, Emmanuel, *Radical Islam: Medieval Theology and Modern Politics*, New Haven, Connecticut: Yale University Press, 1985.

Slonim, Shlomo, *Jerusalem in America's Foreign Policy*, 1947-1997, New York: Kluwer Law International, 1999.

Smelser, Neil J., *The Faces of Terrorism: Social and Psychological Dimensions*, Princeton, New Jersey: Princeton University Press, 2007.

Smith, Barbara J., *The Roots of Separatism in Palestine: British Economic Policy*, 1920-1929, Syracuse, NY: Syracuse University Press, 1993.

Smith, Charles D., *Palestine and the Arab-Israeli Conflict*, New York: Bedford/St. Martin's, 1995.

Smith, Charles D., *Palestine and the Arab-Israeli Conflict, 6th Edition*, Boston, MA: Bedford/St. Martin's, 2007.

Smith, Lee, *The Strong Horse: Power, Politics, and the Crash of Arab Civilizations*, (New York: Random House, 2009)

Smith, Wilfred Cantwell, *Islam In Modern History*, New York: The New American Library, 1957.

Sofer, Sasson, *Zionism and the Foundations of Israeli Diplomacy*, New York: Cambridge University Press, 1998.

Sohar, Ezra, *A Concubine in the Middle East: American-Israeli Relations*, Jerusalem: Gefen Publishing House, 1999.

Soshuk, Levi and Azriel Eisenberg, eds., *Momentous Century: Personal Eyewitness Accounts of the Rise of the Jewish Homeland and State 1875-1978*, New York: A Herzl Press Publication, 1984.

Spencer, Robert, *The Politically Incorrect Guide to Islam (And the Crusades)*, Washington, D.C.: Regnery Publishing, Inc., 2005.

Spencer, Robert, *The Myth of Islamic Tolerance: How Islamic Law Treats Non-Muslims*, Amherst, New York: Prometheus Books, 2005.

Spencer, Robert, *The Truth about Muhammad: Founder of the World's Most Intolerant Religion*, Washington, D.C.: Regnery Publishing, Inc., 2006.

Spiegel, Steven L., *The Other Arab-Israeli Conflict: Making America's Middle East Policy, from Truman to Reagan*, Chicago, Illinois: The University of Chicago Press, 1985.

Sprinzak, Ehud, *Brother Against Brother: Violence and Extremism in Israeli Politics from Altalena to the Rabin Assassination*, New York: Free Press, 1999.

Sprinzak, Ehud, *The Ascendance of Israel's Radical Right*, New York: Oxford University Press, 1991.

Stanislawski, Michael, *Zionism and the Fin de Siècle: Cosmopolitanism and Nationalism from Nordau to Jabotinsky*, Berkeley, Ca: University of California Press, 2001.

Stanley, Arthur Penrhyn, *Sinai and Palestine: In Connection With Their History*, New York: A.C. Armstrong and Son, 1895.

Stav, Arieh, ed., *Israel and A Palestinian State: Zero Sum Game?* Shaarei Tivka: Israel, 2001.

Stav, Arieh, *Peace: The Arabian Caricature: A Study Of Anti-Semitic Imagery*, New York and Jerusalem: Gefen Publishing House, 1999.

Stein, Kenneth W., *Heroic Diplomacy: Sadat, Kissinger, Begin, and the Quest for Arab-Israeli Peace*, New York: Routledge, 1999.

Stein, Kenneth W., *The Land Question in Palestine, 1917-1939*, Chapel Hill: University of North Carolina Press, 1984.

Stein, Leonard, *The Balfour Declaration*, London: Valentine Mitchell, 1961.

Stein, Leonard, *The Palestine White Paper of October 1930*, London: Jewish Agency For Palestine, 1930.

Stern, Kenneth S., *Anti-Zionism: The Sophisticated Antisemitism*, New York: The American Jewish Committee, September 1990.

Sternhell, Zeev, *The Founding Myths of Israel*, Princeton, NJ: Princeton University Press, 1997.

Stone, Julius, *Israel and Palestine: Assault on the Law of Nations*, Baltimore, MD: Johns Hopkins University Press, 1981.

Storrs, Ronald, *Orientations*, Bristol, England: Purnell and Sons, 1939.

Storrs, Ronald, *The Memoirs of Sir Ronald Storrs*, New York: G.P. Putnam's Sons, 1937.

Sultan, Cathy, *Israeli and Palestinian Voice: A Dialogue with Both Sides*, Minneapolis, MN: Scarletta Press, 2006

Sykes, Christopher, *Cross Roads To Israel: Palestine From Balfour To Bevin*, London: Nel Mentor, 1967.

Symes, Stewart, *Tour of Duty*, London: Collins, 1946.

Syrkin, Marie, ed., *A Land of Our Own: An Oral Autobiography by Golda Meir*, New York: G.P. Putnam's Sons, 1973.

Szereszewski, Robert, *Essays on the Structure of the Jewish Economy in Palestine and Israel*, Jerusalem, Israel: Maurice Falk Institute For Economic Research in Israel, 1968.

Talmon, Jacob L., *Israel Among the Nations*, London: Weidenfeld and Nicolson, 1970.

Teitelbaum, Joshua, *The Rise and Fall of the Hashimite Kingdom of Arabia*, Washington Square, New York: New York University Press, 2001.

Tekoah, Yosef, *In the Face of the Nations: Israel's Struggle For Peace*, New York: Simon and Shuster, 1976.

Tessler, Mark A., *A History of the Israeli-Palestinian Conflict*, Bloomington, Indiana: Indiana University Press, 1994.

Teveth, Shabtai, *Ben-Gurion: and the Palestinian Arabs: From Peace to War*, New York: Oxford University Press, 1985.

Teveth, Shabtai, *Moshe Dayan: The Soldier, the Man, the Legend*, London and Jerusalem: Weidenfeld and Nicolson, 1972.

Theissen, Gerd, *Sociology of Early Palestinian Christianity*, Philadelphia, PA: Fortress Press, 1978.

Thompson, Thomas L., *The Mythic Past: Biblical Archaeology and the Myth of Israel*, New York: Basic Books, 1999.

Tiller, Charles, *The Politics of Collective Violence*, New York: Cambridge University Press, 2003.

Timmerman, Kenneth R., *Preachers of Hate: Islam and the War on America*, New York: Crown Forum, 2003.

Touval, Saadia, *The Peace Brokers: Mediators in the Arab-Israeli Conflict*, 1948-1979, Princeton, NJ: Princeton University Press, 1982.

Toynbee, Arnold J., *A Study of History*, New York: Dell Publishing Company, 1946.

Trachtenberg, Joshua, *The Devil and the Jews: The Medieval Concept of the Jew and Its Relation to Modern Antisemitism*, Philadelphia, PA: Jewish Publication Society, 1989.

Trevor, Daphne, *Under The White Paper: Some Aspects of British Administration in Palestine from 1939 to 1947*, Jerusalem: The Jerusalem Press, Ltd., 1948.

Troen, Ilan S., *Imagining Zion: Dreams, Designs, and Realities in a Century of Jewish Settlement*, New Haven, Connecticut: Yale University Press, 2003.

Turki, Fawaz, *The Disinherited: Journal of a Palestinian Exile*, New York: Monthly Review Press, 1972.

Twain, Mark, *The Innocents Abroad*, New York: Hippocrene Books, 1989.

Urofsky, Melvin I., *American Zionism from Herzl to the Holocaust*, Lincoln, NE: University of Nebraska Press, 1975.

Usher, Graham, *Dispatches from Palestine: The Collapse of the Oslo Agreement*, London: Pluto Press, 1999.

Usher, Graham, *Palestine in Crisis: The Struggle for Peace in Political Independence After Oslo*, London: Pluto Press, 1995.

Van Paassen, Pierre, *The Forgotten Ally*, Top Executive Media, 2005.

Verrier, Anthony, ed., *Agents of Empire: Anglo-Intelligence Operations 1915-1919 Brigadier Walter Gribbon, Aaron Aaronsohn and the NILI Ring*, London: Brassey's (UK) Ltd., 1995.

Victor, Barbara, *Army of Roses: Inside the World of Palestinian Women Suicide Bombers*, Emmaus, PA: Rodale Books, 2003.

Victor, Barbara, *A Voice of Reason: Hanan Ashrawi and Peace in the Middle East*, New York: Harcourt Brace, 1994.

Vincent, R.J., ed., *Foreign Policy and Human Rights: Issues and Responses*, New York: Cambridge University Press, 1986.

Vital, David, *The Future of the Jews: A People at the Crossroads?* Cambridge, MA: Harvard University Press, 1990.

Vital, David, *The Origins of Zionism*, New York: Oxford University Press, 1975.

Vital, David, *Zionism: The Crucial Phase*, New York: Oxford University Press, 1987.

Vital, David, *Zionism: The Formative Years*, New York: Oxford University Press, 1988.

Vogel, Lester I., *To See a Promised Land: Americans and the Holy Land in the Nineteenth Century*, University Park, Pennsylvania: Pennsylvania State University Press, 1993.

Wallach, Janet and John Wallach, *Arafat In The Eyes Of The Beholder*, New York: A Lyle Stuart Book, 1990.

Walzer, Michael, *Just and Unjust Wars: A Moral Argument with Historical Illustrations*, New York: Basic Books, 1977.

Warraq, Ibn, *Defending The West: A Critique of Edward Said's Orientalism*, Amherst, New York: Prometheus Books, 2007.

Warren, Christopher, *Chances of A Lifetime: A Memoir*, New York: Scribner, 2001.

Wasserstein, Bernard, *Divided Jerusalem: The Struggle for the Holy City*, New Haven, CT: Yale University Press, 2001.

Wasserstein, Bernard, *Herbert Samuel: A Political Life*, New York: Oxford University Press, 1992.

Wasserstein, Bernard, *Israelis and Palestinians: Why Do They Fight? Can They Stop?* New Haven, Connecticut: Yale University Press, 2003.

Watson, Geoffrey R., *The Oslo Accords: International Law and the Israeli-Palestinian Peace Agreements*, New York: Oxford University Press, 2000.

Weisgal, Meyer, *So Far: An Autobiography*, New York: Random House, 1971.

Weizmann, Chaim, *Trial and Error: The Autobiography of Chaim Weizmann*, New York: Harper and Brothers, 1949.

White, Ben, *Israeli Apartheid: A Beginner's Guide*, New York, New York: Pluto Press, 2009.

Williams, Francis, *A Prime Minister Remembers: The War and Post-War Memories of the Rt. Hon Earl Attlee*, London: Heinemann, 1961.

Wilson, Evan M., *A Calculated Risk: The U.S. Decision To Recognize Israel*, Cincinnati, OH: Clerisy Press, 2008.

Wilson, R. Dare, *Cordon and Search With 6th Airborne Division in Palestine*, Nashville, TN: The Battery Press, 1984.

Windschuttle, Keith, *The Killing of History: How Literary Critics And Social Theorists Are Murdering Our Past*, New York: The Free Press, 1996.

Wise, Stephen S. and Jacob De Hass, *The Great Betrayal*, New York: Brentano Publishers, 1930.

Wisse, Ruth R., *If I Am Not For Myself: The Liberal Betrayal of The Jews*, New York: The Free Press, 1992.

Wisse, Ruth R., *Jews and Power*, New York: Schocken Books, 2007.

Wistrich, Robert S., *Anti-Zionism and Antisemitism in the Contemporary World*, New York: New York University Press, 1990.

Wistrich, Robert S., *Hitler's Apocalypse: Jews and the Nazi Legacy*, New York: St. Martin's Press, 1985.

Wistrich, Robert S., *Muslim Anti-Semitism: A Clear and Present Danger*, New York: The American Jewish Committee, 2001.

Wistrich, Robert S., *The Shaping of Israeli Identity: Myth, Memory and Trauma*, London: Frank Cass & Company, 1995.

Wistrich, Robert S., *Terms of Survival: The Jewish World Since 1945*, New York: Routledge, 1995.

Wistrich, Robert S., ed. *The Left Against Zion: Communism, Israel and the Middle East*, Totowa, New Jersey, 1979.

Wistrich, Robert S., *A Lethal Obsession: Anti-Semitism from Antiquity to the Global Jihad*, (New York: Random House, 2010)

Wistrich, Robert S. and David Ohana, eds., *Antisemitism: The Longest Hatred*, New York: Schocken Books, 1991.

Whitelam, Keith W., *The Invention of Ancient Israel: The Silencing of Palestinian History*, New York: Routledge, 1996.

Woodward, E.L. and Rohan Butler, *Documents on British Foreign Policy 1919-1939, First Series*, 1919, Vol. 4, London: Her Majesty's Stationery Office, 1952.

Yaari, Ehud, *Strike Terror: The Story of Fatah*, New York: Sabra Books, 1970.

Yablonka, Hanna, *The State of Israel vs. Adolf Eichmann*, New York: Schocken Books, 2004.

Yaphe, Judith S., ed., *The Middle East in 2015: The Impact of Regional Trends on U.S. Strategic Planning*, Washington, D.C.: National Defense University Press, 2002.

Ye'or, Bat, Eurabia: *The Euro-Arab Axis*, Madison, New Jersey: Fairleigh Dickinson University Press, 2005.

Ye'or, Bat, *Islam and Dhimmitude: Where Civilizations Collide*, Madison, New Jersey: Fairleigh Dickinson University Press, 2002.

Yodfat, Aryeh Y., and Yuval Arnon-Ohanna, *PLO Strategy and Tactics*, New York: St. Martin's Press, 1981.

Zaken, Mordechai, *Jewish Subjects and Their Tribal Chieftains in Kurdistan*, Leiden, The Netherlands: Brill, 2007.

Zartman, I. William, ed., *Elusive Peace: Negotiating An End To Civil War*, Washington, D.C.: The Brookings Institute, 1995.

Zartman, I. William, *Ripe For Resolution: Conflict and Intervention In Africa*, New York: Oxford University Press, 1985.

Zebel, Sydney H., *Balfour: A Political Biography*, New York: Cambridge University Press, 1973.

Zenner, Walter P., *Minorities in the Middle: A Cross Cultural Analysis*, Albany, New York: State University of New York Press, 1991.

Zertal, Idith, *From Catastrophe to Power: Holocaust Survivors and the Emergence of Israel*, Berkeley, California: University of California Press, 1978.

Zertal, Idith, *Israel's Holocaust and the Politics of Nationhood*, New York: Cambridge University Press, 2005.

Zipperstein, Steve J. and Ernest Frerichs, eds., *Zionism, Liberalism, and the Future of the Jewish State: Centennial Reflections on Zionist Scholarship and Controversy*, Providence, RI: The Dorot Foundation, 2000.

ARTICLES

Aaronsohn, Alexander, "Saifna Ahmar, Ya Sultan!" *The Atlantic Monthly* (July 1916).

Abramov, S.Z., "Was the Conflict Unavoidable," *Midstream* (December 1964): 63-73.

Abu-Ghazaleh, Adnan, "Arab Cultural Nationalism in Palestine during the British Mandate," *Journal of Palestine Studies 1*, no. 3, (Spring 1972):37-63.

Alami, Musa, "The Lesson of Palestine," *The Middle East Journal*, vol. 4, no. 4, (October 1949): 373-405.

Albin, Cecilia, "Securing the Peace of Jerusalem: On the Politics of Unifying and Dividing," *Review of International Studies 23*, (1997): 117-142.

Al-Husseini , Hajj Amin, "Forum Interviews: Hajj Amin al-Husseini," *Middle East Forum*, vol. 35, no. 8, (October 1959): 17.

Alroey, Gur, "Journey to Early-Twentieth-Century Palestine as a Jewish Immigrant Experience," *Jewish Social Studies*, vol. 9, no. 2 (January 2003): 28-64.

Alter, Robert, "Zionism for the 70's," *Commentary*, (February 1970):47-57.

Alterman, Jon B., "The False Promise of Arab Liberals," *Policy Review*, no. 125, (June and July 2004) http://www.hoover.org/publications/policyreview3438441.html.

Arendt, Hannah, "To Save The Jewish Homeland: There Is Still Time," *Commentary*, (May 1948): 398-406.

Arendt, Hannah, "The Jewish State: Fifty Years After: Where Have Herzl's Politics Led," *Commentary* (May 1946): 1-8.

Aridan, Natan, "Abba Eban, The Toynbee Heresy," *Israel Studies*, vol. 11, no. 1 (April 2006), 91-107.

Avineri, Shlomo, "Self-Determination and Realpolitik: Reflections on Kurds and Palestinians," *Dissent* (Summer 2005).

Avineri, Shlomo, "Zionism as a National Liberation Movement," *The Jerusalem Quarterly*, no. 10 (Winter 1979): 133-144.

Avineri, Shlomo, "The Palestinians and Israel," *Commentary*, 42, no. 6 (June 1970): 31-44.

Barsamian, David, "Edward Said," *The Progressive* (April 1999), http://www.progressive/0901/intv1101.html.

Barsky, Yehudit, "Hamas: The Islamic Resistance Movement of Palestine," The American Jewish Committee (New York 2006), *http://www.cpt-mi.org/pdf/Hamas-Islamic_Resistance_Movement.pdf*.

Baumel, Judith Tydor, "Bridging Myth and Reality: The Absorption of She'erit Hapletah in Eretz Yisrael, 1945—48," *Middle East Studies*, vol. 33, no. 2 (April 1997): 362-382.

Ben Gurion, David, "Ben-Gurion and De Gaulle: An Exchange of Letters," *Midstream* (February 1968): 11-26.

Ben-Israel, Hedva, "Debates With Toynbee: Herzog, Talmon, Friedman," *Israel Studies*, vol. 2, no. 1 (April 2006): 79-90.

Ben-Israel, Hedva, "Zionism and European Nationalisms: Comparative Aspects," *Israel Studies*, vol. 8, no. 1 (April 2003): 91-104.

Beres, Louis Rene, "Response to John Quigley," *The American University Journal of International Law and Policy* (Washington, D.C.: Washington College of Law, The American University, 1997).

Bialer, Uri, "Top Hat, Tuxedo and Cannons: Israeli Foreign Policy From 1948 to 1956 as a Field Study," *Israel Studies*, vol. 7, no. 1 (Spring 2002), http://iupjournals.org/Israel/iss7-1.html.

Bostom, Andrew G., from "Communism as the 20th Century Islam, to Islam as the 21st Century Communism," *andrewbostom.org/blog* (December 5, 2009)

Bostom, Andrew G., "Jihad and Islamic Antisemitism," *Frontpagemag.com* (May 22, 2008)

Brailsford, H.N., "Solution for Palestine: A British View," *Commentary* (February 1946): 51-55.

Brecher, Michael, "Jerusalem: Israel's Political Decisions, 1947-1977," *The Middle East Journal*, 32, no. 1 (Winter 1978): 13-34.

Brown, Cameron S., "Answering Edward Said's The Question of Palestine," *Israel Affairs*, 13, no. 1 (January 2007): 55-79.

Bruck, Connie, "The Wounds of Peace," *The New Yorker* (October 1996): 64-90.

Caplan, Neil, "Arab-Jewish Contacts in Palestine After the First World War," *Journal of Contemporary History*, 12, (1977): 635-668.

Carpi, Daniel, "The Mufti of Jerusalem, Amin el-Husseini and His Diplomatic Activity During World War II (October 1941-July 1943)" *Studies in Zionism*, no. 7 (Spring 1983): 101-131.

Cohen, Lloyd, "The Israeli Lust for Peace: Illusion, Tragedy and Prospect," *Israel Affairs*, 11, no. 4 (October 2005): 737-763.

Cohen, Michael J., "British Strategy and the Palestine Question 1936-39," *Journal of Contemporary History 7*, no. 3 & 4 (July-October, 1972): 157-183.

Cohen, Michael J., "Truman, the Holocaust and the Establishment of the State of Israel," *The Jerusalem Quarterly*, no. 23 (Spring 1982): 79-94.

Coleman, M. Donald, "Churchill and the Jews," *Midstream* (May to June 1999): 10-14.

Cooper, Elias, "Nazi Policy in the Middle East, 1935-1945," *Midstream* (June 1964): 61-75.

Cotler, Irwin, "The Legitimacy of Israel," *Middle East Focus* (January 1981): 9-14.

Crossman, Richard H.S., "The Balfour Declaration 1917-1967," *Midstream* (December 1967): 21-28.

Crossman, Richard H.S., "Gentile Zionism and the Balfour Declaration," *Commentary* (June 1962): 487-494.

Crossman, Richard H.S., "Framework For The Jewish State: The New Boundaries of Zionist Aspirations," *Commentary* (November 1947): 401-407.

Dawn, C. Ernest, "The Amir of Mecca Al-Husayn Ibn-'Ali and the Origin of the Arab Revolt," *Proceedings of the American Philosophical Society*, 104, no. 1 (February 1960): 11-34.

Dowty, Alan, "Is Israel Democratic? Substance and Semantics in the 'Ethnic Democracy' Debate," *Israel Studies*, 4, no. 2 (1999).

Duker-Fishman, Rivkah, "'Jerusalem: Capital of the Jews': The Jewish Identity if Jerusalem in Greek and Roman Sources," *Jewish Political Studies Review*, 20:3-4 (Fall 2008): 119-140.

Efraim Inbar, "Israel's Palestinian Challenge," *Israel Affairs*, 12, no. 4, (October 2006), 823-842.

El-Najjar, "Zionism: The Highest Stage of Imperialism," *Aljazeerah* (May 15, 2002).

Elpeleg, Zvi, "Why Was 'Independent Palestine' Never Created in 1948?" *The Jerusalem Quarterly 50* (Spring 1989), (http://www.mfa.gov.il/MFA/Peace+Process/Guide+to+the+Peace+Process/Why+Was+Independent+Palestine-+Never+Created+in+1.htm.)

Epstein, Eliahu, "Middle East Munich," *The Nation* (March 9, 1946): 287-288.

Ettinger, Shmuel, "Anti-Semitism in Our Time," *The Jerusalem Quarterly*, no. 23 (Spring 1982): 95-113.

Feldman, Louis H., "Some Observations on the Name of Palestine," *Hebrew Union College Annual 61* (1990): 1-23.

Fishman, Joel S., "Democratic Universality and its Adversaries," Jerusalem Viewpoints, *Jewish Center for Public Affairs*, no. 533 (August 1, 2005).

Fishman, Joel S., "Ten Years Since Oslo: The PLO's 'People's War" Strategy and Israel's Inadequate Response," *Jerusalem Viewpoints*, no. 503 (September 1-15 2003).

Fishman, Joel S., "The Big Lie and the Media War Against Israel: From Inversion of the Truth to Inversion of Reality," *Jewish Political Studies Review*, 19, Jerusalem Center for Public Affairs, nos. 1&2 (Spring 2007)

Forman, Geremy, "Settlement of Title in the Galilee: Dowson's Colonial Guiding Principles," *Israel Studies*, 7, no. 3 (October 2002): 61-83.

Fraenkel, Carlos, "Teaching Plato in Palestine: Can Philosophy Save the Middle East?" *Dissent* (Spring 2007), http://www.dissentmagazine.org/article/?article=769.

Friedman, Isaiah, "Lord Palmerston and the Protection of Jews in Palestine 1839-1851," *Jewish Social Studies*, 30, no. 1 (January 1968): 23-41.

Friedman, Isaiah, "The McMahon-Hussein Correspondence and the Question of Palestine," *Journal of Contemporary History*, 5, no. 2 (1970): 83-122.

Friedman, Isaiah, "Arnold Toynbee: Pro-Arab or Pro-Zionist?" *Israel Studies*, 4, no. 1 (Spring 1999).

Friedman, Isaiah, "How Trans-Jordan was severed from the territory of the Jewish National Home," *The Journal of Israeli History*, 27, no. 1 (March 2008): 65--85.

Friedman, Saul S., "The Myth of Arab Toleration," *Midstream* (January 1970): 56-59.

Friling, Tuvia and S. Ilan Troen, "Proclaiming Independence: Five Days in May from Ben Gurion's Diary," *Israel Studies*, 3, no. 1 (April 1998): 170-194.

Gans, Chaim, "Is There a Historical Right to the Land of Israel?" *Azure* (Winter 2006), http://www.azure.org.il/magazine/magazine.asp?id=354.

Garfinkle, Adam, "History and Peace: Revisiting Two Zionist Myths," *Israel Affairs*, 5, no. 1 (Autumn 1998): 126-148.

Gavish, Dov and Ruth Kark, "The Cadastral Mapping of Palestine, 1858-1928," *The Geographical Journal*, 159, no. 1 (March 1993): 70-80.

Gavison, Ruth, "Ruth Gavison Offers a Vision of a Democratic, Jewish Israel." (Los Angeles, CA: UCLA Ronald W. Burkle Center For International Relations, February 12, 2004), *http://www.international.ucla.edu/burkle/news/article.asp?parentid=7876.*

Gavison, Ruth, "The Jews' Right To Statehood: A Defense," *Azure*, no. 15 (Summer 2003).

Gavison, Ruth, "A Constitution for Israel: Lessons from the American Experiment," *Azure*, no. 12 (Winter 2002).

Gavison, Ruth, "Jewish and Democratic? A Rejoinder to the 'Ethnic Democracy' Debate," *Israel Studies*, 4, no. 1 (1999): 44-67.

Gazit, Mordechai, "The Israel-Jordan Peace Negotiations (1949-51): King Abdallah's Lonely Effort," *Journal of Contemporary History 23* (1988): 409-424.

Gerber, Haim, "'Palestine'" and Other Territorial Concepts In the 17th Century," *International Journal of Middle East Studies 30*, no. 4 (November 1998): 563-572.

Gerstenfeld, Manfred, "Anti-Israelism and Anti-Semitism: Common Characteristics and Motifs," *Jewish Political Studies Review*, 19: 1-2 (Spring 2007), (http://www.jcpa.org/JCPA/Templates ShowPage.aspDRIT=3& DBID=1&LNGID=1&TMID=111&FID=253&PID=0&IID=1673&TTL=Ant i-Israelism_and_Anti Semitism:_Common_Characteristics_and Motifs)

Gerstenfeld, Manfred, "Rewriting Germany's Past-A Society in Moral Decline," *Jerusalem Center for Public Affairs*, no. 530 (May 1, 2005). http://www.jcpa.org/jl/vp530.htm.

Gerstenfeld, Manfred, "Jews against Israel," *Jerusalem Center for Public Affairs*, no. 30 (March 1, 2005), http://www.jcpa.org/phas/phas-30.htm.

Gerstenfeld, Manfred, "An Interview with Meir Litvak: The Development of Arab Anti-Semitism," *Jerusalem Center for Public Affairs*, no. 5 (February 2003), http://www.jcpa.org/phas/phas-5.htm.

Golan, Arnon, "The Transformation of Abandoned Arab Rural Areas," *Israel Studies*, 2, no. 1 (Spring 1997).

Gold, Dore and Jeff Helmreich, "An Answer To The New Anti-Zionists: The Rights Of The Jewish People To A Sovereign State in their Historic Homeland," Jerusalem Viewpoints, *Jerusalem Center for Public Affairs*, no. 507 (November 16, 2003)

Goren, Asher, "The Palestinian Position on Israel: Some Assumptions and Evaluations," *The Jerusalem Review*, 1, no. 1 (2006-2007): 108-111.

Grief, Howard, "Legal Rights And Title Of Sovereignty Of The Jewish People To The Land Of Israel And Palestine Under International Law," *NATIV Online: A Journal of Politics and the Arts*, 2 (2004).

Gutmann, David, "The Palestinian Myth," *Commentary* (October 1975): 43-47.

Haass, Richard N, "The New Middle East," Foreign Affairs (November to December 2006), (http://www.foreignaffairs.org20061101faessay85601/richard-n-haass/the-new-middle-east.html)

Haim, Sylvia, "Arabic Antisemitic Literature." *Jewish Social Studies*, 17, no. 4 (October 1955): 307-312.

Halevi, Ran, "The Jewish State's Existence is an Affront to Postnationalism," *Policy Review 14* (April and May 2004) http://www.hoover.org/publications/policyreview/3438566.html.

Halkin, Hillel, "Was Zionism Unjust," *Commentary* (November 1999): 29-35.

Halkin, Hillel, "Why the Settlements Should Stay." *Commentary* (June 2002): 21-27.

Halkin, Hillel, "Does Sharon Have a Plan," *Commentary* (June 2004): 17-22.

Hatina, Meir, "The 'Ulama' and the Cult of Death in Palestine," *Israel Affairs*, 12, no. 1 (January 2006): 29-51.

Helmreich, Jeffrey, "Diplomatic and Legal Aspects of the Settlement Issue," *Institute for Contemporary Affairs*, 2, no. 16 (January 19, 2003).

Hertz, Eli L., "UN Resolution 181-The Partition Plan November 29, 1947 A 'Green Light' for Jewish Statehood-A 'Dead' Blueprint for Peace," (November 26, 2008.)

Hertz, Eli L., "The 86th Anniversary of the Mandate for Palestine," *MythsandFacts.Com* (July 24, 2008.)

Hertz, Eli L., "The U.S. Congress in 1922," *MythsandFacts.Com*. (March 7, 2008.)

Hertzberg, Arthur, "A Small Peace for the Middle East," *Foreign Affairs*, 80, no. 1 (January/February 2001): 139-147.

Inbar, Efraim, "Arab-Israeli Coexistence: The Causes, Achievements and Limitations," *Israel Affairs*, 6, no. 2-3 (Spring/Summer 2006): 256-270.

Israeli, Raphael, "Anti-Jewish Attitudes in the Arab Media, 1975-1981" in *Anti-Zionism and Antisemitism in the Contemporary World*, Robert S. Wistrich, ed., (New York: New York University Press, 1990), 74-84

Jabotinsky, Vladimir, "The Iron Wall," (Original in Russian, 1923) Translated by Jewish Herald (November, 26 1937), *http://www.marxists.de/middleast/ironwall/ironwall.htm*.

Jacobson, Abigail, "Sephardim, Ashkenazim and the 'Arab Question' in pre-First World War Palestine: A Reading of Three Zionist Newspapers," *Middle Eastern Studies*, 39, no. 2 (April 2003): 105-130.

Jones, David-Pryce, "Jews, Arabs, and French Diplomacy: A Special Report," *Commentary* (May 2005).

Karsh, Efraim, "Revisiting Israel's 'Original Sin,'" *Commentary* (September 2003): 46-50.

Karsh, Efraim, "1948, Israel, and the Palestinians," *Commentarymagazine.com Web Exclusive* (May 2008).

Karsh, Efraim, "The Collusion that Never Was: King Abdalla, the Jewish Agency and the Partition of Palestine," *Journal of Contemporary History*, 34, no. 4 (1999): 569-585.

Karsh, Efraim, and Inari Karsh, "Myth in the Desert, or Not the Great Arab Revolt," *Middle East Studies 33*, no. 2 (April 1997): 267-312.

Karsh, Efraim, "Peace Despite Everything," *Israel Affairs*, 3, nos. 3 & 4 (Spring to Summer 1997): 117-132.

Karsh, Efraim, "Introduction: From Rabin to Netanyahu," *Israel Affairs*, 3, nos. 3& 4 (Spring to Summer 1997): i–vii.

Karsh, Efraim, and Inari Karsh, "Reflections on Arab Nationalism," *Middle East Studies*, 32, no. 4 (October 1996): 367-392.

Katz, Jacob, "Zionism vs. Anti-Semitism," *Commentary* (April 1979): 46-52.

Kedourie, Elie, "Where Arabism and Zionism Differ," *Commentary* (June 1986): 32-36.

Kerstein, Benjamin, "What Noam Chomsky Really Wants." FrontpageMagazine (November 9, 2004), *http://frontpagemagazine.com/ Articles/Printable.asp?ID=15845*.

Khalidi, Walid, "Thinking The Unthinkable: A Sovereign Palestine State," *Foreign Affairs*, 56, no. 4 (July 1978): 695-713.

Khalidi, Walid, "Thinking the Unthinkable: A Sovereign Palestinian State," *Foreign Affairs*, (July 1978), (http://www.foreignaffairs. org/19780701faessay9869/walid-khalidi/thinking-the-unthinkable-a-sovereign-palestinian-state.html.)

Khalidi, Walid, "The Palestine Problem: An Overview," *Journal of Palestine Studies*, 21, no. 1 (Autumn 1991): 5-16.

Khalidi, Walid, "The Jewish-Ottoman Company: Herzl's Blueprint for the Colonization of Palestine," *Journal of Palestine Studies*, 22, no. 2 (Winter 1993): 30-47.

Khalidi, Walid, "The Fall of Haifa," *Middle East Forum*, 35, no. 10 (December 1959).

Khalidi, Walid, "Toward Peace in the Holy Land," *Foreign Affairs* (Spring 1988), (http://www.foreignaffairs.org/19880301faessay7895/walid-khalidi/toward-peace-in-the-holy-land.html.)

Kimche, Jon, "British Labor's Turnabout on Zionism," *Commentary* (December 1947): 510-517.

Klein, Claude, "Zionism Revisited," *Israel Affairs*, 11, no. 1 (January 2005): 238-253.

Kochavi, Arieh J., "Israel and the International Legal Arena." *The Journal of Israeli History*, 25, no. 3 (March 2006): 223-244.

Kochavi, Arieh J., "Britain's Image Campaign Against the Zionists," *Journal of Contemporary History*, 36, no. 2 (April 2001): 293-307.

Koestler, Arthur, "Letter to a Parent of a British Soldier in Palestine," *New Statesman* (Original: August 16, 1947; Reprinted: January 15, 2007), http://www.newstatesman.com/society/2007/01/palestine-british-jews-jewish.

Kollat, Israel, "The Zionist Movement and the Arabs," *Studies in Zionism*, no. 5 (1982): 129-157.

Kramer, Martin, "Is Zionism Colonialism? The Root Lie," *Jerusalem Center for Public Affairs*, no. 35 (August 1, 2005).

Küntzel, Matthias, "Hitler's Legacy: Islamic Antisemitism in the Middle East," (November 30, 2006), *(http://www.matthiaskuentzel.de/contents/hitlers-legacy-islamic-antisemitism-in-the middle-east)*.

Küntzel, Matthias, "The Roots of Delusion," (February 2005). *http://www.matthiaskuentzel.de/contents/the-roots-of-delusion*.

Küntzel, Matthias, "The 'Protocols of the Elders of Zion' at the Frankfurt Book Fair," (October 24, 2005), *(http://www.trans-int.com/blog/archives/60-The-Protocols-of-the-Elders-of-Zion-at-the-Frankfurt-Book-Fair.html)*.

Küntzel, Matthias, "National Socialism and Anti-Semitism in the Arab World," Jewish Political Studies Review, *Jewish Center For Public Affairs*, 17, nos. 1 & 2 (Spring 2005), http://www.jcpa.org/phas/phas-kuntzel-s05.htm.

Küntzel, Matthias, "European Roots of Antisemitism in Current Islamic Thinking," (November 2004), *(http://www.matthiaskuentzel.de/contents/ european-roots-of-antisemitism-in-current-islamic-thinking)*.

Küntzel, Matthias, "National Socialism and Anti-Semitism in the Arab World," *Jerusalem Center for Public Affairs*, Jewish Political Studies Review 17, nos. 1 & 2 (Spring 2005).

Kushner, David, "Zealous Towns in Nineteenth- Century Palestine," *Middle Eastern Studies 33*, no. 3 (July 1997): 597-612.

Landes, David S., "Palestine Before The Zionists," *Commentary* (February 1976): 47-56.

Lapidoth, Ruth, "UN Resolution 242," *The Weiner Library Bulletin*, 26, nos. 1 & 2; New Series: nos. 26/7 (1972): 2-8.

Lewis, Bernard, "The Palestinians and the PLO: A Historical Approach," *Commentary* (January 1975): 32-48.

Lewis, Bernard, "The Anti-Zionist Resolution," *Foreign Affairs* (November 1976): 54-64.

Lewis, Bernard, "Palestine: On the History and Geography of a Name," *The International History Review*, 2 (January 1, 1980): 1-12.

Lewis, Bernard, "The Decline and Fall of Islamic Jewry," *Commentary* (June 1984): 44-54.

Lewis, Bernard, "The Arab World Discovers Anti-Semitism," *Commentary* (May 1986): 30-34.

Lewis, Bernard, "Freedom and Justice in the Modern Middle East," *Foreign Affairs* (May to June 2005).

Lewis, Samuel, "The United States and Israel: Evolution of an Unwritten Alliance," *Middle East Journal*, 53, no. 3 (Summer 1999): 364-378.

Lichtheim, George, "Winston Churchill and Zionism." *Midstream* (Spring 1959): 19-29.

Lichtheim, George, "Behind Bevin's Hostility To Israel: Britain is Not Yet Reconciled to the Realities," *Commentary* (March 1949): 246-251.

Linowitz, Sol, "Analysis of a Tinderbox: The Legal Basis for the State of Israel," *American Bar Association Journal*, 43 (June 1957): 523-525.

Lochery, Neill, "Peacemaking in Israel and Northern Ireland," *Israel Affairs*, 12, no. 2 (April 2006): 234-252.

Lustick, Ian, "To Build and to Be Built By: Israel and the Hidden Logic of the Iron Wall," *Israel Studies*, 1, no. 1 (Spring 1996), http://iupjournals.org/Israel/iss1-1.html.

Makovsky, David, "Middle East Peace Through Partition," *Foreign Affairs* (March to April 2001): 28-45.

Mandel, Neville, "Attempts at an Arab-Zionist Entente: 1913-1914," *Middle Eastern Studies* (April 1965): 238-267.

Manor, Yohanan, "Contemporary Anti-Zionism," *Encyclopaedia Judaica Year Book 1983-1985*, (1985): 128-137.

Manor, Yohanan, "The New Anti-Zionism," *The Jerusalem Quarterly* (Spring 1985): 125-144.

Marcus, Itamar and Barbara Crook, "Visual Hate Messages in the PA Media - May 2005," *PMW* (June 15, 2005).

Marlowe, John, "How Deal With Arab Nationalism? Enforcement of Partition Will Strengthen Progressive Forces," *Commentary*, (April 1948): 317-333.

McTague, John T., "The British Military Administration in Palestine, 1917-1920," *Journal of Palestine Studies*, vol. 7 no. 3 (Spring 1978): 55-76.

Medoff, Rafael, "The Mufti's Nazi Years Re-Examined," *The Journal of Israeli History*, 17, no. 3 (1996): 317-333.

Medoff, Rafael, "Herbert Hoover's Plan for Palestine: A Forgotten Episode in American Middle East Diplomacy," *American Jewish History*, 79 (Summer 1990): 449-76.

Medoff, Rafael, "The Influence of Revisionist Zionism in America during the Early Years of World War Two," *Studies in Zionism*, 13 (Autumn 1992): 187-90.

Milson, Menachem, "Countering Arab Antisemitism," *Institute of the World Jewish Congress* (2003): 3-17.

Milton-Edwards, Beverly, "Political Islam and the Palestinian Conflict," *Israel Affairs*, 12 (January 2006): 65-85.

Morgenstern, Arie, "Dispersion and the Longing for Zion, 1240-1840," no. 12 (Winter 2002).

Morris, Benny, "The Harvest of 1948 and The Creation of The Palestinian Refugee Problem," *The Middle East Journal 40*, no. 4 (Autumn 1986): 671-685.

Morris-Reich, Amos, "Arthur Ruppin's Concept of Race," *Israel Studies*, 11, no. 3 (October 2006): 1-30.

Mosse, George, "Can Nationalism Be Saved? About Zionism, Rightful and Unjust Nationalism," *Israel Studies*, 2, no. 1 (Spring 1997): 156-173.

Muir, Diana and Paul S. Appelbaum, "The Gene Wars," *Azure*, no. 27 (Winter 2007).

Naor, Arye, "A Matter of Distoriography: Efraim Karsh, the 'New Historians' of Israel, Their Methodology and Perspective," *Israel Studies*, 6, no. 2 (July 2001): 139-150.

Naor, Arye, "Neo-Nazi pro-Arabs and Arabs Antisemites," *Patterns of Prejudice*, (March-April 1968): 13-14, 28.

Nevo, Joseph, "The Arabs of Palestine 1947-48: Military and Political Activity," *Middle Eastern Studies*, 23, no. 1 (January 1987): 3-38.

Nevo, Yosef, "How Many Palestinians?" *New Outlook* ,12, no. 4 (May 1969): 28-31.

Niebuhr, Reinhold, "Our Stake in the State of Israel," *The New Republic* (February 4, 1957): 9-12.

Nisan, Mordechai, "Israel 1948-98: Purpose and Predicament in History," *Israel Affairs 8*, no. 1 & 2 (2002): 3-13.

Nordbruch, Goetz, "The Socio-Historical Background of Holocaust Denial in Arab Countries: Reactions to Roger Garaudy's The Founding Myths of Israeli Politics," *The Vidal Sassoon International Center for the Study of Anti-Semitism* (2001).

Odeh, Adnan Abu, "Two Capitals in Undivided Jerusalem," *Foreign Affairs*, 71, no. 2 (Spring 1992): 183-188.

Oren, Michael B., "Jews and the Challenge of Sovereignty," *Azure*, no. 23 (Winter 2003).

Ottolenghi, Emanuele, "The Isaiah Berlin Public Lectures in the Middle East Dialogue: An Introductory Note," *Israel Studies 10*, no. 2 (July 2005): V-IX.

Perlmann, Moshe, "Arabic Antisemitic Literature: Comment on Sylvia G. Haim's Article," *Jewish Social Studies*, 17, no. 4: 313-314.

Perlmann, Moshe, "Chapters of Arab-Jewish Diplomacy, 1918-22," *Jewish Social Studies*, 66, no. 2 (April 1944): 123-153.

Pipes, Daniel, "Arab vs. Arab Over Palestine," *Commentary* (July 1987): 17-25.

Pipes, Daniel, "Israel, America and Arab Delusions," *Commentary* (March 1991): 26-31.

Pipes, Daniel, "Israel's Moment of Truth," *Commentary* (February 2000): 19-25.

Pipes, Daniel, "The Muslim Claim to Jerusalem," *Middle East Quarterly*. (Fall 2001), www.meforum.org/article/490.

Pipes, Daniel, "The Politics of Muslim Anti-Semitism," *Commentary*, (August 1981): 39-45

Podeh, Elie, "Rethinking Israel in the Middle East," *Israel Affairs*, 3, nos. 3 & 4 (Spring 1997): 280-295.

Podhoretz, Norman, "The State of World Jewry," *Commentary* (December 1983): 37-45.

Porath, Yehoshua, "The Land Problem in Mandatory Palestine," *The Jerusalem Quarterly*, no. 1 (Fall 1976): 18-35.

Possony, Stefan T., "Language As A Communist Weapon: Consultation With Dr. Stefan T. Possony," *Government Printing Office* (Washington, D.C.; Committee on Un-American Activities House of Representatives, Eighty-Sixth Congress First Session March 2, 1959).

Reichman, Shalom, Yossi Katz and Yair Paz, "The Absorptive Capacity of Palestine 1882-1948," *Middle Eastern Studies*, 33, no. 2 (April 1997): 338-361.

Ro'i, Yaacov, "Relations Between Rehovot And Its Arab Neighbors, 1890-1914," Carpi, Daniel and Gedalia Yogev. *Zionism: Studies in the History of the Zionist Movement and of the Jewish Community in Palestine* (Tel-Aviv: Massada Publishing Company, Ltd. 1975): 337-388.

Rose N.A., "Palestine's Role in Britain's Imperial Defence: An Aspect of Zionist Diplomacy, 1938-39," *The Weiner Library Bulletin* 22, no. 4, New Series, Number 13 (Autumn 1968): 32-35.

Rostow, Eugene V., "The American Stake in Israel," *Commentary* (April 1977): 32- 46.

Rostow, Eugene V., "Bricks and Stones: Settling for Leverage; Palestinian Autonomy," *The New Republic* (April 23, 1990).

Roth, Andrew, "The Mufti's New Army," *The Nation* (March 9, 1946), 551-552.

Rouhana, Nadim N. and Daniel Bar-Tal, "Psychological Dynamics of Intractable Ethnonational Conflicts: The Israeli-Palestinian Case," *American Psychologist* (July 1998): 761-770.

Rubenstein, Danny, "The People of Nowhere," *Palestine-Israel Journal*, no. 2 (Spring 1994): 79-85.

Rubin, Uri, "Muhammad's Night Journey (Isra') to Al-Masjid Al-Aqsa Aspects of the Earliest Origins of the Islamic Sanctity of Jerusalem," *Al-Qantara 29* (2008): 147-264.

Sacher, H., ed.. "Zionism and the Future Jewish State," *John Murray* (1917)

Scholch, Alexander, "Britain in Palestine, 1838-1882: The Roots of the Balfour Policy," *Journal of Palestine Studies*, 22, no. 1 (Autumn 1992): 38-53.

Schvindlerman, Julian, "Yerushalayim versus Al-Quds," *Midstream* (September to October 2000): 26-28.

Seener, Barak M., "Israeli Arabs between a Palestinianization and Islamism," *Jerusalem Center for Public Affairs*, no. 560 (January 1, 2008).

Shapira, Anita, "The Failure of Israel's 'New Historians' to Explain War and Peace: The Past is Not a Foreign Country," *The New Republic* (December, 1, 2000) http://ontology.buffalo.edu/smith/courses01/rrtw/Shapira.htm.

Shapira, Anita, "The Jewish-people deniers," Review Essay, *The Journal of Israeli History*, 28, no. 1 (March 2009): 63-72.

Shapira, Shimon, "Has Hezbullah Changed?" *The 7th Hizbullah General Conference and Its Continued Ideology of Resistance*, vol. 9, number 15, Jerusalem Center for Public Affairs (December 15, 2009)

Sharabi, Hisham, "An Interview with Lord Cardon," *Journal of Palestine Studies*, 5, nos. 3 & 4 (Spring to Summer 1976): 142-152.

Sharansky, Natan, "On Hating Jews," *Commentary* (November 2003): 26-34.

Sharett, Moshe, "Israel's Position and Problems," *Middle East Affairs 3*, no. 5 (May 1952): 133-149.

Sharkansky, Ira, "The Potential of Ambiguity: The Case of Jerusalem," *Israel Affairs*, 3, nos. 2 & 4 (Spring 1997): 187-199.

Shlaim, Avi, "Interview with Abba Eban, 11 March 1976," *Israel Studies*, 8, no. 1 (Spring 2003): 153-177.

Sinanoglou, Penny, "British Plans for the Partition of Palestine, 1929-1938," *The Historical Journal*, 52, no. 1 (Cambridge University Press, 2009), 131-152.

Sivan, Emmanuel, "Islamic Fundamentalism, Antisemitism, and Anti-Zionism," in *Anti-Zionism and Antisemitism in the Contemporary World*, Robert S. Wistrich, ed., (New York: New York University Press, 1990), 74-84

Smith, Anthony D., "Sacred Territories and National Conflict," *Israel Affairs*, 5, no. 4 (Summer 1999): 13-31.

Smith, Charles D., "The Invention of a Tradition: The Question of Arab Acceptance of the Zionist Right to Palestine during World War I," *Journal of Palestine Studies*, 22, no. 2 (Winter 1993): 48-61.

Spector, Sam, "Nathan Sharansky: 'Peace Will Only Come after Freedom and Democracy,'" *Middle East Quarterly* (Winter 2005).

Stein, Kenneth W., "The Intifada and the 1936-39 Uprising: A Comparison," (Summer 1990): 64-85.

Stein, Kenneth W., "Palestine's Rural Economy, 1917-1939," *Studies in Zionism*, vol. 8 no. 1 (1987): 25-49.

Steinberg, Gerald M., "Zionism as Affirmative Action," (April 20, 2001), *http://www.freeman.org/m_online/may01/steinberg.htm*.

Stone, I.F., "The Case of the Mufti," *The Nation* (May 4, 1946), 526-527.

Taheri, Amir, "Is Israel the Problem?" *Commentary* (February 2007), (https://www.commentarymagazine.com/viewarticle.cfm/is-israel-the-problem—10829?page=all.)

Tal, David, "The Forgotten War: Jewish-Palestinian Strife in Mandatory Palestine, December 1947-May 1948," *Israel Affairs*, vol. 6 no. 3 & 4 (Spring-Summer 2000): 3-21.

Talmon, J.L., "The New Anti-Semitism," *The New Republic* (September 18, 1976): 18-23.

Teveth, Shabtai, "Charging Israel with Original Sin," *Commentary* (September 1989): 24-33.

Trevor-Roper, H.R., "Jewish and Other Nationalisms," *Commentary* (January 1963): 15-21.

Troen, Ilan S., "Frontier Myths and Their Applications in America and Israel: A Transnational Perspective," *Israel Studies*, vol. 5 no. 1 (April 2000): 301-329.

Turki, Fawaz, "To be a Palestinian," *Journal of Palestine Studies*, vol. 3, no. 3 (Spring 1974): 3-17.

Urian, Dan, "The Emergence of the Arab Image in Israeli Theatre, 1948-82," *Israel Affairs*, vol. 1 no. 4 (Summer 1995): 101-127.

Viton, Albert, "Why Arabs Kill Jews," *The Nation* (June 3, 1936).

Volkov, Shulamit, "Readjusting Cultural Codes: Reflections on Anti-Semitism and Anti-Zionism," *Journal of Israeli History*, vol. 25 no. 1 (March 1, 2006): 51-62.

Weltsch, Robert, "What Chance for Arab-Jewish Accord? The Basic Issues Must Be Resolved," *Commentary* (July 1948): 8-17.

Whitelam, Keith W., "The Identity of Early Israel: The Realignment and Transformation of Late Bronze-Iron Age Palestine," *Journal for the Study of the Old Testament*, vol. 19, no. 63 (1994): 57-87.

Ya'ari, Ehud, "The Israeli-Palestinian Confrontation: Toward a Divorce," *Jerusalem Issue Brief*, vol. 2, no. 2 (June 30, 2002).

Yaalon, Moshe, "Israel and the Palestinians: A New Strategy." no. 34, *Azure* (Autumn 2008).

Yakobson, Alexander, "Jewish Peoplehood and the Jewish State, How Unique? - A Comparative Survey," *Israel Studies*, vol. 13 no. 2 (Summer 2008): 1-27.

Zimmerman, John, "Radio Propaganda in the Arab-Israeli War 1948," *The Weiner Library Bulletin*, vol. 27, no. 30 & 31 (1973-1974): 2-8.

Zimmerman, Moshe, "From Radicalism to Anti-Semitism," *The Jerusalem Quarterly*, no. 23 (Spring 1982): 114-128.

Index